THE BLACK PRESENCE

IN THE

KOREAN WAR 1950 - 1953

THE BLACK PRESENCE

IN THE

KOREAN WAR 1950 - 1953

ROBERT EWELL GREENE

R. E. GREENE, PUBLISHER - FORT WASHINGTON, MARYLAND, 2003

Copyright © 2003 by Robert Ewell Greene
ALL RIGHTS RESERVED
PUBLISHED IN 2003 BY R. E. GREENE PUBLISHER
Fort Washington, Maryland

Library of Congress Control Number 2003091869
ISBN 0-954733-17-8

ILLUSTRATION CREDITS

I sincerely thank you again my loving sister, Ruth Greene Richardson, for another outstanding cover painting. I am honored to have you prepare this cover for my twenty-sixth book.

May God continue to bless you, your hand and brush.

TO DAVID ARTHUR FRIEDRICH GREENE, the memory of Robert Ewell Greene II.

and

to those courageous and heroic Black Defenders, other Americans and the United Nations command troops of the Korean War who answered the final call of taps so bravely when they gave their lives for this country.

TABLE OF CONTENTS

AUTHOR'S PREFACE

ACKNOWLEDGMENTS

CHAPTER	PAGE
1 A Brief Sketch of Korean History	2
2 Eight US Army and The Far East Air Force (FEAF)	4
3 Segregated African American Units	8
4 Selected Veterans	50
5 Reported Military Wounded In Action	65
6 Prisoners of War (POW's)	70
7 Missing In Action	77
8 Reported Killed In Action	79
9 Heroic Acts of Courage	81-2
10 Ethiopian Profile and the Kagnew Battalions	93
11 Thurgood Marshall and Military Service	104
12 Integration of US Military Service In Korea	108
APPENDIX	114
BIBLIOGRAPHY	120
INDEX	132

PREFACE

This book will attempt to balance out the omissions which by design or otherwise have prevented accurate portrayal in study after study and volume after volume the historical true facts of the African American's heroic and courageous performances during the Korean War 1950 – 1953. There has been minimal coverage of the Black American's positive performances during the Korean War in the majority of written literature on the War. The unfavorable reports have been magnified by some authors and allowed to remain unmodified by more commendable performances of the Black military service men and women.

African Americans during the Korean War combat, flew sorties over North Korea, many were drafted and some volunteered. They experienced the beginning of integration in the military in the Fall of 1951. The Black Americans were the victors because against the odds they survived and proved to others that their performance was superb during the Korean War.

This is the time to recapture the historical events of the Korean War and re examine the pluses versus the minuses of the African American's presence in the War. There is also a need for non Blacks to include immigrants of all ethnic groups to become aware of some positive attributes of the Black military.

The Korean War should be remembered for the laudatory decision made by some concerned and courageous civilian and military leaders to integrate the United States Military Service in Korea. I believe that those leaders finally realized that in combat conditions:

> "Fleecy locks and Black complexions cannot alter nature's claim skins may differ but affliction dwell in Black and White the same"

Robert Ewell Greene
March 2, 2003

ACKNOWLEDGEMENTS

I wish to express my sincere gratitude and appreciation to my very dear and caring fiancé, Sylvia L. Rogers for her patience, understanding and most outstanding contributions to this manuscript. Her superb administrative assistance, grammatical editing, proofreading and stenographic expertise has been most commendable.

I also wish to thank the following people for their contributions in making this book a reality.

David Carlisle
Bill Grant
David Greene
Norval Lacy
Ruth G. Richardson
Lisa C. Rogers
Sylvia L. Rogers

My gratitude is also hereby expressed to those wonderful persons who have assisted me and may have been inadvertently excluded.

A BRIEF SKETCH OF KOREAN HISTORY

CHAPTER I

The members of the Engineer officer: Basic course (EOBC) in the fall of 1955 received their first active duty assignment. I received orders to a country, Korea. At that time I had no knowledge of Korea except that a war or conflict ended with an armistice in 1953. Ironically, I would be assigned another thirteen month tour in Korea in 1971 as a Chemical Officer, U. S. Army. Fortunately, by that time I was privileged to learn a great deal of facts about a great country with a very rich historical legacy and culture, the "Land of the Morning Calm", Korea.

Korea is a country that is geographically one hundred miles wide, located on the East Asian Coast, 1,000 miles long at its extremities, to the west is the Yellow Sea. The Northern areas of the country are situated near the Chinese provinces of Manchuria and near Russia. Japan lies across the strait of Tushima. The country's terrain is rugged mountains and heavy forestry. The major harbors in Korea are in the cities of Pusan, Wonsan, Hungnam, and Inchon.

It is believed that the Korean's genetic heritage dates back to the Tungusic branch in Manchuria, a Sub-brachycephalic type of the Mongolian race. After many waves of migration to the Korean peninsula more than 4,000 years ago, one of the oldest civilized races in the world settled in a land area that is called today the country of Korea.

The Korean language is a member of the Altaic family which is subdivided into three branches, Turkic, Mongolian, and Tungusic. The Turkic branch embraces the numerous languages and extends from Asia Minor to the Japan Sea. The Mongolian branch is subdivided into Chalcha, Kalmuks and Buryad. It is the third branch, the Tungusic that the Korean is believed to belong.

The history of Korea spans some 4,000 years and possibly began with a number of primitive tribes unified into a single Kingdom in the year, 2333 BC. These tribes included the Kija, Silla, Koguryo, Paekje, and other Kingdoms.

In 668 AD the Silla Kingdom which was founded in 57 BC united the entire country for the first time and ruled until replaced by the Kirkyo Dynasty in 918 AD. The Silla Dynasty was over thrown and replaced by the Yi Dynasty in 1392, which weakened over the years. Some of the factors causing this were increasing diplomatic and political interventions by China, Russia and Japan. The Russo-Japanese War and the Portsmouth Treaty mediated by President Theodore Roosevelt gave Japan a free hand in Korea. They eventually annexed Korea in 1910 and ruled until World War II.

Some other significant events in Korean history were, in 372 Buddhism was adopted. From 644 – 668 the Tang forces invaded Korea. The Mongols conquered Korea in 1267 and Confucianism was introduced in 1392. In 1852 Commodore C. Perry of the United States sailed a squadron to Japan and initiated procedures to open Asian International trade. Some US Merchant ships sailed up the Taedong River to Pyonyang in 1866 where some crew members became intoxicated and looted the homes of several local residents. The crew was imprisoned, some killed and the ship burned. A US Navy Flotilla arrived in 1871 and retaliated against the earlier actions of the Koreans. The Flotilla fired on Korean forts and landed Marines to siege several of the Forts. When confronted by King Kojangs' troops they left the area. In the 1880's the United States and Korea signed a treaty that opened Korea to foreign trade.

The major agricultural products are rice, barley, beans, wheat, millet, minerals, gold, silver, graphite and tungsten. The Korean currency is called Won. The traditional Korean music is court and folk music. A popular instrument is the Kayagum and the others are the Keomango and Tangum all of which are long stringed instruments. The reed instrument is the Bipa which is a kind of fiddle and also the drum. An instrument similar to the Japanese Kota is the Kayagum which has twelve strings. It was invented by U-ruk a sixth century musician. The Korean court music is called an "A-ak, developed from Tang-ak and Song-ak, related to Chinese classical music. Korean folk music is called Hyang-ak.

Some Koreans believe in Shamanism, a protection from the supernatural evil spirits through Shaman Incantation with the assistance of a medicine man.

At the conclusion of World War II, Korea was independent of the Japanese rule in the country. In 1945 the Soviet Union and the United States occupied Korea to accept the Japanese government's surrender. In 1948 the Soviet Union denied the United Nations access to North Korea where a communist government was being established. In the south, the South Koreans were forming a democratic style government with the assistance of the United States and other allies. Under this new government their first president was S. Rhee who was born in North Korea in 1875 and educated in the United States. He received a B.A. degree from George Washington University, a M.A. degree from Harvard University and a PhD degree in Theology from Princeton. The Korean army was trained by the U.S. Military Assistance Group in a program called KMAG.

In June, 1950 when the North Koreans invaded South Korea, the first major conflict of the Cold War Era commenced. President Harry S. Truman was able to obtain the support and assistance from concerned members of the United Nations (UN). When the United States declared war against the North Koreans and came to the immediate aid of South Korea, the following foreign countries contributed troops for the United Nations Military Command or United Nations Command (UNC). The ground forces were Australia, Belgium, Canada, Columbia, Ethiopia, Greece, Republic of Korea, Luxembourg, France, Netherlands, New Zealand, Philippines, Thailand, United Kingdom, United States and the Union of South Africa. The Medical units were Denmark, India, Italy, Norway and Sweden. It should be noted that Italy and the Republic of Korea in 1950 were not members of the United Nations. The United Nations Command was officially established on July 24, 1950.

CHAPTER 2

EIGHTH US ARMY and the FAR EAST AIR FORCE (FEAF)

The 8th US Army was organized in Korea, July 13, 1950. African Americans served in some of the major units of the 8th Army. The major units were 1st Cavalry Division, 2nd US Infantry Division, 3rd US Infantry Division, 7th US Infantry Division, 24th US Infantry Division, and the 25th US Infantry Division.

There were some African Americans who served in the Far East Air Force Units. The Major organizational structure of Far East Air Force was the Fifth Air Force FEAF, Bomber Command FEAF, FEAF Combat Cargo Command (Provisional) and 315th Air Division (combat cargo). The types of planes flown during the early phases of the war were the C-47, F-80 and F-51; the Albatross aircraft was used for rescue.

Two National Guards Units arrived in Korea in 1942, Pennsylvania's 40th Infantry Division and Oklahoma's 45th Infantry Division. When these all White division arrived in Korea, there was an agreement that prevented African Americans from being assigned to these units. Later they would integrate.

The United States Marine Corps were represented in Korea by the presence of the 1st Marine Division. The ground combat division had support and service units. The organization consisted of three rifle battalions, Headquarters and Headquarters Service Company, Anti tank Company and 4.2 inch Mortar Company. The three regiments were the First Marines, Fifth Marines, and the Eleventh Marines. There was also an aircraft squadron attached with helicopter and observation aircrafts. The Marines were present at Hongchon, Musan, Pohang and Wonju Korea.

The United States Navy operated ships in the Korean waters and did provide tactical support during the Korean War. They also played a significant role in transport services of personnel and material. The United States Navy Nurse Corps provided outstanding service in operating the medical facilities and administering care to the wounded military on hospital ships docked mainly in the Pusan Harbor. Unfortunately, the separate but equal policy was enforced by the Navy because my research has supported an initial inference that no African American Nurses served on the hospital ships or were present for duty in Korea.

Segregation is a practice that separated an individual or group from another and has been enforced by law in the US since the infamous Supreme Court ruling, Plessy V. Ferguson in 1896. In the 1960's a positive response to the problem was accomplished by several Congressional legislative acts.

The United States Military as late as May 1950, two months prior to the start of the Korean War practiced segregation without any regrets. In May, 1950 a young officer of color reported for his first assignment following graduation from Officer's Candidate School, he was not allowed on the Post's all White Officers Club. The food for African American Officer's was prepared in the White Officers Club kitchen and placed in field thermite cans and trucked to a small annex where the Black Officers ate their meals. This policy and other segregated restrictions enforced in the

United States Military was sanctioned by law and the continuance of it was supported idealistically and mentally by so called honorable officers and gentlemen that had attained the rank of general officer and were assigned to a high level command. The one general officer who possessed these characteristics served in World War II and the Korean War was General Almond. He served as the Commanding General X Corps, Korea. General Almond expressed his personal views concerning an idealism about the Black soldier's abilities to fight in combat and his opposition to an integrated army.

In a conversation with General Douglas Mac Arthur, Almond said "General, there is nothing you did to me would disturb me emotionally because I once commanded the 92nd Infantry Division in World War II", (The 92nd Infantry Division was an old Black division with both White and Black Officers. There were some problems and allegations of racist leadership by General Almond).

During the Korean War there was an incident involving an X Corps Black Artillery Unit. A Black Artillery Unit was immediately exposed to combat action near Yong Hung, Korea and experienced a serious assault by the enemy, possibly due to improper infantry support. When General Almond received a report of the incident, he blamed the Black Unit as being incompetent and positioned the Unit in a non-artillery mission. However when he was in immediate need of artillery support, he would use the "Black Cannon Fodder or the Black Artillery Unit to confront a serious Chinese offensive. Even though Almond believed Blacks were incompetent to fight in combat, the US X Corps had a considerable number of African Americans assigned or attached, the majority in segregated units. The combat units were the 58th Armored Field Artillery Battalion, 999th Field Artillery Battalion, 64th Tank Battalion and some Infantry troops. The all Black X Corps service units were medical, ambulance companies, ordinance, maintenance companies, signal construction companies, salvage companies, bakery company, petroleum support company, laundry company and truck companies.

General Almond has his own perception about the genetic diversity of Puerto Ricans. He probably was alluding to the biological facts that a great majority of Puerto Ricans are endowed with a genotype that is representative of their Spanish, Tiano Indian and African genetic heritage, a multiracial triangle of genes.

When General Almond was visiting the 65th Puerto Rican Infantry Regiment, he engaged in an interesting conversation with the regimental commander, LTC. Harris. Almond told Harris that he did not have much confidence in colored troops because of his bitter experience with them in Italy during WW II, and he did not trust them. LTC. Harris said "these troops are not Colored, they are White", now I do have some Colored Virgin Islanders. It is interesting that Harris did not explain who Virgin Islanders really are. (They are citizens of the US Virgin Islands that comprise St. Croix, St. Thomas and St. John. The population as of the 1990's consisted of a small percentage of Puerto Ricans, White, and a considerable number of Blacks. Over the years the country has been ruled by Spain, England, France and Denmark. The Islands were sold to the US in 1917. The late Judge William Hastie was the first African American governor of the Virgin Islands). LTC. Harris also remarked that he had some Colored Puerto Ricans. There was no response from the General.

General Almond once stated that integration might improve military efficiency, but it also could weaken it because there is no question of the inherent differences in races. Almond said those individuals who supported integration did not understand the problem. He served as X Corps Commanding General until July 15, 1951. He returned to the US and served as the Commandant of the Army War College, Washington, DC until his retirement in 1953.

There was another high ranking general officer who also expressed his views about the potential combat abilities of African Americans. He was General Mark Clark. Clark wrote "Most Negro units have spotty records from WW II and in the early fighting in Korea. Because of the way the Negro fought in the integrated army in Korea, it would be worthwhile to review the judgment of the leadership problem". Clark believed that there should not be an indiscriminate mixing of Black and White soldiers in the army. He did think that integration could be tried at lower levels. General Mark Clark did realize that Blacks had proven to be better soldiers when fighting alongside White soldiers. Clark possibly really opposed discrimination but he was cautious about how integration should be implemented.

When the battle worn soldiers returned to rear areas after many days exposed to severe combat conditions, many would ask for a change of scenery other than rear area rest areas. Headquarters Eighth Army and the Japan Military Logistical Command commence a program in December, 1950 called "Operation Relax for service men" or little R, "REST and RECUPERATION," "R & R". The program was intended to enhance morale for a five day rest and recuperation period. The troops would normally receive an R and R during their sixth or seventh month of the combat tour in Korea. The men were transported to Japan and were provided special services, hotels and recreational facilities. They would leave from Kimpo Airfield, Seoul, Korea on C-54 Transport airplanes. They would go to Camp Kokuru near Ashlya Airbase on Kyushu, Camp McNealy near Haneda Airbase in the Tokyo-Yokohama area. In 1951 a third processing center opened at Itami Airbase, Osaka, Japan.

The soldiers were paid in Japanese currency at the processing center. They were given clean clothes, uniforms and fed steak dinner. The men left their boots, weapons and uniforms at the center to be cleaned and repaired. The soldiers were able to enjoy entertainment in the town and some would arrange for their families and girl friends to meet them in Japan. The service men would spend their R and R dining, dancing sightseeing, watching movies and purchasing presents and souvenirs.

The Fifth Air Force in the Far East had a none-flexible program than the Army. When airmen could be available, they were allowed to go to Japan on flights without being processed.

The International and American Red Cross which was present in Korea and Japan assisted the service people in arranging emergency leaves and maintained some rest centers behind the front lines. Ironically, in 1955, the Rest and Recuperation Program was present in a modified form for those personnel who were serving a thirteenth month tour in Korea.

TROOP ROTATION SYSTEM

During the Korean War, a rotation system was devised based on points. Each military personnel received four points for every month spent in a combat zone. Three points were given for being located within the area between regimental headquarters and the combat front lines. Two points were given for rear echelon duties. Those who served in Japan were given one point per month except for soldiers wounded in combat.

When a soldier accrued thirty points he was rotated home and discharged unless he preferred to re-enlist. The average infantry man returned home within one year of survived battle and weather conditions. The rotation had its shortcomings. The individual rotation did weaken unit cohesion and effectiveness. Sometimes experienced troops were replaced by reservists, national guardsmen and draftees sometimes were unfamiliar with the Korean terrain and mountain combat techniques.

A SPECIAL SERVICES SERVICE CLUB

In Japan during the Korean War, there was a Special Services Club located on the Tokyo, Japan U. S. Army Quartermaster Depot. The Club was operated on an interracial basis and had a superb program for military personnel. It was supervised by Ms Ethel Payne who served as the Club's Director. She was assisted by Ms Kathryn M. Davenport, Program Director from Norristown, PA, Ms Dorothy Mitchell, Philadelphia, PA, Recreational Director and Ms June Wells, Savannah, GA, also a Recreational Director. Ms Payne maintained a journal of her observations of discrimination against Black servicemen while serving as the Club Director during the period 1949 – 1950.

Ms Ethel L. Payne was noted for achievements other than the director of the Special Services Club. She was the first Black female commentator on network television and had served as a columnist for the Chicago Defender and Afro American newspapers during the period 1952 – 1982. While covering news conferences at the White House, Ms Payne would often ask questions on civil rights issues. At a conference in 1954, she asked about a possible executive order to end train segregation in interstate and out travel. President Eisenhower responded in a somewhat tense mood and said "What makes you think that I am going to give special favoritism to special interests? I am the President of all the people". Ms Payne also covered news conferences in Bandung, Indonesia in 1956 and she died on May 28, 1991.

"THEY WERE THERE"

Major tactical and combat situations that some African Americans were present in combat and or service roles were: The establishment of the Pusan Perimeter August, 1950; first Battle of the Naktong Bridge, August, 1950; Inchon Landing, September, 1950; recapture of Seoul, September, 1950; the United Nations crossing of the 38th Parallel, October, 1950; the retaking of Seoul, March, 1951; the Battle of Pork Chop Hill, April, 1953; Pile driver operation, the last United Nations offensive of the Korean War that occurred in the vicinity of the towns of Chorwon and Kim Hwa, Korea.

African Americans were also present in the following combat situations or events: Operation Dauntless, established the Utah line; the Battle of Bloody Ridge; Operation Ripper, the offensive to cross the Han River; Operation Rugged, the advance to the Line Kansas; participated in combat operations in the Iron Triangle; the geographical areas north of the 38th Parallel, central part of the Korean peninsula; the invasions swept from north to south. The three major areas of the Iron Triangle were Kumhwa East, Chorwom West, and Pyong Gang North. There was also African American military presence during the combat operation along the Hamhung – Hungnam perimeter, December, 1950.

The segregated and later integrated African American military personnel made an enormous contribution while serving in units that provided considerable combat and service related support to the United States 8th US Army Far East Air Forces, US Marine Corps and the US Navy during the Korean War Era, 1950-1951.

CHAPTER 3

SEGREGATED AFRICAN AMERICAN UNITS

Among the approximately 2,834,000 U. S. personnel who served in Korea, 1950 – 1951, there were some African American personnel who were represented in segregated combat and service units in the U.S. Army. A very small number of Blacks were assigned to integrated units in the US military services. The majority of African Americans were assigned to the following segregated units prior to September, 1951:

- 2nd Ranger Co.(airborne)
- 3rd Battalion, 9th US Infantry Regiment
  - 2nd US Infantry Division
- 15th US Infantry Regiment, 3rd US Infantry Div.
- 24th US Infantry Reg., 25th US Infantry Div.
- 58th Field Artillery Battalion
- 64th Tank Battalion
- 73rd Engineer Combat Battalion
- 76th Anti Aircraft Artillery Automatic weapons Battalion
- 77th Engineer Combat Co.
- 96th Field Artillery Battalion
- 159th Field Artillery Battalion
- 503rd Field Artillery Battalion
- 933rd Anti Aircraft Artillery Automatic Weapons Battalion
- 999th Armored Field Artillery Battalion
- 25th Chemical Decontamination Unit
- 28th Transportation Truck Co.
- 39th Medical Dispensary Co.
- 42nd Transportation Truck Co.
- 46th Transportation Truck Co.
- 48th Transportation Truck Co.
- 49th Transportation Truck Co.
- 51st Military Police Criminal Investigation Detachment
- 54th Transportation Heavy Truck Co.
- 55th Ordnance Ammunition Co.
- 55th Engineer Treadway Bridge Co
- 57th Ordnance Recovery Co.
- 58th Quartermaster Salvage Co.
- 59th Medical Dispensary Unit
- 60th Transportation Truck Co.
- 65th Ordnance Ammunition Co.
- 69th Transportation Truck Co.
- 70th Transportation Truck Co.
- 71st Chemical Smoke Generator Co.
- 74th Transportation Truck Co.
- 375th Chemical Smoke Generator Co.
- 376th Engineer Construction Co.
- 402nd Transportation Truck Co.
- 403rd Signal Construction Co.
- 505th Quartermaster Reclamation & Maintenance Co.
- 506th Quartermaster Petroleum Sup. Co.
- 512th Military Police Co.
- 513th Transportation Truck Co.
- 514th Transportation Truck Co.
- 515th Transportation Truck Co.
- 519th Veterinary Food Inspection Detachment
- 529th Quartermaster Petroleum Sup. Co.
- 539th Transportation Truck Co.
- 540th Transportation Truck Co.
- 541st Transportation Truck Co.
- 546th Engineer Fire Fighting Co.
- 548th Engineer Service Battalion
- 549th Quartermaster Laundry Co.
- 549th Veterinary Food Inspection Ser.
- 551st Transportation Truck Co.
- 553rd Transportation Heavy Truck Co.
- 556th Transportation Heavy Truck Co.
- 558th Medical Collecting Separate Co.
- 558th Medical Ambulance Co.
- 560th Medical Ambulance Co.
- 563rd Medical Ambulance Co.
- 567th Military Police Co.
- 568th Medical Ambulance Co.
- 570th Engineer Water Supply Co.
- 571st Engineer Dump Truck Co.
- 573rd Engineer Pontoon Bridge Co.
- 576th Engineer Service Co.
- 577th Ordnance Co.
- 584th Transportation Truck Co.
- 595th Engineer Dump Truck Co.
- 611th Transportation Port Co.

THE BLACK PRESENCE IN THE KOREAN WAR 1950 - 1953

- 78th Transportation Truck Co.
- 91st Ordnance Medium Automotive Maintenance Co.
- 93rd Engineer Construction Battalion
- 95th Transportation Car Co.
- 112th Army Postal Unit
- 118th Malaria Control Detachment
- 130th Quartermaster Bakery Co
- 167th Transportation Truck Battalion
- 212th Military Police Co.
- 216th Medical Detachment
- 231st Transportation Truck Battalion
- 250th Quartermaster Laundry Detachment
- 619th Ordnance Ammunition Co.
- 630th Ordnance Ammunition Co.
- 636th Ordnance Ammunition Co.
- 646th Ordnance Co.
- 665th Transportation Truck Co.
- 696th Ordnance Ammunition Co.
- 715th Transportation Truck Co.
- 726th Transportation Truck Co.
- 803rd Regional Post Engineer Units
- 811th Engineer Aviation Battalion
- 822nd Engineer Aviation Battalion
- 849th Quartermaster Petroleum Sup. Co.
- 862nd Transportation Port Co.
- 866th Transportation Port Co.
- 945th Quartermaster Service Co.

Some of these units could have been located in Japan or Korea at a later time. In addition there were seven bands, the 15th, 16th, 19th, 55th, 56th, 289th and 291st. The major segregated combat unit during the Korean War was the US 24th Infantry Regiment, 25th Infantry Division.

TWENTY FOURTH INFANTRY REGIMENT

A HISTORICAL SKETCH

The 1866 Act involving the reorganization of the regular US Army included a provision for four Black Infantry regiments. However in 1869, they were reduced to two. The Twenty-fourth Infantry Regiment was created by the consolidation of the Thirty-eighth Infantry Regiment with the Forty-first Infantry Regiment. The Twenty-fourth Infantry Regiment was present in the "Winning of the West", Spanish American War and the Philippine Insurrection. In 1867, the regiment was assigned a reinforcement mission to fight some attacking Indians. When Lt. William R, Shafter led an expedition of soldiers from Barilla Springs, Ft. Davis and Ft. Stockton, Texas, a detachment of the Twenty-fourth Regiment was with the expedition in June, 1871. They traveled to the Pecos, White sands region.

In 1871 the Regiment was assigned duties of patrolling areas during the Indian Campaigns. The soldiers patrolled the Carrizo Mountains, Alamo Springs, Eagle Springs, and Van Horn Wells mail station where they sometimes confronted Indian warriors.

The Twenty-fourth Infantry Regiment was present in field searching missions during the Indian Wars. On May 16, 1873, Colonel Mac Kenzie departed from Ft. Clark, Texas to search for some Indian Warriors. His search force consisted of his regiment and a detachment of the Twenty-fourth Infantry Regiment. When Colonel Shafter commanded an expedition that left Ft. Concho on July 14, 1875 to pursue some Indian warriors, his command included two companies of the Twenty-fourth Infantry.

In July 1876, Lt. Bullis and soldiers of the Twenty-fourth Infantry marched 110 miles in 23 hours and were successful in surprising a camp of 23 Indian lodgers. The Indians were from the Lipans and Kickapoo Tribes, who were camped near Saragossa, Mexico. There were some Indian casualties and the soldiers captured many horses.

During the Victoria War, Colonel Grierson, commanding officer, Tenth US Cavalry Regiment was searching for Victoria and the Indian warriors near Rattlesnake Springs around July 30, 1880. Company H of the Twenty-fourth Regiment was part of the search force. The soldiers of the Twenty-fourth Infantry served as escorts for army supply trains in the 1880's. When a supply train was approached by a band of Apache Indian warriors, they received an element of surprise because hidden inside of the wagon train were the soldiers. They immediately commenced firing and were able to force the Indians to retreat.

In 1898, the Twenty-fourth Infantry provided some support for the Tenth Cavalry Regiment during the battle of San Juan Hill, Cuba. Lt. Lyon of the Twenty-fourth Infantry and his men provided a hotchkiss gun in support of the advancing Tenth Cavalry Regiment. The members of this Regiment were also assigned in August, 1806 to assist the Philippine constabulary in the pursuit of some rebels at Leyte. The 3rd Battalion of the Twenty-fourth Regiment had also been stationed at Colona Dublan, New Mexico where they were treated with kindness by the Mexicans. Later they were transferred to Columbus, New Mexico. In addition, this Regiment experienced some racial hatred, discrimination and racial violence during their tours of duty at some Forts and the nearby towns and cities. A racial incident in 1917 gained national attention and a serious concern for African Americans who were still faced with racial segregation and "second class citizenship".

THE BLACK PRESENCE IN THE KOREAN WAR 1950 - 1953

The Houston, Texas Riot of 1917 occurred on July 29, 1917. The 3rd Battalion of the Twenty-fourth Infantry Regiment was stationed in Houston to perform some special guard duties. When they arrived in Houston, they were "insulted deliberately by the white inhabitants of the city. Saloons and taverns had signs reading Dogs and Nigras not allowed here. One evening in July, 1917, a First Sergeant of Company A and some other soldiers were present in the town and decided they would not tolerate any more insults. Some confrontations occurred between the soldiers and white citizens. The situation appeared to develop into a riot when people were wounded and the sheriff and some people were killed. The Governor of Texas declared martial law and ordered the Texas National Guard to assist local law enforcement officers in maintaining law and order in Houston. The First Sergeant, who led the men into town committed suicide when he "sat down on a railroad track" and decided to kill himself.

There was a shortage of officers as well as noncommissioned officers in the battalion who were in a training school at Fort Des Moines, Iowa. It is believed that lack of Officer leadership in the battalion could have been a contributing factor in the events that occurred. An investigation revealed that the First Sergeant led 150 soldiers into town and that they began to fire on the white people at random killing some and wounding others. An investigation officer stated that the soldiers had defied their officers and obtained their weapons with ammunition and departed for Houston. The investigation report stated that the white officers "showed gross negligence and insufficient leadership". The two officers were recommended to be court-martialed for the violation of an article for gross neglect of duty. The commanding officer of the company involved in the race riot was Lt. James. He was very upset over the incident and considered himself a disgrace. The night after he accompanied his men back to Columbus, Mexico he returned to his living quarters and committed suicide rather than face the disgrace of having commanded a rebellious unit. A battalion of the white Sixty-fourth Infantry Regiment was ordered to guard the Twenty-fourth Infantry Regiments campsite. Later they obtained a train and escorted the Black soldiers back to Columbus, Mexico. Sixty-three men were charged, 169 witnesses appeared for the prosecution and 27 witnesses for the defense. Thirteen Black soldiers were executed on December 11, 1917. The Black communities throughout the country demonstrated their support for the accused soldiers of the regiment's 3rd Battalion. The NAACP and other leaders requested some consideration be given for these soldiers. Numerous signature petitions were forwarded to the Department of the Army. However, the Secretary of the Army, Newton Baker and other higher ranking officials were determined to see that these men would be tried and executed.

The inglorious and glorious performances of duty of those "Real Buffalo Soldiers" of yester year were tinted by some unfavorable actions in combat by their successors during the Korean War.

On June 25, 1950 South Korea was attacked by North Korean troops along the Onjin Peninsula northwest of Seoul, the South Korean capital. Seoul was taken on June 29th and on June 30th the first US ground forces entered the conflict as part of a United Nations police action to force North Korean troops back beyond the 38th parallel. Black soldiers were a part of the war, first in the segregated 1st, 2nd, and 3rd battalions of the Twenty-fourth Infantry Regiment, twenty-fifth Infantry Division. After October, 1951 the US Army started to implement President Truman's order to integrate the Armed forces.

Various accounts have been published about the poor performance of some members of the Twenty-fourth Infantry Regiment during combat operations in Korea. There are books, periodicals, newspapers, government and military publications that give accounts of the regiments' unfavorable combat actions during the Korean War. My thorough research on this subject revealed the following accounts that are available in 2003 to the various layperson and researcher about the Twenty-fourth Infantry Regiment's combat record in Korea:

In July 1950, the Twenty-fourth Infantry Regiment was situated at the town of Kumchon. The 2nd Battalion was involved in a joint operation with the 17th South Korean Regiment near the village of Idang, West of Sangju on the road to Poun when the 2nd Battalion came under heavy enemy fire, some men started to withdraw on their own, without receiving an official order for withdrawal.

On July 22, 1950, some members of E Company, Twenty-fourth Infantry Regiment received some enemy mortar and automatic weapons fire. The men took cover alongside the road and then decided to withdraw without an official order. The men were in a state of confusion and had abandoned their machine guns and a rocket launcher.

A North Korean force attacked C Company, Twenty-fourth Infantry Regiment on August 6, 1950 killing twelve men. Some of the men were in a state of panic and eventually the enemy was able to overpower the Company's position. This occurred near the town of Pil-bong.

On 29 August 1950 during some intense fighting, the Twenty-fourth Infantry Regiment unit left their position without an official command because of rumors received. Some members of the Twenty-fourth Infantry Regiment's 2nd Battalion wasted their ammunition on false targets. When the enemy attacked their positions some men were short of ammunition and they decided to leave their positions without permission.

On August 12, 1950 some men of the 3rd Battalion Twenty-fourth Infantry Regiment were accused of fleeing to the rear of the combat line. The North Koreans surprised some soldiers of this Regiment on August 3rd and two companies of the Regiment retreated leaving mortars and a 75 recoilless rifle to be destroyed by the enemy. This action could have contributed to the North Koreans capturing the town of Haman.

When the North Koreans conducted an assault on "Battle Mountain's" ridges in August, two companies of the Twenty-fourth Infantry Regiment were instructed to hold their position. However one platoon decided to move to the rear without official orders and the men ran. This Regiment also demonstrated a cowardly performance when exposed to combat conditions at San Gju. When some of the regiment's troops came under a heavy enemy assault, many men ran and abandoned their equipment. Because of their tendency to panic under extreme combat conditions, they were labeled the "Bug Out Unit". Some of the Regiments soldiers had a pattern of running toward the rear and would become hysterical once they faced an enemy attack. It was necessary to construct a road block in order to stop the "Stragglers" of the regiment. The members of the regiment who left their positions in a combat situation were "psychologically and physically unruly for these young combat soldiers became frightened when out numbered by the North Koreans and Chinese soldiers.

On 4 September 1950, the 2nd Battalion of the Regiment's companies G, H and E were located to the west of Haman, Korea. When the enemy attacked their positions, some soldiers abandoned their machine guns and withdrew without official orders. A white Inspector General (IG) stated his appraisal of the African American Soldiers in the Twenty-fourth Infantry Regiment. He said "Black soldiers as a group were hardly as alert as white soldiers and tended to sleep while on duty. They were stragglers and would leave their individual positions.

During the Korean War an article appeared in a popular white weekly magazine about the performance of Black troops. The author stated that a (white) LTC. Russell Blair, Commanding officer, 3rd Battalion, 24th Infantry Regiment said that he was driving down a Korean road and observed some Black troops assembled around a small fire singing. The Lt. Colonel asked the men what was the song they were singing? A soldier replied, Sir this is the official song of the Twenty-fourth Regiment, "The Bug Out Boogie." The Colonel ordered the soldiers to sing the song. The verse was as follows:

> "When the Chinese mortars begin to thud
> The old deuce four begin to bug"

It is believed that LTC. Blair later instructed his officers that there would be no more singing of that song in his battalion. A former white lieutenant who was a platoon leader in this Regiment challenged the allegations about troops singing the Bug Out Boogie song. He said "it was ludicrous and that there was never a time when his troops left their positions and withdrew voluntarily."

It is interesting how the terms retreat, move to the rear and withdraw have no similarity what so ever to the term "bug out". There has been reported some accounts of non Black units during the retrograde or withdrawal movement without official designation by some people as "Bug Out". This is in no way to justify the inefficient and most devastated performances by some members of the Twenty-fourth Infantry Regiment during the Korean War. However these accounts should be known also.

On or about January 1, 1951, the 3rd Battalion, 35th Infantry withdrew from the Imijin River line without receiving any imminent enemy attack". A scholarly military historian, who researched a book for the U. S. Army Center of Military History, stated in his manuscript that the 7th U. S. Infantry Division's 31st Infantry Regiment was given the combat mission to guard an area near a blown bridge, Chosin Reservoir in the winter, 1950. It was observed that some men of this Regiment's 3rd Battalion deserted their position and were running down the road toward the rear safe areas. There were some Junior Officers among the troops who ignored a senior officers' command to stop. It is quite interesting that this all White infantry unit was not characterized as a "Bug Out Unit". Just another "Nutritional Reasoning." There is a photograph in a book on the Korean War that depicts some soldiers of the 2nd U. S. Infantry Division traveling down a Korean road near the town of Pyongyang. The weary appearing soldiers have just confronted a strong Chinese assault and they were leaving the battle front for safer ground. The majority of the members of this Unit appear to be non Black. However the author has a caption under the picture that read "The Great Bug Out".

There were probably some white units that did sing the Bug Out song. The following song did not specify any relevance to the Twenty-fourth Infantry Regiment:

> "Hear the Pitter-patter of tiny feet
> It's the US Army in full retreat
> They are moving on it won't be long
> It's getting cold and they are
> Moving back to Seoul
> A thousand North Koreans coming down the pass
> Playing burp gun – Boogie on a doggy butt it's getting
> And they are
> Moving back to Seoul"

The soldiers of this Regiment had at one time 469 cases of frost bite. It was alleged that some men had intentionally froze their feet by pouring water into their combat boots in order to be transferred to a medical facility in the rear area for treatment. When the Regiment officers became aware of the scheme, they started a daily inspection of the soldiers' feet. The immediate action did reduce the number of reported frost bite cases. There were some military officials who were acquainted with a research study by Norwegian scientists on frost bites. The scientists had learned that "dark complexioned Norwegians tended to develop frost bite of the ears and face more often than blond individuals, when exposed to identical circumstances. The results were not conclusive. Some U.S. scientists postulated from this preliminary research that "Blacks as a group were more susceptible to cold injury than whites, because Blacks had frost bite exposure during a shorter period and experienced injury at temperatures higher than their white counterparts."

In view of those findings and analysis, I pose the question, "Did the U.S. Medical personnel consider in their protocol study that the African American's genetic make up or geneotype is heterogeneous?" Some population biologists have develop an approach to explain race by analyzing genetic marks in selected populations.. They have learned that there are more genetic differences within one race than there are between that race and another. Some of these genetic differences are difficult to explain. An example would be if one would select at random any two Black Americans and an analysis is conducted on their 23 pairs of chromosomes, the results would show that their genes have less in common than do the genes of a randomly selected white person. This research adds some support that African Americans are probably the most diverse individuals on this planet as a biological group. A Caucasian physician and geneticist, who is a professor at a renowned university told me during a telephone conversation in 1992 that there has been research that concluded that 'the average African American probably has 20 – 25 percent of mixed European or white genes and that the more the Black is racially mixed with whites the percentage would increase. The reality in America is that white Americans, Europeans, Hispanics, Asians and African Americans themselves identify American Blacks by distinctive physical features, such as hair, skin color, lips, nose, and eye color. It is quite obvious that they do not consider the African American's ethnicity from a biological or genetic perspective. It is interesting how some of America's other minorities today possess some of the similar physical descriptions of Blacks except the hair texture and they are of course called by the name of their ethnic group in their country. A case in point would be the very dark skinned "untouchables or Dalits from India. Just another "Nutritional Reasoning". Would the frost bite studies apply to the Dalits?

Credit must be given to a small number of historians and writers on the Korean War who did address some positive actions or performances by the men of the Twenty-fourth Infantry Regiment. Some significant accounts were as follows:

When the town of Namwon was secured by United Nation Troops, the 1st Battalion, 24th Infantry Regiment was successful in securing the town of Kunsan without difficulty and they performed well. - - In August, 1950, the North Koreans attacked and entered the position of Company I, 1st Battalion, 24th Infantry Regiment, but the Company was most successful in repulsing the enemy. - - Companies E and G of the 24th Infantry Regiment accomplished their mission in an exemplary manner when they assisted the 9th Infantry Regiment during a withdrawal movement. - - When Company F, 24th Infantry Regiment was involved at the Han River crossing, they were located to the left of the 27th Infantry Regiment. The Company was commanded by 1st Lt. George Shuffer. His Company had the mission to establish and secure a beach head. The Company had experienced some swift currents during the crossing. Lt. Shuffer was able to successfully secure the beach head on the western edge of a hill. While serving as the Director of the U. S. Army

THE BLACK PRESENCE IN THE KOREAN WAR 1950 - 1953

Race Relations School in Germany, I had the opportunity to meet Brigadier General George Shuffer. He was the Assistant Deputy Chief of Staff for Personnel of the U.S. Army in Europe. At that time I had no knowledge of the outstanding performance of duty of General Shuffer when he was a lieutenant in the 24th Infantry Regiment during the Korean War.

There were some civilians and military persons of all races who were seriously concerned about the past performances of the 24th Infantry Regiment's combat record in Korea. Those persons were successful in having the Secretary of Army, the Honorable John Marsh, Jr. in 1987 to direct the U. S. Army center of military history to conduct a study of the Regiment's daily journals, operational orders, messages memoranda of records, war diaries, maps, graphs, and overlays as well as oral interviews with white and Black veterans who had served in Korea.

Some of the significant lessons learned from the study were: The 24th Infantry Regiment had encountered some problems while stationed in Gifu, Japan. The troops had lower classification test scores than the white troops. The senior commanders of the Regiment were white. Some white officers viewed Black soldiers as inferior and incompetent. The officer positions changed constantly to ensure that Black officers would not command white officers. Some of the white leadership were incompetent and possessed limited combat experience. There were some white leaders who actually believed the Black soldiers' failures were due to the stereotypes that African Americans were afraid of the dark, would not dig fox holes and failed to keep their equipment in good operational order. The 24th Infantry Regiment did sustain a large number of casualties in combat operations in the vicinity of Sangju and Battle Mountain. Sometimes orders received through the chain of command were not always clear to the average soldier.

There were two panel members involved in this study that I had the privilege of knowing personally. They were the late Four Star General Roscoe Robinson, the first Black Four Star General, in the U. S. Army. The late Colonel John Cash, a graduate of Rutgers University where he received degrees in history and the University of Wisconsin where he received a degree in Latin American Studies. During his active military service, he served as a Unit Commander in Vietnam and served as Defense Attache` in El Salvador and Brazil. He also served as a military historian at the U. S. Army Center of Military History and taught history at the U. S. Military Academy, West Point, New York. Colonel Cash wrote a book, <u>Seven Fire Fights in Vietnam</u> and contributed to the manuscript, the <u>Exclusion of Black Soldiers From The Medal of Honor in World War II.</u> Colonel John Cash, a soldier, scholar and a very personable individual was admired by all made a most notable contribution to the published book by the Center of Military History's final results of the 24th Infantry Regiment's study, <u>Black Soldier – White Army: The Twenty-fourth Infantry Regiment in Korea.</u> He taught History at Morgan State University, Baltimore, Maryland and I was able to discuss with him on numerous occasions about his definitive research and interviews of many veterans of the 24th Infantry Regiment.

There was another person who made some contributions in the campaign to have the United States Army to review the combat record of the 24th Infantry Regiment. He was the late David K. Carlisle, a West Point graduate, class of 1950, Corps of Engineers. Carlisle served in Korea in 1950 with the 77th combat Engineer Company. In civilian life he was a businessman in Los Angeles, CA.

David Carlisle diligently requested the Department of the Army for some years to re examine the Army's official historical account of the 24th Infantry Regiments' combat record in Korea. He also wanted the Army to award the Regiment an presidential unit citation and award a medal of honor to a Black Officer, LTC. Charles Bussey who performed heroic deeds during the first U. S. Victory of the war at Yechon, Korea. Carlisle also challenged the Army's official historical manuscript that discussed in detail about some of the poor performances of the 24th Infantry Regiment. David Carlisle wrote articles, letters to the press, made phone calls and tried to solicit support from Congress and the President of the United States to correct what he believed was an incorrect combat record of the 24th Infantry Regiment in Korea.

I did not have the opportunity to meet David Carlisle, but I did receive several telephone calls from him as well as correspondence. I am including in this chapter a letter dated August 13, 1981, that was addressed to a former professor and mentor of mine at Howard University, the late Dr. Harold O. Lewis.

"Dear Dr. Lewis:

It was a real pleasure to chat with you on the phone this morning.

I came across the volume, Black Defenders of America, 1775-1973, in the library yesterday for the first time. I spent several hours reading the book last night, along with the appendices and bibliography. Major Greene has done a tremendous job and a real service in placing a virtual encyclopedia of knowledge between two covers—and I sincerely congratulate him for doing so. I was particularly interested in the several bibliographies of black general officers in the South Carolina national guard during the 1870's inasmuch as my mother (a native of Anderson, SC) has recently been relating to me some of the little know facts about our family history and the general situation in her home state of her personal recollection and as passed on to her by her relatives.

And, of course, I was very much interested in the references to West Pointers, to World War I during which my father served in the 367th Infantry Regiment, 92nd Infantry Division, winning a Croix de Guerre and serving at one point as his company first sergeant; and during which my two maternal uncles served respectively in the 365th Infantry Regiment and the 319th (?) Engineer Battalion; and World War II; and particularly Korea. Somewhat humorously, my mother recalls when her mother went to the Red Cross during WW I to check on an allotment due to come to her from the engineer soldier-son she was told that her son couldn't be serving in the 319th Engineers—that was a "white" outfit. My uncle, John Robert Kay, not only served in the 319th Engineers; he also became an aircraft mechanic in Europe during WW I, raced at Indianapolis as a mechanic during the period when there were two-man cars in the mid-1920's; and worked as a movie electrician and L. A. police vice squad officer in Hollywood—long before "we" were supposed to have done these things. My uncle, James Howard Kay, served before WW I in the "white" US Navy and during WW I in the black 365th Infantry without too many references to his earlier days as a boxing champion in the Pacific fleet.

I believe that you and Major Greene will be very interested in some additional factual discussion on the role of black units and black soldiers in Korea that comes from my personal experience as a newly-commissioned West Point graduate, Class of 1950. (Coincidentally, my West Point roommate was named Robert W. Green—he and I graduated on June 2, 1950; spent our two months' graduation leave largely together at my home in Los Angeles and his in Oakland, CA; read the news of the first UN victory over the North Koreans at Yechon together at a newsstand a few blocks from my home; left by train and boat to Pusan; and together reported to the 24th Infantry Regiment where the CO, Colonel John T. Corley, Bob's West Point tactical officer, tried to "commandeer" both of us for assignment to his regiment; and finally arriving at our first unit, the 77th Engineer Combat Company, 25th Infantry Division, and going immediately into a frontline defensive position in the Pusan Perimeter.)

THE BLACK PRESENCE IN THE KOREAN WAR 1950 - 1953

Another coincidence: our first company CO, Captain Charles M. Bussey, had grown up with my brother, and Bussey and his brothers and my brother and I had all gone to Sunday school together as youngsters. During the late 1930's, as fellow trainees at the Citizens Military Training Camp, Ft. MacArthur, CA, Bussey and by brother were the two finalists in the camp wide manual of arms competition. As trainee after trainee dropped out, leaving them the only two standing, I could recall how excited I was when Bussey made one false movement, leaving my brother the camp champion. Shortly after this training session, Bussey enlisted in the Army, underwent pilot training at Tuskegee Institute, and became a qualified fighter pilot in the 332nd Fighter Group, ETO. My brother, denied permission to enlist by our parents, joined the California State Guard which was "federalized" during WW II and wound up as battalion sergeant-major, 1401st Engineer Combat Battalion, Ft. Lewis, Washington, during the Korean conflict.

(My brother laughingly relates how Korean engineer veterans, rotating back to the States and joining his unit at Fort Lewis, reported to him that they had been made to keep their boots shined at the frontline by his brother in the 77th Engineers.)

I suggested that Major Greene's treatment of the Korean War, Page 213, needs to be expanded to include references to other Black units including the 159th Field Artillery Battalion and 77th Engineer Combat Company, 25th Infantry Division; and to other semi-integrated organizations including the 9th Infantry Regiment, 2nd Infantry Division; and the 65th Regimental Combat Team which arrived in Korea during, perhaps, October, 1951, and was assigned or attached to the 3rd Infantry Division. Although I personally observed the 65th RCT moving north to its initial combat assignment in Korea I no longer recall seeing any Black Puerto Ricans in the unit—but it must be a fact that Black soldiers were present in the 65th. Marine and national guard units were also integrated.

The 9th Infantry Regiment was semi-integrated—I don't know exactly how. The regimental CO, Colonel Charles C. Sloane, was a West Pointer well known throughout the Army as the originator of the "aggressor" concept in training situations. The regiment had a very fine reputation in Korea—unfortunately, it took very heavy losses at the hands of the Chinese when they entered the was in late 1950, overrunning the 9th Infantry along the eastern shore of the Chongchon River and then decimating the 2nd Infantry Division during the Battle of Kunuri—all written up by the military historian, Brigadier General S. L. A. Marshall, in the book, The River and the Gauntlet.

In his preface, Major Greene writes "(the 24th Infantry's) glorious career ended with integration but not before the Regiment had achieved the honor of being the first to engage the enemy in combat". The first US divisions into Korea were the 1st Cavalry Division and the 24th Infantry Division- -I believe they had both been heavily involved before the 24th Regiment left for Korea on July 9, 1950. But one battalion of the 24th Regiment (with one platoon of the 77th Engineers at the point of the attacking battalion) did win the first UN and US victory over the invading North Koreans at the village of Yechon in late July.

During this battle the CO of the 77th Engineers, then 1st Lieutenant Charles M. Bussey, coming up to check on the wellbeing of the platoon earlier attached to the infantry battalion, observed a large body of men outflanking the attacking battalion and fired over the head of the suspected enemy with a .50 caliber machine gun mounted on one of the trucks left behind by the attacking American battalion. Bussey, along with two infantrymen manning a .30 caliber truck-mounted machine gun, began firing directly at the men now identified as enemy by Bussey. Enemy mortar fire was placed on the two trucks; one of the infantrymen was killed one wounded; but Bussey unharmed kept firing. When he ceased firing, 258 North Koreans (by actual count accomplished immediately afterward) lay dead!

Bussey was recommended for a DSC for this action. Colonel Corley (who was not his line superior nor in any way involved with the separate engineer company administratively) called Bussey in and told him that, for certain reasons of a racial discriminatory nature, he would receive a Silver Star instead. Bussey was awarded a Silver Star on a divisional general order for this action.

Within the past few years, working with Bussey on a history of the 77th Engineer Combat Company, "IN A HIGHER TRADITION", I learned for the first time what had actually transpired at Yechon. I subsequently sent a telegram to the President of the United States citing Bussey's actions and suggesting that it would be appropriate to review all of the foregoing with the idea that Bussey should actually receive the Congressional Medal of Honor. I am in touch with the Army's military awards branch concerning the possibility of this award and enclose this correspondence along with a copy of "IN A HIGHER TRADITION" and another work, "SOARING LIKE EAGLES – WALKING WITH TURKEYS", that I recently did. This latter work is the story of one battalion of the 24th Infantry Regiment as seen by three engineer officers. Most importantly, for the interest I share with you and Major Greene, the story serves to suggest why the 24th Infantry Regiment performed as it did in Korea- -i.e., in a spotty manner, both good and bad- -and actually proves in a limited sense the suggestion.

Some incidental information about the 24th Infantry Regiment:

- The original regimental CO and his successor CO could not "cut the mustard—one because, being willing and capable, he was too old and feeble; the other, being unqualified in every sense of the word.

- The Third CO chronologically, Colonel John T. Corley, USMA '39, served in Europe during WWII with the 1st Infantry Division as a battalion CO and was the most decorated Regular officer—Audie Murphy being the most decorated officer, period. Corley won a DSC and five Silver Stars in WWII and received another DSC and three additional Silver Stars, not all earned by the way, in Korea. He became a brigadier general after Korea and died a few years ago. Colonel Corley had an intense rivalry with Colonel John H. Michaelis USMA '36, CO of the 27th "Wolfhound" Regiment who was the boy friend of the New York Herald – Tribune's Marguerite Higgins and thereby the most famous regimental commander in Korea. (During the Battle of Kunuri, I happened to be alone with these two regimental COs both out of touch with the division commanding general. They discussed how to handle matters and then got into a heated argument over who, being senior to the other, was going to tell the other what to do. I stepped up to stop one or the other from throwing the first punch but, fortunately, comparing dates of temporary promotions throughout their respective careers, both realized that Corley was actually senior to Michaelis. Instantly, Michaelis came to attention, saluted, said, "Very well, John", and left to carry out Corley's orders.

- The regimental officers were mixed Black and White—Whites being senior staff officers and battalion COs and largely company COs. Among the outstanding Black officers were Major Richard D. Williams, Regimental S-2; Captain Roger Walden, Company F CO who years before as a sergeant had been the first Black paratrooper; and Captain "Heavy" Mike Keiler, Heavy Mortar Company CO. Williams and Walden had previously been officers in the 3rd Battalion, 505th

Parachute Infantry Regiment, Fort Knox, Kentucky. Walden's company was generally considered to be the best in the regiment; and Williams had been promoted in Korea after being recognized as perhaps the best company-grade officer in the regiment. (about one year earlier, while the new West Point first class was touring Army posts during the summer, Williams' and Walden's friend, Captain Baker, had loaned me his car and his uniform shirt to take his girl friend out on a date one evening!) Perhaps the 3rd Battalion 505th was assigned to Fort Bragg, Kentucky. Then—I forget now.

- The non-commissioned officers in the regiment were largely outstanding- -in many instances they could and did act to replace the company-grade officers, white and Black, who were killed or wounded and out of action; and, in a few instances, they would act to rectify errors committed by those among the company-grade officers who were less than qualified.

- By and large, the regiment performed only as well as any organization could when officered by a group of officers that was, largely, incompetent. Colonel Corley's immediate predecessor and his immediate successor as regimental CO were both wholly incompetent. His successor compounded things by being a drunkard as well. (I have personally received combat instructions by Corley's successor, Colonel Henry C. Britt, USMA '32, when he was too drunk and/or too confused even to know on which bank of an important river- -friendly or enemy side, that is- -one of his battalions was located.)

- The regiment's predicament was somewhat compounded by the presence of a battalion CO, Lieutenant Colonel Melvin Russell Blair, winner of two DSC's during WWII with Merrill's Marauders in the CBI Theatre, who was perhaps a legitimate hero during WWII but was a coward, an incompetent, a liar, and in most every way a troublemaker while serving in Korea with the 24th Infantry. He was quoted extensively in the Saturday Evening Post during 1951, making derogatory statements about the Black soldiers under his command, when he himself happened to be the sorriest soldier in the battalion. (It so happened that I was the individual most familiar with his derelictions—asleep while his rifle companies were heavily engaged, unknowing and uncaring about their predicament, failing to discharge his command responsibility, failing to communicate the whereabouts of his HQ and his battle dispositions to the regimental CO—at a critical juncture during the Battle of Kunuri and perhaps the individual Army officer closest to the scene when this sad sack was arrested during 1958 while unsuccessfully attempting to rob the box office at the Bing Crosby golf tournament at Pebble Beach, California.)

The 159th Field Artillery Battalion was a thoroughly professional organization officered almost entirely by whites. The noncommissioned officers and enlisted men- all Black— were superb soldiers. I myself did not have too much contact with the artillery battalion, but it deservedly enjoyed a top notch reputation.

Our unit, the 77th Engineer Combat Company, was perhaps the finest unit in the entire Army. (By the way, there is a small error on Page 214: William Benefield, a winner of the DSC posthumously, was an officer in the 77th (not 74th) Engineers as was Chester J. Lenon, another DSC winner on Page 215.) The company had actually received perhaps more decorations among individual officers and men than any other unit in Korea during the early days of the Korean conflict—i. e., before Bob Green and I joined it in late August, 1950. In my platoon I had an assistant squad leader who had earlier in his service been a regimental sergeant-major. There was probably not a finer bunch of NCOs anywhere in the Army. Although the T/O strength for a divisional engineer combat company was five officers and 153 EM, we had nine officers and 253 men present for duty—every EM a Regular Army soldier. Two of our officers were white—Lt. Paul D. Wells of Texas, an ex-infantry officer who actually outranked Bussey but who had been instructed and agreed to serve as Bussey's second-in-command and did a fine job; and Lt. Carroll N. LeTellier, a 1949 graduate of The Citadel, who eventually became a major general, Corps of Engineers, Regular Army, before being retired for disability a few years ago. (When Carroll's father, a professor at The Citadel, died just a few years ago, Carroll went through his personal possessions and found in his wallet a letter that Bussey had written to his father about his son in Korea back in 1950!)

The 77th Engineers were a separate unit, assigned to the 25th Infantry Division and sometimes attached to the 65th Engineer Combat Battalion (Which had only three lettered companies to accommodate the 77th as a fourth company), 25th Infantry Division. Actually we functioned much like a battalion ourselves—we turned out as much engineering work as the rest of the 65th Engineers. But we normally functioned in support of (and sometimes attached to) the 24th Infantry Regiment.

I have frequently observed Bussey (and, after I became company CO myself, I have myself) received three sets of mutually conflicting operational orders—one from the division headquarters, one from the 65th Engineers, and one from the 24th Infantry. On various occasions he would elect to do the most important job the next day, or the most dangerous, or the safest, or the most fun—it was up to him to decide. And, of course, there was never any repercussions.

Occasionally, when he chose to put his men's interest foremost, Bussey would "con" someone into giving him the assignment he preferred. Once, after being hit by the Chinese during the winter of 1950, we fell back with the whole of the Eighth US Army into a defensive line well north of Pyongyang. That morning, for the first and only time in my experience, we received a message from General MacArthur addressed to field organization and unit commanders telling us that "one million Chinese (it was actually only half a million –our intelligence was faulty as usual) had entered the field against us and we had to hold the positions we were in or risk being annihilated"—that's almost a direct quote. Bussey did not want to be assigned with his company to a frontline defensive position by the CO of the 24th Infantry Regiment—a normal assignment which could be expected. Instead he went to Corley and asked him, inasmuch as we were sitting in the middle of the division sector and it would be some three to five miles to go laterally to reach a main north-south route in the event we had to evacuate the regiment's position, how would Corley like us to construct an "escape" route for him. Corley asked how long it would take. (Now, we had no heavy equipment at all at this juncture—no bulldozers, no truck-mounted air compressor, nothing but hand tools.) Bussey said he would construct a road by improving a narrow trail overnight, but he would have to have a couple of tanks assigned to use as earthmovers, essentially as bulldozers. Corley said, fine, go to it and issued orders to Lt. Francis "Fritz" Nordstrom, a legendary armor officer (who had been a tank company commander since the North African Theatre phase of WWII but had never made captain since he refused to get along amicably with any battalion commander superior to him), to let us have two tanks. Working through the night, we had the road passable to infantry vehicular traffic (i.e., 2 – ½ ton trucks towing 1-ton trailers) by daylight.

That afternoon Bussey fortuitously received orders for us to move south to begin preparing new defensive positions. We left just about dusk, electing to drive some five miles westward along the MLR to intersect the MSR southward. Shortly after we pulled out the Chinese attacked in strength, forcing the 24th Infantry Regiment and other friendly forces to withdraw. The regiment withdrew in good order down the newly-constructed "escape" route.

As occasionally would happen, early during the Korean conflict, the North Koreans would drive our forces back and disrupt normal command procedures. Whenever this happened Bussey would seek (or be sought by) the 24th's Heavy Mortar Company and the tank company—D Company of the 89th Medium Tank Battalion under Lt. Colonel Welborn G. Dolvin, USMA '39 (see Major Greene's reference to him on Page 213, ninth line from the bottom)- - commanded by Nordstrom. These three units would form an informal task force- -armor, (Nordstrom); infantry (Bussey, combat engineers); and artillery (Keiler, heavy mortars) - -and literally take on anything the North Koreans could throw at them.

On this page I am making the point about informal decision processes and spontaneous organization deliberately. These features became a way of life with us in the 77th Engineers- -so much so, that whenever Bussey and then I would receive an operational order by telephone from some "superior" officer; we would invariably acknowledge the order but, before acting on it, we would call another "superior" officer to verify that what we had been told was known and agreed to by the other(s).

Years later- -talking with a Black West Point graduate who served in combat in Vietnam- -I was told that the successful combat units in Vietnam were known as "Blood" Units- -i.e., they tended to verify everything in the way of operational orders and to spontaneously take actions appropriate to circumstances, developments, situations either unknown to or unanticipated by their superiors or higher headquarters. I was not in Vietnam, but it was my impression from my Korean experience that the US Army was going to have to develop the capability for fighting "informally" at the unit level if it were going to prevail successfully over unorthodox enemy forces in future wars.

Bussey and I have written about our combat engineer unit without reference to official Army documents or histories, primarily so that there would be no possibility of our being "muzzled" as we told our story. Fortunately, "IN A HIGHER TRADITION" has been well received by the Pentagon. A former Army chief of public affairs, Major General Robert B. Soloman (a personal friend of our ex-company fellow officer, Major General Carroll N. LeTellier, retired), being assured by Carroll of our story's authenticity, has referred to the work as the "most stirring account of unit achievement and individual heroism" to come out of the Korean conflict. General Soloman some three years ago pledged the Pentagon's full cooperation in assisting our efforts to produce the work. Somewhat amusingly, he assured us that whenever we were ready he would have the Army make available to us as many Black soldiers as we required for filming- -you may realize that the Army now refuses anyone's request to make all-White units available for filming.

However, we did (and continue to) run into flak as we attempted to have the Army's chief military historian review and correct the official version of the Battle of Yechon published in

From the Naktong to the Yalu, one of five volumes in the Army's official history of the Korean conflict. This brigadier general – chief historian actually stated (in reply to a communication from my Congressman, Julian C. Dixon, Black) that the author of this volume, being a historian, had the prerogative of interpreting events as he chose. Congressman Dixon, instead of replying that the Army and its historians had no right to misrepresent actual facts and make disparaging remarks about official war correspondents such as the Pittsburgh Courier's James B. Hicks, received this assertion without comment and informed me that I could do more research into these matters. Clearly it's the Army which needs to do further research!

That's about where matters stand. It's now Monday, August 17. I reached Major Greene by phone yesterday and discovered how dedicated an outstanding an individual he is. I believe that there is more important work for Major Greene to do- -to establish and perhaps direct the functioning of a center for Black American military history. I have some thoughts along this line which I shall convey to him and, if you are interested, to you as well; and I believe that it will be possible to obtain public funds to establish and support such an activity as an academic adjunct to a functioning department of history at a predominantly Black college/university within convenient commuting range of Federal archives in Washington, DC. I also believe that it will be possible to obtain the full cooperation of the US armed forces and perhaps the various service academies as well. I happen to have extensive experience in contributing to the establishment of academic undertakings similar to this on predominantly Black campuses, and I would be pleased to make my services available for this purpose. What do you say?

I would be very pleased to hear from you once you have had the opportunity to read and digest all of the enclosures I am sending. And I am delighted to have had the opportunity of chatting with you and getting to know you by phone last week.

    Every good wish,

    DAVE

Carlisle wrote me the following letter on August 16, 1981.

August 16, 1981

Dear Bob,

I very much enjoyed our telephone conversation this morning.

Rather than write a long, detailed letter to you to accompany the various enclosures I mentioned to you, I'm sending you this short note along with a copy of the letter I had started to Harold Lewis.

Charles Bussey and I would very much appreciate any assistance you choose to render to us vis-à-vis "IN A HIGHER TRADITION" or "SOARING LIKE EAGLES - WALKING WITH TURKEYS". Both of these works are registered with the Writers Guild of America and we are, therefore, fully protected. I believe that "IN A HIGHER TRADITION" can become the basis for a television special or mini-series; I don't really see it as a motion picture. We are seeking to have it produced for the widest possible general viewing audience. We have had several expressions of interest from Black production companies that have seen it as a run-of-the-mill Black violence "shoot 'em up" movie- -we are not at all interested. We see the production, on television, of a quality equal to "PATTON" or "THE LONGEST DAY" or whatever.

Obviously there may prove to be interest in a more modest production for public television or whatever. This possibility led me to dash off "SOARING LIKE EAGLES..." about a year ago.

We both have a genuine interest in one day being able to publish "IN A HIGHER TRADITION" as a professionally researched, fully documented, comprehensive history of the 77th Engineers in Korea. Neither of us has been able to devote the time and effort to a task of this magnitude and, because of the distance between us and the official records presumably in Washington, DC, we have done what we could do to this point.

The effort I undertook several months ago in connection with a Congressional Medal of Honor for Bussey is separate and distinct from the task of writing the two works. Because I recognized that a base of support in Washington would be helpful I contacted my Congressman, Julian C. Dixon, who is Black. Nothing happened of a positive nature for several months so I began checking into things to find that someone was either not at all interested or "scared" to attempt to get the Army's chief military historian to correct the official version of the Battle of Yechon contained in FROM THE NAKTONG TO THE YALU. (See the enclosed correspondence with Dixon et al.) Checking with Dixon himself, I was put in touch with one of his staff members- - a young lady- -who told me he was keenly interested in working on assignment from Dixon toward a positive result because she grew up with Lt. William Benefield's daughter in Kansas. Well, it's about 18 months later and, despite some 10 telephone calls from me (one of which the young lady returned). I haven't heard a damn thing. So about three months ago I suggested that Dixon's office simply return the various materials to me.

Whatever ideas you have along either direction- -the military award for Bussey or getting either of the works published/produced- - please let me know. If something does develop from your efforts you will have an interest in whatever monetary rewards come to us equal to mine or

Bussey's. (By the way, we have an agreement to put one-half of whatever comes to us into a nonprofit foundation/organization designed to render assistance directly to any former member of the 77th Engineers in need of assistance.)

I want to make one point strongly; Bussey and I do not contend that the story of the 77th Engineers is to be considered as the only or best or ultimate story of a Black military unit in combat. We submit that it is probably typical of a number of Black combat units that have proven to be truly outstanding in the field where it counts but have, subsequently, never had their true story recorded. So we have labored to record the true story of our unit as illustrative of what an outstanding Black unit has accomplished- -fortunately, as COs of the unit, we have been able to achieve a documented and further documented chronological history which is probably unique in Black American military annals. We consider our work as a tribute to every Black American military unit and to every Black American soldier/sailor/marine/airman.

Now to a basic point: I have been interested for several years in assisting in the establishment of a center of Black American military history. (Back in 1971, being contacted by Lieutenant General William A. Knowlton, than West Point superintendent, about practical methods for increasing the enrollment of Blacks as cadets, I suggested that the most fundamental requirement would be for West Point's department of military history to accomplish a comprehensive study of the contributions of Black units/individuals to American military history. Being familiar with the work of Colonel Campbell C. Johnson, see your work, Page 313 for his photo, my wife's late uncle, in recording the exploits of Blacks in the military, I realized that the Regular Army by and large did not accept such "special" studies.) I believe it will prove to be possible, given your demonstrated interest in and achievements in this field, to interest the US Army and USMA in working jointly with, say, Howard University's History Department, to establish such a center as a formal academic undertaking in the Washington area convenient to the archives; I believe that funds can be made available for this purpose from the Federal Government to establish and support such an undertaking. And I am more than willing to assist you obtain such funds with the thought that you- -should you be so inclined- -would become involved in such an undertaking on a fulltime, paid basis. There must necessarily be the condition that you would find support for such an undertaking from a given academic institution (say Howard University - -what do you say?

(I say the foregoing, knowing of the parallel efforts toward establishing at West Point both a Jewish chapel and museum of American – Jewish military history principally championed by my good friend and Class of '49 companymate, Richard D. Rosenblatt. I believe it to be a given that, contrary to the largely private funds which Dick obtained for his purpose and a West Point – located center, we would have to depend almost entirely on public funds. Further, for successful research, such a center would almost certainly have to be located at least initially in the Washington area.)

And, of course, we should certainly attempt to have such an effort receive the full participation of the DOD, not just the Army.

I'll close here and get this in the mail to you and to Harold Lewis.

Every good wish,

DAVE

I was very pleased and honored when Captain David R Carlisle sent me a copy of his article, "Black Combat Units In Korean War Action" and suggested that I incorporate it in my published works. It is a privilege and honor to include this article in this book. I dedicate it as a memorial to David whose efforts to review the records of the regiment were not in vain.

BLACK COMBAT UNITS IN KOREAN WAR ACTION

The Korean War (1950 to 1953) was the last American conflict involving segregated units of the armed forces, i.e., the US Army. Three American Infantry Divisions - -the 25th, the 2nd, and the 3rd- -contained Black combat units during 1950/51.

Among the 25th Division's three infantry regiments was the Army's last black 24th Infantry, the largest black unit to serve in Korea. (The 24th Infantry was also the Army's only three-battalion regiment in action during initial weeks of the war. Other American regiments first committed to action from peacetime occupation duty in Japan contained only two battalions.) Accompanied by the black 159th Field Artillery Battalion and the black 77th Engineer Combat Company, the 24th Infantry arrived in the Korean Combat Zone beginning July 13. On July 20 the 24th's 3rd Battalion, reinforced by a battery of the 159th and a platoon of the 77th, was the first 25th Division element to go into action at Yechon. In an extraordinary two-day action hailed around the world as the US' initial Korean War victory, the reinforced battalion drove the enemy from the town and recaptured it at a cost of two Americans killed and 10 wounded in action to at least 258 enemy dead.

Subsequently, the 24th Regimental Combat Team

- Held the most vital part of the Pusan Perimeter August/September, taking and retaking Battle Mountain 19 times in 30 days

- Led portions of 25th Division's breakout and advance west northward to the outskirts of Seoul mid-September

- Advanced in North Korea to within a few miles of the Yalu River during late November, and then staged a fighting withdrawal as the Chinese entered the war astride the Chongchon River and in the vicinity of Kunu-ri

- Crossed the Han River near Seoul with two other 25th Division regiments on March 7, 1951 (an important part of what UN Supreme Commander General Matthew B. Ridgway characterized years later as "the most successful single action fought by troops under my command during either World War II in Europe, or in Korea")

- Crossed the Hantan River northeast of Seoul alone April 11 in the face of determined resistance from a superior enemy occupying the commanding terrain

- Stormed the heights above Mando and ejected the enemy from fortified positions with a bayonet charge and hand to hand fighting with hand grenades, med-September, 1951

During early August, 1950, the 9th Infantry Regiment's black 3rd Battalion and the black 503rd Field Artillery Battalion arrived in Korea with other 2nd Division elements. Initially, the Black battalion, a Black artillery battery, a tank company, and a company of engineers were detached and withheld from front line action and assigned to guard a airfield near Pohang. In early September heavy combat losses among the 9th Infantry's two white battalions led to the assignment of some 200 black soldiers as individual replacements, a practice heartily endorsed by the regimental commander, Colonel Charles C. Sloane, Jr. During mid-September, having been introduced gradually to combat action near Pohang and elsewhere, the 3rd Battalion rejoined in time to strengthen the 9th Infantry in attempting to break out from the Pusan Perimeter. During late November the last segregated 24th Infantry (on the right of the 25th Division) and the first integrating 9th Infantry (on the left of the 2nd Division) advanced in northern most North Korea side by side astride the Chongchon River. On November 25, hit more heavily (than the 24th, the hardest hit of the 25th Division's regiments) by the Chinese, the 9th Infantry fought extraordinarily well as two integrated and one segregated battalion, the latter temporarily reinforced two nights running by two rifle companies separated from the 24th's fighting 2nd Battalion. By the night of November 29 the 9th Infantry had been reduced to some 600 effectives as had its sister 38th Infantry. On the morning of November 30, these 600, spearheading the 2nd Division's desperate attempt to withdraw south from Kunu-ri, surrounded by the enemy, were virtually wipe out and the 2nd Division was effectively destroyed. But a rebuilt 9th Infantry Regiment, thoroughly integrated, thereafter acquitted itself well in action after action during 1951.

The 3rd Infantry Division, complete with the black 3rd Battalion, 15th Infantry Regiment, disembarked at Wonsan in northeast Korea in mid-November, 1950, joining X Corps commanded by Major General Edward M. Almond, notorious for his racist attitudes commanding the Black 92nd Infantry Division in Italy during World War II. The division included, in addition to the Puerto Rican 65th Infantry Regiment, the black 64th Tank Battalion while the Corps-level Black 58th and 999th Field Artillery Battalions provided supporting firepower. After acquitting itself well in a defensive role during the evacuation of Hagaru and Hungnam, the 15th's 3rd Battalion excelled in early February, 1951, and on May 19/20 at Pungnam.

The performance of Black artillery and armor battalions in Korea was consistently superior. The 25th Division's 159th Field Artillery never lost a gun to the enemy, a record that few other 105-mm. gun battalions could match. The 77th Engineer Combat Company- -eventually the last black combat unit of the US Army ever to engage an enemy of the US- -was perhaps the most decorated single American unit in Korean War action. Two of its officers, 2nd Lts. Chester M. Benefield and Chester J. Lenon, earned Distinguished Service Crosses during the initial weeks of the war, Benefield posthumously.

The 24th Infantrymen, Private First Class William Thompson and Sergeant Cornelius H. Charlton, posthumously were awarded the first Medals of Honor to black fighting men since Spanish-American war days (excepting, as of April, 1991, the Medal of Honor awarded to a heroic World War I black 371st Infantryman). Another 24th Infantryman, Corporal Levi A. Jackson, the US Army's heavyweight boxing champion, was posthumously awarded the Distinguished Service Cross. Yet another Distinguished Service Cross wearer, 24th Infantryman Sergeant Curtis Pugh, is alive and well. The 77th Engineers' commander, 1st Lt. Charles M. Bussey, was recommended for (but, apparently, wrongfully denied) both the Medal of Honor and the Distinguished Service Cross before having time enough in combat to be promoted to his World War II rank of captain. (Bussey, a fighter pilot in the pioneering black 332nd Fighter Group, flew 70 missions and scored two "kills", two probables, and two damaged enemy aircraft in aerial combat.) Another Distinguished Service Cross was awarded to 1st Lt. Ellison C. Wynn who took command of the 9th Infantry's integrated B Company and led it heroically until he was seriously wounded during bitter fighting in late November, 1950, astride the Chongchon River. No account of Black combat units and heroes in Korea would be complete without mentioning the late Major Richard

W. Williams, S-2, 24th Infantry Regiment, who served during World War II as a pioneering officer of the Black 555th Parachute Infantry Battalion; or of Captain Roger S. Walden, CO, F Company, 24th Infantry, the second longest-serving rifle company commander in frontline action in Korea (who also served during World War II as a pioneering NCO of the Black 555th Parachute Infantry Battalion). Or, finally, of the late 1st Lt. Harry E. Sutton, platoon leader, I Company, 15th Infantry, Silver Star at Hungnam, killed in action February, 1951, another pioneering Black paratrooper.

But the performance of some of these black combat units came into question, unjustly and unwarrantedly, during the war and afterward. The 24th Infantry Regiment was accused, even by the late Army Chief of Staff General J. Lawton Collins of "repeatedly breaking and running until the regiment was deactivated 1 October, 1951". (But the late General of the Army Omar N. Bradley's co-author of A General's Story, Clay Blair, himself a distinguished military historian, has recently informed the Army chief of military history in personal correspondence that he knows that, had General Bradley known of the true facts concerning the 24th Infantry's Korean War outstanding service, he would have rewritten portions of his autobiography in tribute to these brave American soldiers.) In early September, 1950, the 25th Infantry Division's commander, Major General William B. Kean, recommended to Eighth Army headquarters that the 24th Infantry be relieved of frontline combat service. This recommendation was ignored by the late General of the Army Douglas MacArthur and, subsequently, the record shows that the 24th Infantry fought at least as well as other American regiments during the remainder of its last tour of duty until deactivated October 1, 1951. During 1951, back in the US, the 24th's famous commanding officer, the late Brigadier General John T. Corley, sought to dispel others' criticism by pointing out that in action "exceeding in roughness" anything he had witnessed in Europe 24th Infantrymen had fought as well as his own 1st Infantry Division soldiers during World War II. But then-Colonel Corley was ordered to cease demonstrating his regard for his Korean War regiment by General Mark W. Clark because, reportedly, "some people in high places" were beginning to become alarmed.

Among some factors worth noting concerning the 24th Infantry's initial weeks' commitment to Korean War actions are

- On his first day in Korea in July, 1950, the original regimental executive officer feigned a heart attack and cowardly had himself medically evacuated

- There was not a physically fit/professionally competent regimental commanding officer until Lt. Colonel Corley succeeded to command September 6

- During its first three months in action the 24th Infantry experienced 13 changes (of which only two were casualty related) in battalion commanders as compared to one and three changes, respectively, in the 25th Division's other (i.e., White) regiments

It is interesting to note that none of these factors nor any of the 24th Regiment's outstanding combat successes has ever been officially recorded. But it has been recorded in the first of the Army's three volume official Korean War History covering the first five months of the war (including only the first four months of the 24th's 14 1/2-month Korean War Service) That black 24th Infantrymen "broke and ran", "ran away from the enemy", "threw down their weapons", "withdrew without a fight", "broke ranks", repeatedly, whereas these terms are not used in reference to other (i.e., White) US regiments whose initial weeks' combat performance was no better. Curiously, although the first volume was published in 1961 and the third volume in 1966, the second volume was not published until 1990. How, then, could a separate official history,

Integration of the Armed Forces 1940-65, published in 1982, assert that the 24th Infantry's overall KW performance was "poor" and the proximate factor in the decision to begin integrating Eighth Army in Korea? Particularly when the second volume's evenhanded treatment of US combat units, Black and White, in action from mid-November, 1950, to mid – 1951 (corresponding with another eight months of the 24th Infantry's service) indicates that this Black regiment performed its frontline combat duties as well as others.

During 1988, responding to representations by then-Congressman Gus Hawkins* and House Armed Services Committee Chairman Les Aspin, Secretary of the Army John O. Marsh, Jr. chartered a special board of review to determine the truth about the 24th Infantry Regiment in Korea. In another year or so this board will render a report to Secretary of the Army Michael PW Stone including an unprecedented official regimental-level history, the 24th Infantry during 1950/51.

(NOTE TO ROBERT GREENE: Because of your demonstrated singular quality of loyalty to black American fighting men and your unfailing selfless dedication to finding and recording the historical truth, I am pleased to submit this "Black Combat Units in Korean War Action" to you and your publishers for incorporation in any form without any obligation for acknowledging or otherwise recompensing me for my contributed material. (At the same time I am proud of my work and am perfectly willing to be identified as the author.) I offer this material to you as a small tribute to the memory of your late beloved son.)

DAVID K. CARLISLE, April 19, 1991

---

*It will be recalled that in 1972, Congressman Hawkins caused President Nixon to restore to the Army's honor rolls 165 Black 25th Infantrymen who wrongfully had been discharged without honor following their alleged involvement in 1906 in the infamous "Brownsville (Texas) Incident", by which time only two of these soldiers remained alive.

SELECTED BLACK UNITS THAT SERVED IN KOREA

3rd BATTALION 9th INFANTRY REGIMENT 2nd INFANTRY DIVISION

The 3rd Battalion was one of the integrated US Army Infantry units during the Korean War. The racial composition in B Company was 30 per cent Black, 60 per cent white and 10 per cent ROK (Republic of Korean soldiers).

It is quite possible that some of the African American officers and enlisted men were present and involved in the following combat tactical operations:

1. Pusan and Naktong area, 31 July, September, 1950
2. Pusan to Kunu`ri withdrawal of the Chinese offensive 25-28 November
3. Withdrawal, Sunchon North Korea, south of Pyongyang 1 December 1950
4. Chunghwa, North Korea, south of Pyong Yang, major withdrawal, 24 December 1950
5. Withdrawal movements at times near Seoul, Munsan Ni, Inchon and Yong dong Po, December 1950
6. Redeployment, areas of Changju and Chechon, 25-31 December 1950
7. Patron engagements in the areas of Wonju, Hoengsong, Chipyong`Ni, and Kwiron, 1 January – 20 February, 1951
8. The 3rd Battalion was a part of a task force, September, 1950 during the enemy penetration of Piohang-dong westward to Taegu and the Naktong river

On January 13, 1951 the 3rd Battalion was involved in a combat operation with the 187 Airborne Regimental Combat Team (RCT) near the towns of Punggi and Tanyang. It was reported that the 3rd Battalion lead the attack and was able to occupy a position on the side of the mountain pass.

Some personnel that were assigned to the 9th Infantry regiment and performed well during various combat operations were Private First Class (PFC) Laurence Smith, a squad leader. While leading his squad at Chongchon, Korea, Smith was wounded. Master Sergeant Herbert Smith, Savannah, GA, PFC George Chapel, PFC Whitehurst, PFC Brasfield, Corporal (CPL) Walter Crawford, South Boston, Virginia, PVT James Warmley, PVT Robert Noel, PVT Charles Murray, PVT John Howard, Lt. Ellison Wynn, PVT Paul Frost, Capt. Eldridge Carter, Cleveland, Ohio, and Capt. William Wallace were present for duty with the 9th Infantry Regiment in Korea.

The 3rd Battalion, 9th Infantry Regiment made significant contributions to the overall success of the 2nd Infantry division during the Korean War.

SECOND INFANTRY RANGER COMPANY AIRBORNE

The US Army decided on July 23, 1950 to create an all Black Ranger Company. The Unit was activated on September 29, 1950, and the men entered the Ranger training program at Fort Benning, GA on October 9, 1950. The Unit trained along with the all white 4th Rangers. The first commanding officer of the Second Rangers was First Lieutenant (1Lt.) Warren E. Allen of Los Angeles, CA. He was a veteran of WWII. Upon completion of their training in December, 1950, the Second Rangers departed for Camp Stoneman, CA. Later they sailed for the Far East aboard the USS General Butner with stops at Pearl Harbor and Yokohoma, Japan enroute to Korea. Upon their arrival in Korea, the Unit was attached to the Seventh Infantry Division.

The basic weapons of the Ranger Co. were 30 caliber carbine, automatic pistol .45 caliber, 30 Caliber Browning automatic rifle, 30 caliber M1918A3 45 caliber sub machine gun M3A1, crew served weapons, 3.5 inch rocket launchers 60 MM mortar, 30 caliber machine gun and three 57 MM recoilless rifles.

In commemoration of the 50th Anniversary of the conclusion of the Korean War, numerous books, brochures and articles have been published on the Korean War. Unfortunately this vast amount of literature has not addressed the heroic exploits of the Second Ranger Co. The following accounts of the Ranger's combat actions during the war substantiates that fact and eradicates any myths that African Americans cannot and are afraid to fight under extreme combat conditions.

When the Second Rangers were attached to the 17th Regimental Combat Team (RCT) during the capture of Chechon, Korea, they were their assisting in the combat operations. It was reported that Ranger James Oakley was caught in a current and drowned.

The 187th RCT had the 2nd and 4th Ranger Companies attached in operation Tomahawk as well as eight US Army's airborne support for operation Ripper. The Second Ranger Co. participated in the air combat jump on March 23, 1951, at Munsan`Ni, Korea. Its mission was to siege Hill 151. There were two men injured in the jump and received medical assistance from the Indian Field Ambulance Unit.

Several heroic acts occurred near the Second Ranger's assembly area. 1[St] Sergeant West observed a North Korean machine gunner about to commence firing on their position. Immediately 1st Sgt. West executed a surprise attach on the enemy's position and was able to capture some men and weapons from the 36th Regiment, 19th North Korean division.

A durable Chinese force conducted a counter attack near the Second Rangers' position and their covering force was practically depleted. The only member that possibly survived was Ranger William E. Rhodes of Bridgeport, CT. As some Chinese were moving toward Rhodes he assumed a prone position as though he was dead. The Chinese began to gather their casualties and confiscation of weapons and Rhodes' rifle, watch and ammunition belt was taken. When the Chinese left the area, Rhodes was able to travel toward his command post; however, some Chinese troops observed him and fired several rounds. Again he was far away from the enemy to play dead again. This time the Chinese took his socks, boots, wallet, cap and coat. When it appeared safe, Rhodes continued to move toward his Unit's position. He was able to receive assistance from a South Korean couple for three days. Some allied troops arrived in the village and Rhodes was able to report to his Company.

Some North Korean troops made a serious attempt to assault and move through a Second Ranger Company's roadblock. The Rangers successfully repulsed the enemy but did sustain some casualties. It was reported that SFC. Isaac Baker was killed. The wounded were Rangers Burke Webb, Craig Paulding, and Wheeler Small.

On January 9, 1951 the Second Ranger Co. was in a combat action near the town of Changnim-Ni and Ranger Sherman Daniels was wounded.

The Ranger Co. was given a mission on January 14, 1951 to capture the Village of Majori. They confronted a very hostile enemy force in the village and became involved in a firefight in which enable them to force the enemy to withdraw from the village. The Chinese tried to counter attack and the Rangers sustained some casualties while defending their positions. The reported casualties were Rangers Milton Johnson, Frank King, J. Holley, Richard Glover, Charles Scott, Robert StThomas, Herman Rembert and Laurence Williams.

The Second Rangers, with aerial fire support of F-51 Air Force fighters and 81 MM mortar directed by Lt. James Queen, Executive Officer, were able to assault a strategic hill and defensive position. The rewarding results were assisting in restoring a stable and friendly atmosphere in the village of Sangdokso'ri. The Rangers had two wounded SFC Daniel Boatwright and Sgt. Smead Robertson.

During a fierce battle with the Chinese on a hill, the Second Rangers were able to inflict fifty Chinese casualties and wounded ninety Chinese soldiers. There was one death Ranger Ralph Sutton and several wounded. The most serious wounded was Ranger Herman Jackson. The Company provided support to the 5th Marine Regiment and the 31st Regimental Combat Teams near the Hongchon Gang River where the action occurred.

A mission was assigned to three Rangers of the Second Co. to provide security for the US 7th Infantry division's outpost. The Rangers were PFC Sherrell Smith, Houston, TX, Sgt. Howard Squires, Pittsburgh, PA and Corporal Marion Alston, Nashville, NC

The members of the Ranger Company represented many cities and states. Some of them were: Baltimore, MD Corporal Samuel Payne; Washington, DC, Lt. James Queen; Chattanooga, TN, 1st Sgt. Laurence West; New York, NY, Pfc. Jose A. Escarela; New York City, NY Corporal William Hanes; Bridgeport, CT, William Rhodes; Columbus, OH, Sgt. Robert Watkins; Detroit MI, Lt. Albert Cliette; Chicago, IL, Corporal Roy Rhone; New Brunswick, NJ, Sgt. John Jones; Houston, TX, Pfc. Scherrell Smith

The 2nd Ranger Infantry Company participated in the Chinese Communist soldiers' first intervention, the first UN Command counter offensive, Chinese spring offensive, UN Command Summer – Fall offensive. The Company received the Korean Presidential Unit Citation and the Combat Infantry Streamers. The Commanding General, Major General Ferenbaugh 7th US Infantry division made some inspiring and commendable remarks about the 2nd Ranger Co.. He stated: "On every occasion the performance of the 2nd Ranger Co. has been highly praised by Commanders who have assigned missions to the organizations. Their specialized training and high esprit de corps due to their volunteer status makes the assignment desirable to augment one's fighting unit."

The 8th US Army's general order number 584, dated July 25, 1951 inactivated the 2nd Ranger Co. along with the other Ranger Units effective August 1, 1951. Prior to the inactivation, it was reported that some white soldiers were assigned to the Company. Therefore it is believed that the following roster of the 2nd Ranger Co. should be inclusive of its original African American soldiers

ROSTER OF THE ALL BLACK RANGER UNIT IN THE KOREAN WAR
2nd RANGER INFANTRY COMPANY AIRBORNE

ADAMS, EDWARD
ADAMS, LOUIS
ADELL, ALLEN
ADKINS, LEGREE
ALLEN, DONALD
ALLEN, WARREN
ALSTON, MARION
ANDERSON, JESSIE
ANDRADE, ANTHONY
ANDREA, TEEDIES
ANTHONY, ANTONIO
ARNOLD, EUGENE
BAKER, ISAAC
BANKS, NELSON
BARTON, RICHARD
BEDLEY, BETHEL
BELL, JOHN
BEVERLY, WILLIAM
BIVENS, GEORGE
BOATWRIGHT, DANIEL
BROWN, JAMES
BRISCOE, RICHARD
BUFORD, DAVID
BURSE, THOMAS
BUSH, HOMER
BYNUM, GEORGE
BYRD, LLEWELLYN
CAMPBELL, MACK
CAMPOS, VICTOR
CARRELL, JAMES
CLARKE, DAVID
CLEVELAND, CLINTON
CLEAVELAND, VARLEY
CLIETTE, ALBERT
COCKAYNE, JOHN
COLEMAN, EUGENE
COLEMAN, WILLIE
COLLINS, NORMAN
COLLINS, VIRL
COURTS, CURTIS
DANIELS, SHERMAN
DAVIS, JAMES
DAVIS, RICHARD
DEFRAFFINREED, PAUL
DIAS, HERCULANEO

JOHNSON, HAROLD
JOHNSON, MILTON
JONES, JOHN
JULIUS, VICTOR
KELLY JOSEPH
KING, FRANK
LAND, ELMORE
LANIER, WILLIAM
LEARY, FRED
LEE, HOSEY
LEGGS, RALPH
LESURE, DAVID
LEWIS, CHARLES
LEWIS, GORDON
LOFTON, MATTHEW
LOUNDES, JOHN
LUCUS, ERNEST
LYLES, PAUL
MASON, JACOB
MATHIS, WILLIAM
MCBRIDE, CLEAVEN
MCLEAN, LESLIE
MCPHERSON, WILLIAM
MILLER, NED
MITCHELL, GEORGE
MOLSON, GEORGE
MONTE, JAMES
NEEL, GORDON
NEWMAN, RICHARD
NIXON, SAMUEL
NUNLEY, JOHN
OAKLEY, JAMES
OLIVER, HOWARD
OLIVER, JOE
PARKS, NATHAN
PAULDING, CRAIG
PAYNE, SAMUEL
PETTERESS, JAMES
PLATER, JAMES
POPE, JAMES
POSEY, EDWARD
PRYOR, BERNARD
QUEEN, JAMES
RACALERA, JOSE
RANKINS, GEORGE

ENGLEMAN, HARVEY
ESCARELA, JOSE
ESTELL, LAURENCE
EVANS, JAMES
FELDER, DONALD
FEREBEE, ROBERT
FIELDS, JAMES
FLETCHER, HENRY
FORD,, JOHN
FOSTER, ALBERT
FREEMAN, JAMES
FULTON, ROBERT
GALINGTON, OLIVER
GARLAND, LESTER
GERMUN, GERARD
GIBSON, CULVER
GLOVER, RICHARD
GORDON, ANDREW
GORDAN, MORGAN
GOULD, JOHN
GRAHAM, EARL
GRASTY, ISAAC
GRAY, WALTER
GREEN, HERMAN
GUDE, JAMES
GURIA, JOHN
HALL, CARL
HARDY, JIM
HARGROVE, WILLIAM
HARRIS, ELLSWORTH
HARRIS, WILLIAM
HARRISON, HERMAN
HARVEY, JAMES
HAWKINS, WILLIE
HENDERSON, JAMES
HIGGENBOTHAM, MCBERT
HILL, ROLAND
HODGE, ROLAND
HOLLAND, FLOYD
HOLLEY, J.
HOLINGER, WILLIAM
HOSEY, LEE
HOWARD, BENNIE
JACKSON, EARL
JACKSON, HERMAN
JACKSON, WINSTON
JENKINS, GLENN
JOHNSON, BRUCE
JOHNSON, EMMET

REESE, EARNEST
REMBERT, HERMAN
RHODES, WILLIAMS
RHONE, RAY
RIDDELL, WILLIAM
ROBERTSON, SNEAD
ROGERS, MONTELL
SCOTT, CHARLES
SCOTT, SAMUEL
SHADE, WILLIAM
SIMMS, WILLIAM
SMALL, WHEELER
SMITH, ROBERT
SMITH, SCHERRELL
SMITH, SUMERRELL
SQUIRES, HOWARD
ST. MARTIN, JUDE
ST. THOMAS, ROBERT
STROTHERS, STEWART
SUTTON, RALPH
TATE, BILLIE
TAYLOR, JAMES
TERRELL, JOHN
THOMAS, GEORGE
THOMAS, WILLIAM
TUCKER, ORRIE
VAILS, ROBERT
VALERY, CLEVELAND
VAN DUNK, WILLIAM
VICTOR, JULIUS
WADE, VIRGIL
WALKER, JAMES
WASHIHGTON, WILLIAM
WATKINS, ROBERT
WEATHERSBEE, WILLIAM
WEBB, BURKE
WELLS, JOSEPH
WEST, DONALD
WEST LAURENCE
WEST, RAMON
WHITE, LEROY
WHITEMORE, JOSEPH
WILBURN, VINCENT
WILLIAMS, AIKINS
WILLIAMS, LAURENCE
WILLIAMSON, OTIS
WILSON, HENRY
WILSON, WILLIAM
WODDARD, ISAIAH
WRIGHT, WILLIAM

503ᴿᴰ FIELD ARTILLERY BATTALION
2ᴺᴰ US INFANTRY DIVISION

The 503rd Field Artillery Battalion (FAB) was activated in 1947 as an all Black unit, on December 27 at Fort Lewis, Washington replacing the 12th FAB. The Unit's history goes back to the 351st Field Artillery Regiment, 1917, WW I.

The 503rd arrived in Pusau, Korea on August 16, 1950, aboard the ship USS General William Mitchell. The Unit's strength was 607 enlisted men and 40 officers. The first combat role was near the Naktong river area where artillery support was being provided to assist in the destruction of a North Korean Force. Some 2500 rounds were fired and no casualties were sustained.

In September, 1950 while providing support to the 9th Infantry Regiment, the 503red received some casualties. They were Corporal L. E. Johnson and Corporal James W. Dixon of Battery C; in addition, Battery A's Corporal Gabriel Mackall was killed and Pfc. Bernard Scott was wounded in action. Sgt. Russell Vann, Chief of Howitzer Section Battery C was also wounded.

Battery A of the battalion was involved in a combat situation on September 4, 1950. Lt. Raymond Gilbert and his men Corporal Norman Crawford and Pfc. Charles Taylor were able to adjust their fire power on an enemy target where many were killed and an ammunition dump destroyed. During the month of September the 503rd fired approximately 11,000 rounds inflicting damage on the enemy in support of the infantry.

On October 10, 1950, the 503rd was located near Anyang-Ni Korea in a reserve position training and maintaining their equipment. Some members of the Unit were instructed to drive their one half ton cargo trucks to assist the truck companies in moving supplies from Seoul to Pyongyang, Capital of North Korea.

The 503rd Field Artillery Battalion along with the 2nd US Infantry Division "suffered one of the greatest defeats in the history of the US. The 503rd had a total loss of 327 officers and enlisted men as well as equipment loss of 18 Howitzers and other equipment left on the road to Kunu-ri. The following account actually occurred: The Chinese Peoples Liberation Army began an assault offensive on 25 November, 1950. The Chinese inflicted many casualties on some US and South Korean Infantry troops. The Chinese attacked the 61st Field Artillery Battalion but were halted by the 23rd Infantry Regiment. The battle positions of the 503rd Battalion on 26 November were separate the main body had withdrawn five miles north toward a valley and Batteries B and C were supporting the 9th and 23rd Infantry Regiments while Battery A was still with the 38th Field Artillery Battalion.

The Chinese PLA's continual advances and assaults upon the US 2nd Infantry Division and the ROK corps caused the 2nd Infantry Division's commanding General, Lawrence B. Keiser to order the division to withdraw to the area of Kunu-ri in order to halt the advancing Chinese troops. The 503rd was instructed to establish positions in the vicinity of Kunu-ri. As the battle situation began to change for the worse scenario, the 2nd Division started to withdraw and attempted to develop defensive positions near the village of Chondong. The 503rd Battalion was tasked to move to positions below the town of Kunu-ri. This mission was assigned to Headquarters and Service Batteries. The 2nd Infantry Division continued its advance into North Korea. They confronted a strong Chinese Communist PLA in late October, 1950.

The 503rd was positioned near Sunch'on in November. Battery A was attached to the 38th Field Artillery Battalion, the 2nd Divisions' direct support Battalion. On 24 November Battery A and the 38th Artillery were attacked by some Chinese infantry men, but the two artillery units' gun crews and small arms defense were able to cause the enemy to withdraw. The Chinese troops were an advance party. The artillery units were successful in attacking the advancing enemy battalion and killed approximately one hundred Chinese troops.

The 2nd Division decided to assign some of the battalion to other units during their advance. Headquarters (HQ) Battery and B and C Batteries were given a mission to support the 9th Infantry Regiment. The tactical positions of the 2nd Division's units were along the division's front fifteen miles near the Chongch'on River and the small town, Kunu-ri. The major body of the 503rd was located on the east bank of the Chongch'on River with a battalion of the 23rd Infantry Regiment and the 61st Field Artillery to the North. Batteries B and C supported the retreating infantry regiments before closing in on their regiments' main position.

After assessing the tragic attacks and assaults on the 2nd Infantry Division and its supporting units, the commanding General Keiser had devised a plan for the Division to move south to Sunch'on, Korea. The plan would have the 9th Infantry Regiment attempt to open the main road toward Sunch'on. The 38th Infantry Regiment would be traveling in trucks and tanks toward the south and would eradicate any visible Chinese positions, and later connect with a British battalion that was moving toward the north. The 503rd Artillery was assigned the mission to support any enemy attacks during the infantry efforts to open the road.

The 2nd US Infantry Division was experiencing the beginning of a great defeat in attempting to repulse the advancing Chinese troops, especially when their manpower was affected by numerous casualties and the problems of the 9th Infantry Regiment on November 30. The Regiment was not able to remove some Chinese forces from the surrounding hills. They also faced some difficulties in trying to open the road because it was blocked by the presence of abandoned and damaged vehicles and equipment. It was reported that the British Battalion did not make any significant gains against the Chinese. There were some Chinese troops waiting for the US troops on both sides of the road. It was necessary for the US troops to clear road blocks and at the same time counter act any surprise sporadic attacks by the Chinese. The 503rd artillery was still providing support to the Infantry Units.

As the 2nd Division was withdrawing under very serious combat conditions, there was a designated tactical line of march. The order of march was the 37th Field Artillery Battalion, the 503rd, the 38th Field Artillery Battalion, Battery A of the 82nd AAA Battalion and the 2nd Engineer Battalion. During the course of the withdrawal movements on the main road, "B" Battery leading the 503rd Battalion was assaulted by a Chinese force. The Battery's lead tractor was destroyed, and the majority of the men were either killed or wounded. The 503rd's operations officer, Major John C. Fralish and the battalion commander Major Geoffrey Lavell made an assessment of the situation with concerns about continuing to march on the road. They consulted with the 38th Field Artillery Battalion commander. While the three officer were discussing whether they should continue on the road or destroy their equipment and proceed on foot through the hills to the town of Sunch'on, they received fire from a Chinese machine gun team. The Chinese were also firing on the 503rd's march column. Battery C's Howitzer was hit by a bazooka rocket and made inoperable. There was one casualty. With the assistance of an AAA Battalion's weapons, some Chinese machine guns and small arms fire were silenced. Major Lavell was reported missing and Major Fralish assumed command of the 503rd Battalion. The Battalion encountered weapons fire from the Chinese as they were moving through the pass near Karhyon-dong, the 38th

Regiment and 503rd men were tasked to remove vehicles and destroy Chinese machine guns. When Battery A was cut off from Headquarters and C Battery, the ammunition truck was hit and blown up; sadly, few of Battery A's men escaped as the Chinese attacked.

Major Fralish demonstrated outstanding leadership and efficiency when he was confronted with various obstacles in leading his battalion and some elements of other units to safer ground during the dreadful withdrawal of remaining units of the 2nd Infantry Division and their support forces. Fralish directed some one hundred men into the mountains in order to escape the Chinese soldiers. This contingent consisted of the remaining men of the 503rd, some from the 38th Field Artillery and the 2nd Engineer Battalion. On 1 December, 1950 they were fortunate to be observed by a US Air Force forward air controller. Later a 503rd single engine light observation plane was able to land and provide the group with water, food and directions to Sunch'on. Major Fralish was able to continue their march and eventually met some US soldiers from the 9th and 38th Infantry Regiments. He included them with the other units then continued toward the Taedong river where finally they saw some troops of the 1st Cavalry Division. These troops assisted them in reaching the 2nd Infantry Division assembly area outside of Sunch'on, Korea.

The 503rd Field Artillery Regiment's casualties and loss of equipment was a tremendous blow to the battalion. It was reported that four men were killed in action, three died of wounds, 24 seriously injured, 221 were prisoners of war, and 64 missing in action. Some 121 prisoners of the 221 died from their wounds or disease in the prisoner of war camps. Some 327 officers and enlisted men were casualties of the 503rd Battalion. The Unit lost 18 howitzers and some of the equipment had to be abandoned on the road near Kunu'ri. In December, the 503rd underwent a rebuilding process. The Eighth US Army assigned replacements and provided the battalion with new equipment to include twelve new howitzers and communications equipment. It was not until 13 January 1951 that that 503rd returned to a combat status. The Battalion was given the mission of assisting the 187th Airborne Regimental Combat Team which was trying to prevent a North Korean assault of X Corps' defensive line. The 503rd fired 512 rounds for the 187th and the ROK's 32nd Regiment.

The Eighth US Army organized a Support Force on 21 February 1951. The force consisted of the 15th Field Artillery Battalion, Battery A. 503rd Field Artillery Battalion, a Battery from the 82nd AAA Battalion and an Infantry Battalion. The Support Forces mission was to help the ROK's 8th Division north of Wonju as part of the US X Corps' Operation Roundup. The Chinese counter attacked on 11 February and inflicted a massive assault on ROK's 8th Division causing a loss of "70 per cent of its men and most of its equipment." The 15th Field Artillery Commander evaluated the reports of ROK's 8th Division casualties and loss of equipment and requested the 2nd Infantry Division's Artillery to give him permission to withdraw his troops. There was a delay of approximately 90 minutes by Headquarters' 2nd Infantry Division to give the 15th F A Commander permission to withdraw. However, the delay created a tragic situation for the US troops. The 503rd's Battery A became an early morning target for the Chinese troops. Because it was the lead element in the march column when attacked, the Company Commander, 1st Sergeant and some enlisted soldiers were captured. This action separated Battery A from the other Units of the Support Forces. The 15th FAB was able to stabilize the area after using direct fire on some Chinese positions with their howitzers and assistance from the Infantry Battalion. When the major body reached Company A's position, they found that Battery A had been overpowered with "71 missing and 56 prisoners of war. It was reported later that only 27 survived the war camps. There were only one officer, 21 enlisted men, and some wounded that were able to return to their assembly area.

Battery B, 503rd FAB was attached to the 37th FAB supporting the 23rd Infantry Regiment Combat Team on 1 February 1951. The 23rd Infantry Regiment had a mission to defend the CHIP'Yong'ni perimeter. Captain John A. Elledge, staff officer 503rd FAB was with B Battery, located south of the town. Company G, 23rd Infantry Regiment was situated near B Battery of 503rd. On 13 February 1951 four Chinese Regiments attacked with a mortar shell near the Regimental Combat Team's perimeter where Battery B was located killing two men and wounding six. The mortar shell exploded near an outpost and Captain Elledge and five men from Battery B went to investigate and found a machine gun damaged. Elledge and PFC Leslie Alston returned to the battery position, obtained another machine gun and some ammunition then returned to the outpost. They also brought some wounded men back to the Battery. When some Chinese troops attacked Company G, the 503rd Battery B soldiers assisted the Infantry Regiment in repulsing the Chinese. Capt. Elledge assisted in the rescue of some wounded men, PFC Thomas G. Allison and Isaiah Williams.

In April 1951, the Chinese troops conducted their spring offensive. The 503rd provided assistance to the 2nd Infantry Division and in four days had fired 3,000 rounds. The total number of rounds fired in April was 13,000. The Battalion also provided considerable support for the 2nd Infantry Division tactical combat operations in the battles of Bloody Ridge and Heartbreak Ridge during the months of August and October, 1951.

The 503rd FAB was selected for integration in November 1951. Approximately 538 white enlisted soldiers from various units of the 2nd Infantry Division artillery were transferred into this Battalion. A similar number of Black enlisted soldiers from the 503rd were transferred to other units. On 10 November 1951 the Department of Army designated the 12th Field Artillery Battalion to replace the 503rd FAB and assume its role as the 2nd Infantry Division's general support Artillery Battalion. The 503rd's lineage and honors were consolidated with those of the 12th Field Artillery Battalion.

The 503rd Field Artillery Battalion's meritorious and most commendable performances in combat during their 15 months in Korea attests to the reality that African Americans could and did fight in combat conditions even though they were relegated to a separate and second class status in the US Military during the early phases of the Korean War. They definitely earned the following awards and decorations:

> 19 Silver Stars, 4 Distinguished Flying Crosses and 79 Bronze Stars. The Battalion had 451 casualties, including 151 men who died in Chinese-North Koreans' prison camps and 79 reported missing in action. The 503rd Field Artillery Battalion's Motto was "WE CAN DO IT". However, I must add to it the phrase "ALWAYS IN COMBAT".

159TH FIELD ARTILLERY BATTALION (FAB)

3RD US INFANTRY DIVISION

The 159th FAB was the only African American Field Artillery unit stationed in the Far East prior to July, 1950. The Battalion was located at Nara Honshu, Japan. During the Korean War the 159th was attached to the 3rd US Infantry Division. The Unit assisted the 24th Infantry Regiment during a withdrawal movement by providing artillery weapons support. A platoon leader of the 24th Infantry Regiment remarked "the 159th FAB was a well trained unit whose fire power against the North Koreans frequently made the differences in a combat situation. They had a good record of many heroic actions in Korea.

When Battery A of the Battalion was without infantry support as some North Korean soldiers attempted to black the road linking the towns of Asan and Chingdong, A Battery displayed some heroic actions. The Battery using small arms weapons against the enemy in an intense seven hour battle were able to force the North Koreans to retreat. Private First Class Howard Jackson, Newport, Rhode Island, manned a 50 caliber machine gun aboard an ammunition truck and confronted the enemy. Jackson continued to fire toward the enemy even though he was constantly in the line of enemy machine gun and mortar fire.

An article in the Baltimore Afro American newspaper, 9 September 1950 stated that three batteries of the 159th FAB were credited with the killing of 650 North Korean soldiers in a two day battle. Some 3,000 North Koreans had penetrated a US Infantry Regiment's front line position by September 1, 1950. Another regiment was requested to rescue the unit attacked and they met strong enemy resistance and called for artillery support on a large scale. The 159th FAB was given the task and was able to assist the regiment to advance toward the enemy positions with the coordinated artillery rounds of fire.

The 159th FAB provided the 5th Marine Regiment artillery support in August, 1950. The Battalion fired approximately 1,600 rounds. In December 1951 the 159th FAB was included in a Task Force commanded by the Assistant Division Commander, 3rd Infantry Division. It was reported that the 159th FAB's Medical unit was integrated. The commander was Capt. Sylvester Baker of Pasadena, CA. The unit was responsible for the evacuation of wounded members of the Battalion.

Lieutenant Charles Gethers, Philadelphia, PA was assigned to 159th FAB as an artillery fire coordinator and air observer. He flew a Piper Cub plane over enemy lines and observed enemy concentrations and movements. Other officers of the battalion were Lt. Edward Greer, Battery A, Lt. Welch, West VA, Lt. Marshall Hurley, Chicago, IL and Major Thomas Watson, Lawton, OK.

The soldiers of the 159th FAB were representative of various cities and hometowns in America. Cpl. Walter Allen, Service Battery, aid attendant, 159th Medical Detachment Deland, FL; Pfc. Eugene Alston, Louisburg, NC; Pfc. Theophilius Anderson, Fire Direction Center, Dallas, TX; Cpl. James Andrews, New York City, NY; Pfc. Norman Ard, Chicago, IL; Lt. Morris Armstrong, Forward Observer, Soper, OK; Sgt. Jackson Avery, Chief Gun Section, Asheville, NC; Capt. Charles Barbour, Battalion Intelligence Officer, Junction City, KS; SFC. James Battle, Fire Direction Center, 159th FAB, Texas; Lt. Joe D. Bennett, Ada, OK; Cpl. Sammie Bibbs, Gunner, Valliant, OK; Pfc. Lewis Brown, Gun Charger, Jefferson, TX; Cpl. Charles Brumfield, Battery B, Baton Rouge, LA; Pfc. Clifford Burney, Battery B, Lineville, AL; Cpl. Arthur Calvin, ammunitions, New Orleans, L; Pfc. Alvin Charles, Battery B, St. Rosa, LA; Pfc. Willie Christian,

Houston, TX; Pfc. Hardy Cole, Fire Direction Center, Chicago, IL; Pfc. Timothy Coley, Battery B, Glendale, OH; Capt. Robert B. Coplin, C Battery, Tulsa, OK; Private Embre Cox, Aid Attendant, 159th Medical Detachment, VA; Pfc. Carl Davis, Aid Attendant, 159th Medical Detachment; Cpl. Merrill Dennis, 159th Medical Detachment, Battery B Aid Attendant, Detroit, MI; Cpl. Joseph Diaz, New York City, NY; Pfc. Johnny Dozier, Fire Direction Center, East St. Louis, IL; Cpl. Stacey Ellis, Air Attendant 159th Medical Detachment, Spencer, NC; Pfc. Robert Evans, Aid Attendant 159th Medical Detachment, Battery C, Newberry, NJ; Sgt. Baldwin Farmers, Fire Direction Center, Philadelphia, PA; Cpl. Travis Flournoy, Chicago, IL; Pfc. Albert Gibson, Cleveland, OH; Pfc. Edward Gillis, Fort Worth, TX; Msg. Harvey Ginn, Battery C, Tacoma, WA; Pfc. Claude Girifin, loader, Houston, TX; Pfc. Theodore Greene, New York City, NY; Cpl. Clarence Gordon, Los Angeles, CA; Sgt. O'Neil Harris, Battery B, Waco, TX; Pfc. Robert Jackson, Washington, DC; Sgt. William Jasper, Battery B, Washington, DC; Sgt Thomas Johnson, New Orleans, LA; SFC. Harry Jones, Battery B, Kirkwood, Mo; Pfc. William Jones, Aid Attendant, 159th Medical Detachment, Battery C, Fayetteville, NC; Pfc. Elijah Kendrix, Eldorado, AR; Pfc. Norman Kenny, Aid Attendant, 159th Medical Detachment, Battery B, Washington, DC; Pfc. Ernest King, Headquarters and Headquarters (HQ and HQ) Battery, Supply Truck River, Ridgeville, SC; SFC. Sam Lane, Fire Direction Center, Okechobee, FL; Pfc. Joseph Marshall, Baltimore, MD; Pfc. James Mason, HQ and HQ Battery Baltimore, MD; Pfc. Jake McClary, Jersey City, NJ; Pvt. Archie McEachin, Washington, DC; Pfc. Fred Moore, Battery B, Toledo, OH; Sfc. Albert Patton, Battery B, Memphis, TN; Sgt. Rupert Pope, Ammunition Sergeant, Chicago, IL; Cpl. Wesley Rogers, HQ and HQ Battery, driver, Smyrna Beach, FL; Cpl. Kenneth Shackleford, Fire Direction Center, Washington, DC; Pfc. Thomas Shane, Chicago, IL; SFC. Benny Smedley, Eldorado, AR; Pfc. Herbert Tammons, Fire Direction Center, St. Louis, MO; Cpl. Walls, Air Attendant, 159th Medical Detachment, Battery A, Columbus, OH; Cpl. George Wardell, Air Attendant, 159th Medical Detachment, Battery C, Oliphant Furnace, PA; Pfc. Johnnie C. Washington, Aid Attendant, 159th Medical Detachment, New York City, NY; SFC. Louis Williams, Chief, First Platoon, Fire Direction Center, Fort Worth, TX; Pfc. Leroy Woodard, Battery B, San Francisco, CA; and Col. Henry Woodmore, Dixo Springs, TN.

The Officers and soldiers of the 159th Field Artillery Battalion served in Korea under extreme combat conditions and their serious dedication to duty and the accomplishment of their missions were most commendable.

3RD BATTALION 15TH INFANTRY REGIMENT
2ND US INFANTRY DIVISION

Prior to 1950 the 3rd Battalion was stationed at Fort Benning, GA. The all Black segregated unit except for its White officers had a mission of performing menial tasks and providing some support for the Infantry school. The Battalion Commander prepared his men for combat conditions through extensive training. There were some African American officers assigned as Company commanders and platoon leaders. Harry Sutton, a veteran of WWII was an outstanding officer assigned to the Battalion.

Time Magazine had an article about the heroic performance by the 3rd Battalion near the Hungnam Perimeter. The Magazine stated that when the battalion was attacked by the Chinese troops, I Company fought very valiantly for 11 hours non-stop. Harry Sutton's commendable actions during the combat encounter earned him the Silver Star for the Units' decisive victory.

231ST TRANSPORTATION TRUCK COMPANY

Some members of the Truck Company were, Lt. Col. Vernon Greene, Baltimore, MD; Private First Class James Butler, Washington, DC; Corporal Roy V. Burrough, Baltimore, MD; Lt. W. Emerson Brown, Baltimore, MD; Capt. George Brooks, Baltimore, MD; Lt. Herman Briscoe, Baltimore, MD; Private Jimmie Bowie, San Bernardino, CA; Lt. Joseph Bracy, Baltimore, MD; Webster Boone, Baltimore, MD; Corporal William R. Bland, Baltimore, MD; Private First Class George Battle, Baltimore, MD; Chief Warrant Officer Wilbert Armstead, Baltimore, MD; Private Russell Allen, Baltimore, MD; Sgt. Joseph Locklear, Weston, CT; Corporeal John Lopes, Newport, RI; Corporal Lewis Lowery, Detroit, MI; Private Reginald Lloyd, Bronx, NY; Private First Class Moses Life, New York City, NY; Corporal Charlie King, GA; Corporal Victor Jones, Norfolk, VA; Private William Johnson, San Francisco, CA; Private Sidney Jones, Hartford, CT; Private First Class Robert Ingram, Terre Haute, IN; Capt. Lester Hudgin, Baltimore, MD; Master Sgt. Charles Hurd, Baltimore, MD; Corporal James Hopkins, Baltimore, MD; Master Sgt. Carl Hicks, Baltimore, MD; Corporal James Hill, Baltimore, MD; Henry Hoggalt, Natchez MS; Private John Henry, Oakland, CA; Sgt. Oscar S. Harvey, Baltimore, MD; Sgt. Archie Henderson, Trenton, NJ; Private First Class William Graves, Baltimore, MD; Sgt. Gary Gross, Chicago, IL; Corporal Arthur Griffin, Baltimore, MD; Sgt. William Green, Morton, PA; Sgt. Arthur Golden, Buffalo, NY; Sgt William Floyd, Baltimore, MD; Corporal Richard Dawson, Cumberland, MD; First Lt. George Dawson, Baltimore, MD; Corporal Joseph L. Cole, Baltimore, MD; Sgt. Verdell Clark, Baltimore, MD; Walter Clark, Mount Vernon, NY; Private First Class Jeffries Carey, Baltimore, MD; Major Melvin Cade, Baltimore, MD; Corporal Charles M. Watkins, Baltimore, MD; Sgt. First Class Bernard Thomas, Baltimore, MD; Corporal Anderson Williams, Baltimore, MD; Sgt. Eldred Wilkerson, Baltimore, MD; Corporal Albert White, Los Angeles, CA; Theodore Wilson, New York City, NY; Franklin Youngblood, Chester, PA; James H. Smith, Baltimore, MD; Corporal James Spruell, Baltimore, MD; Capt. Anthony Porter, Baltimore, MD; Private First Class Elijah Person, Newport News, VA; Sgt. Claude Patterson, Baltimore, MD; Major Charles Parker, Baltimore, MD; Sgt. First Class Ralph Murdock, Baltimore, MD; Arthur Russell, Clairton, PA; Private First Class Charles Roman, Washington, DC; Corporal Nathaniel Roand, Southern Pines, NC; Private Henry Robinson, Cincinnati, OH; Corporal Maxio Roe, Baltimore, MD; Sgt. Thomas Randall, Baltimore, MD; and Corporal Henry Rauls, Baltimore, MD.

58th ARMORED FIELD ARTILLERY BATTALION
3RD US INFANTRY DIVISION

The 58th Armored FAB was an all Black unit attached to the 3rd US Infantry Division. The Battalion provided support to the 65th Puerto Rican Infantry Regiment during the Han River crossing in March 1950.

64TH TANK BATTALION

This Battalion was constituted 13 January 1941 in the regular Army as the 78th Tank Battalion, re –designated 8 May 1941, as the 758th Tank Battalion (light), activated 1 June 1941 at Fort Knox, KY. It was re-organized and re-designated 3 May 1945 as the 758th Light Tank Battalion and in-activated 27 September 1945 at Viareggio, Italy. It was re-designated 23 May 1946 as 758th Tank

Battalion. Activated in 1946 at Fort Knox, KY then re-organized and re-designated 15 January 1948 as 758th Heavy Tank Battalion. It was again re-designated in November 1949 as the 64th Heavy Tank Battalion and assigned to the 2nd Armored Division. Relieved August 1950 from assignment to 2nd Armored Division and assigned to the 3rd Infantry Division. It was re-organized and re-designated again 6 March 1951 as the 64th Tank Battalion. On 1 July 1957 at Fort Benning, GA the Battalion was inactivated and relieved from assignment to 3rd Infantry Division and re-designated again 25 June 1963 as the 64th Armor. It was considered a parent regiment under the Combat Army Regimented System.

The Battalion's coat of arms:
- SHIELD: Argent the head of a fighting African Elephant sable tusks proper
- CREST: On a wreath of the colors argent and sable mounted on a trophy base or charged with a Korean Taeguk two elephants proper supporting a Catherine wheel gules charged on the hub with a bezant all in front of a mount of Three beaks
- MOTTO: WE PIERCE
- SYMBOLISM: The elephant symbolizes the heavy assault of a tank battalion. Elephants were used in ancient times to lead the attack in a manner comparable to the present day use of armored organizations.

The Catherine wheel with its hooked spikes symbolizes the armored truck vehicles and its functions. The spikes further representing eight battle honors for the Korean War and the gold disk in the center referring to the award of the Bravery Gold Medal of Greece. The Elephant tusks in a trophy base decorated with a Korean Taeguk are symbolic of the Korean Presidential Unit Citation. The three peaks allude to service in the North Apennines in WW II and the valley between the tusks to the Po Valley campaigns.

The Battalions' participation credits:
- World War II – North Apennines, Po Valley
- Korean War – CCF intervention, First UN counter offensive, CCF spring offensive, UN Summer – Fall offensive, second Korean Winter, Third Korean Winter and Korean Summer, 1953.

The Decorations:
- Republic of Korea – Presidential Unit Citation, Stream embroidered, Uijon-bu corridor to Seoul (64th Tank Battalion cited Department of Army, General Order 29, 1954
- People of Korea Presidential Unit Citation streamer embroidered, Iron Triangle (64th Truck Battalion cited Department of Army, General Order 29, 1954)
- Chryssoun Aristion (Bravery Gold Metal of Greece) streamer embroidered Korea (64th Tank Battalion cited Department of the Army, General Order 2, 1956)

The 64th Tank Battalion's combat and tactical operations' achievements during the Korean War were commendable. On January of 1951, 8th US Army ordered US I Corps to launch an offensive toward the town of Pyong Gang because of many Chinese communist troops concentrated in the Triangle area. The 64th Tank Battalion, 7th US Infantry Division executed an attack near the Han Ton River. The Chinese communist forces were present in well fortified bunkers. However, the enemy was repulsed and some were captured, approximately 48 prisoners. Sgt. Joseph Holden Philadelphia, PA, Corp. Joseph James and Pvt. Clarence Smith, Mt Cross Roads, VA was assigned to the 64th Tank Battalion.

During the X Corps evacuation from the ports of Song jin, Wonsan and Hung nam as well as the Yon po airfield, B Company, 64th Tank Battalion provided some protection for the harbor areas.

76TH ANTI AIRCRAFT ARTILLERY

AUTOMATIC WEAPONS BATTALION (AAAW)

The 76th AAW Battalion was a segregated all Black Unit in Korea prior to September 1951. Corp. Henry Carroll, San Francisco, CA and Lt. Lonnie W. Williams, Norfolk, VA and a graduate of Hampton University were member of this Unit.

74th ENGINEER COMBAT BATTALION (ECB)

The 74th ECB was an all Black Unit during the Korean War prior to September, 1951. Some of the members were, Lt. Charles Brown, Washington, DC. He was a senior aviator attached to the 74th ECB. Brown flew over 400 combat missions and was awarded the Air Medal Korean Service Medal and the Republic of Korean Presidential Citation. Corp. Rudy Buckner, San Francisco, CA, Company B was reported missing in action in April, 1951. Corporals Johnny C. Sawyer and Ronald E. Thompson were also assigned to this Unit.

77TH ENGINEER COMBAT COMPANY (ECC)

The 77th ECC was an all Black Engineer Unit that served in Korea prior to September, 1951. The Company performed heroically during several engagements with the enemy. During operation Ripper in March, 1950, the 77th ECC assisted in some river crossings on the Han River to support the 25th Infantry Division.

A war correspondent for the Baltimore Afro American Newspaper, James L. Hicks, wrote an account of the 24th Infantry Regiment's victory in capturing the town of Yechon, Korea in August, 1950. The article stated the following:

> "The Combat Engineer Unit (77th) commanded by First Lt. Charles Bussey knew their responsibility after the 3rd Battalion, 24th Infantry Regiment had secured the town of Yechon. Their mission was to construct and destroy routes of communication. In the withdrawal from Yechon, it was necessary for the destruction of 40,000 homes and buildings. The Engineers destroyed everything of military and commercial value".

When the 77th ECC was repairing a main bridge cable, the acting company commander, West Point graduate, Lt. David Carlisle ordered his men to use some assault boats for floats and construct a light raft for transporting 2 ½ ton trucks. Unfortunately an enemy mortar round struck the raft and blew it to pieces. However, the men were able to build another raft and cross the river successfully. In April 1951, the 77th ECC were again instrumental in blasting some Chinese troops out of caves and bunkers along the Hantan River.

Some members of the 77th ECC were Corp. James G Boyd, St Louis, MO; Sgt. First Class Herbert Davis, Cincinnati, OH; Pvt. First Class Willis Foster, Richmond, CA; 2nd Lt. Chester Lenon, WW II Veteran reported wounded in action; Warrant Officer Junior grade, Thomas Pettigrew, Pittsburgh, PA; Pvt. Leroy Sellers, Chesterfield, SC; and Lt. James Wilson, Corona, NY.

96TH FIELD ARTILLERY BATTALION (FAB)

The 96th FAB was an all Black Unit until September 1951. It was reported that in 1952, some White replacements were assigned to the unit.

933RD ANTI AIRCRAFT ARTILLERY AUTOMATIC WEAPONS BATTALION, BATTERY A (AAW)

Battery A (AAW) was an all Black unit prior to September 1951. PFC Theodore P. Carter, Boston, MA was assigned to the unit during the Korean War.

999TH FIRLD ARTILLERY BATTALION (FAB)

The 999th FAB was an all Black Unit prior to September 1951. This Battalion's mission was to augment X Corps artillery. The Unit had 18 155mm self propelled Howitzers mounted on Tank Hulls. Their weapons were often employed in the Northeastern area of Korea. When artillery support was requested by I Corps during a combat action near the town of Kumyangiang, the 999th FAB responded to the request. This unit also participated in a combat operation near Ham bung in support of a Task Force.

Private First Class Henry Buckner, San Francisco, CA, was reported missing in action, April 1951. Other members were Corp. James Fetherson, Monroe, NC; Battery A's Capt. Elbert Patterson, Baltimore, MD; and Pvt. 1st Class George L. Simpson, Suffolk, VA also served with the 999th FAB.

866th TRANSPORTATION PORT COMPANY

The 866th Transportation Port Company was an all Black Unit prior to September, 1951. Pvt. 1st Class (PFC) Robert Shelton, Louisville, KY, and PFC William White were assigned to this Unit.

515 TH TRANSPORTATION TRUCK COMPANY

The 515th Transportation Truck Company was an all Black Unit prior to September, 1951. Corp. Nealy Kimble, New Orleans, LA; Corp. William Wallace, Washington, DC; Corp. Bernard Crocker, Norfolk, VA; and Corp. Dannie Gomes, Hutchinson, KS were members of this Unit. Kimble, Wallace and Crocker were all members of a singing gospel group organized in the Company. The group was called the "Gloryland Gospel Singers". They recorded their Sunday programs at the Armed Forces Service Mobile Radio Service in Korea.

930th ENGINEERING AVIATION UNIT

The 930th Engineering Aviation Unit was an all Black Unit prior to September, 1951. Sgt. Wilbur Williams, Greenwood, MS, US Air Force was assigned to the 930th

939th ENGINEER AVIATION GROUP

The 939th Engineer Aviation Group was an all Black Unit prior to September, 1951. Staff Sgt. Hiram Wilkins, a WW II veteran was a chief draftsman in the Unit. The group's mission was to assist in the developing of plans for the construction and repair of forward air bases for tactical aircraft in Korea.

696th ORDNANCE AMMUNITION COMPANY

The 696th Ordnance Ammunition Co. was an all Black Unit prior to September, 1951. Some members of the Unit were PFC Paul Blount, Norfolk, VA; Sgt. Edward Ceasar, New Orleans, LA; Corp. George M. Penn, Lynchburg, VA; PFC. Willie Tiller, Hopewell, VA; PFC Bernie Toppins, Norfolk, VA; and PFC Crenshaw Young, Portsmouth, VA. The overall mission of the 696th was to provide ammunition to frontline troops and artillery units in the I Corps area in Korea.

715TH TRANSPORTATION TRUCK COMPANY

The 715th Transportation Truck Co. was an all Black Unit prior to September, 1951. The "Capital Truck Co." from Washington, DC landed in Pusan, Korea January 5, 1951; it was one of the first National Guard Units to join X Corps. The 715th logged 439, 717 miles in Korea and transported 11,435 troops under the company command of Capt. Maurice J. Burke.

726TH TRANSPORTATION TRUCK COMPANY

The 726th Transportation Truck Co. was an all Black Unit prior to September, 1951. This was the first National Guard Unit to arrive in Korea. They arrived in Pusan on 31 December 1950 with a mission to provide administrative and logistical support to truck companies assigned. Their executive officer was Lt. Joseph Bracey.

822ND ENGINEER AVIATION BATTALION

The 822nd Engineer Aviation Battalion was an all Black Unit prior to September 1951. It was a subordinate unit in Korea under the 417th Engineer Aviation Brigade. The Far East Air Force (FEAF) deployed to Korea engineer aviation units manned by special category army personnel with air force (SCARWAF) troops.

As early as July 1950, the 802nd and 822nd Engineer Aviation Battalions were repairing and extending run ways at Pohang and Taegu, Korea. These Engineer Units also repaired, renovated and expanded air fields at Pyongyang, Pusan, Hoengsong, Chunchon, Chinhae, Chungnu, Kunsan, Seoul and Pyong Taek.

In 1952, the 822nd constructed new run ways for Jet Fighters at Taegu and Kunsan, Korea. Staff Sergeant Lowell Wills, Detroit, MI was assigned to this Battalion.

849TH QUARTER MASTER PETROLEUM SUPPLY COMPANY

The 849th Quarter master Petroleum Supply Co. was an all Black Unit prior to September 1951. Sgt. Fred Holmes, Montgomery, AL was assigned to this Unit.

933RD ANTI AIRCRAFT AUTOMATIC ARTILLERY WEAPONS BATTALION

The 933rd was an all Black Unit prior to September 1951. Theodore Carter, Boston, MA was assigned to Battery A 933rd and served near Pohang Dong.

549TH QUARTER MASTER LAUNDRY COMPANY

Another all Black unit prior to September 1951 was the 549th Quarter Master Laundry Co. This Unit participated in the Inchon landing in August, 1950. They provided support for the 1st Cavalry, 24th and 25th Infantry Divisions under the command of Captain Alfred G. Rollins.

546TH ENGINEER FIRE FIGHTING COMPANY

Prior to September1951, the 546th Engineer Fire Fighting Co. was an all Black Unit. Their mission was to provide fire protection support for units in the Pusan, Korea area. The commanding officer of the Unit was Captain Morris Clay, Enfield, NC. Some members of this Unit were John Alston, Alexandria, VA; Thad Mango, NC; Thomas Atkins, Akron, OH; Nathaniel Banks, College Park, GA; Robert Brown, Pittsburgh, PA; James Price, Phoenix, AZ; Earl Cunningham, Chicago, IL; Tommy Daniels, Houston, TX; Tony English, Oklahoma, Timothy Ferguson, Florida; Carlton Farrell, Anniston, AL; Clyde Fisher, Ladelle, AR; Gerald Fox, Chicago, IL; James Wedgeworth, Samuel Williams, Williamston, NC; Ozzie Williams, Wynn, Arkansas, Theodore Otis, Des Moines, IA; James Price, Danville, VA; Ostell Johnson, Laurel, DE; James Jones, Chicago, IL; Edward Jones, Columbus, OH; Daniel Frazier, Beckley West VA; Willie Smith, Cayce, SC; and Morris Graves, Phoenix, AZ.

558TH MEDICAL COLLECTING SEPARATE COMPANY

Before September 1951, the 558th Medical Collecting Separate Co. was an all Black Unit. The commander of the Unit was Major William Gott. According to a Black weekly newspaper, some members of the 558th had established a small congregation of soldiers in the Unit who were of the Seventh Day Adventist faith. They conduct services in the Company area. Sgt. Henry Fuller, Grand Cave, LA; was the Church's elder and its members were Walter Robertson, Shreveport, LA; Charles Hinton, San Bernardino, CA; and Clarence Baker, Sylacagua, AL.

551ST TRANSPORTATION TRUCK COMPANY

Some members of the 551st were PFC Thomas Ashe, Hanover, NC; Pvt. William Jones, Aberdeen, MD; Pvt. John Ivey, Monroe, NC; PFC Edward Haith, Mebance, NC; PFC Robert Guinyard, Warwick, VA; Pvt. James Gibson, Birmingham, AL; PFC Obie Golston, Washington, DC; PFC Ellis Pitt, Edgecombe, NC; PFC Samuel Paschall, Roanoke, VA; Royal Nickens, Philadelphia, PA; Alexander Myers, Jr., Washington, DC and Pvt. John Morgan, Dunn, NC. The 551st Transportation Truck Co. was an all Black Unit before September 1951.

564TH MILITARY POLICE COMPANY

The 564th Military Police Company was an all Black Unit during the Korean War prior to September 1951. PFC Samuel Evans, Chicago, IL was a Member of this Unit.

567TH MEDICAL AMBULANCE COMPANY

The commander of this Unit was Captain Benjamin D. Reed, Gardner, ME. The Unit supported frontline hospitals, and gave ambulance service to the entire Pusan area including the air fields and dock areas. Prior to September 1951, this Unit was all Black. The 567th was awarded the Meritorious Unit Commendation. The Headquarters Eighth Army award stated that the commendation was awarded for exceptionally meritorious conduct in the performance of outstanding service during the period July 1950 to March 1951. Sgt. Charles E. Thomas served with this Unit in Korea.

568TH MEDICAL AMBULANCE COMPANY

The 568th Medical Ambulance Company was another all Black Unit before September 1951. Sgt. Tommie L. Brown, Birmingham, AL; and Sgt. Albert Samuel, Winston Salem, NC were both part of this Unit.

580TH QUARTER MASTER SALVAGE COMPANY

Sgt. 1st Class Edward Watson of Roderfield, VA was member of this all Black Unit during the Korean War prior to September, 1951.

595TH ENGINEER DUMP TRUCK COMPANY

Corporal Jeremiah Easterling, Norfolk, VA and Sgt. B. L. Wingfield were assigned the 595th Engineer Dump Truck Co. while it was an all Black Unit prior to September 1951.

584TH TRANSPORTATION TRUCK COMPANY

Pvt. John H. Turnipseed, Peoria, IL was a member of the 584th Transportation Truck Co. when it was an all Black Unit prior to September, 1951.

624th TRANSPORTATION COMPANY

Pvt. James Carey, Cleveland, OH served in Okinawa, Japan with this Unit during the Korean War. This too was an all Black Unit prior to September, 1951.

630TH ORDNANCE AMMUNITION COMPANY

Pvt. James C. Williams served in Korea with the 630th Ordnance Ammunition Co. It also was an all Black Unit prior to September 1951.

93RD ENGINEER CONSTRUCTION BATTALION

The mission of the 93rd Engineer Construction Battalion was to construct bridges, dams and roads. This was an all Black Unit prior to September 1951 and Lt. Delon Felder, Chaplain, Baltimore, MD and PFC Dennis Moss were assigned to the Unit.

376TH ENGINEER CONSTRUCTION BATTALION

Some members of the 376th Engineer Construction Battalion were PFC Carl Chambers, Baltimore, MD; PFC Eugene Dawson, Baltimore, MD; Sgt. John Fairfax, Baltimore, MD; PFC Robert Fitz, PFC John Nixon and PFC Wilbur Ophee` were all of Baltimore, MD. This too was an all Black Unit prior to September 1951.

396TH TRANSPORTATION TRUCK COMPANY

Sgt. Morgan Carter was assigned to the 396th Transportation Truck Co. which was an all Black Unit prior to September, 1951.

508TH QUARTER MASTER SALVAGE COMPANY

PFC Benjamin Morton was assigned to this Unit while it was all Black prior to September 1951.

539TH TRANSPORTATION TRUCK COMPANY

The 539th Transportation Truck Co. was an all Black Unit prior to September, 1951. The Company operated an express from Kumchon to Kaesong. Its commander was Captain Ralph Anderson, Washington, DC. Some officers and enlisted men of the company were Lt. Antonio Carr, Cincinnati, OH; Lt. Hollis Posey, Cleveland, OH; Pfc. L. J. Lyons, Newark, NJ; Staff Sgt. Joe Henry, Brooklyn, NY; Pfc. David McMullen, Atlanta, GA; and Lt. Edgar Potts, Cleveland, OH.

540TH TRANSPORTATION TRUCK COMPANY

Another all Black Unit in Korea prior to September 1951 was the 540th Transportation Truck Co. Corporal John L. Smith, Petersburg, VA was assigned to the Unit and served in the area of SunChon, Korea.

27TH TANK RECOVERY ORDNANCE BATTALION

The mission of the Battalion was to recover damaged and disabled tanks. Some members of the Unit were Cpl. James Brock, Akron, OH and Cpl. Willie C. Staples, Tuscaloosa, AL.

45TH MILITARY POLICE COMPANY

Pvt. Willie V. Gorham of Norfolk, VA was assigned to this MP Company while serving his tour of duty in Korea.

There was a critical logistical mission that 8th US Army assigned to many segregated Black Transportation Units and that was to transport supplies, material and troops throughout Korea during the Korean War. They really represented the "Red Ball Express" of the Korean War. During WW II that name was given those segregated Black Transportation Truck Units that moved men and supplies across the European Theater of Operations.

The efficient and dependable African American soldiers assigned to the truck companies and battalions in Korea transported supplies from the Pusan ports around the clock in order to complete the 8th Army urgent logistical requirement. The 2nd Infantry Division provided 320 trucks to supply I Corps tactical operations in the Han river area.

49TH TRANSPORTATION TRUCK COMPANY

Pfc. Lee Thompson, Baltimore, MD was assigned to 49th Truck Co., and also Pfc. Charles McIntosh, East St. Louis, IL.

51ST SIGNAL BATTALION

Pfc. Henry Weaver, Suffolk, VA. was a driver for I Corps 51st Signal Battalion in Korea.

69th ORDNANCE AMMUNITION COMPANY

This Company was responsible for the loading of 9,000 tons of ammunition and 400 unserviceable vehicles (trucks) aboard transport vessels during the final evacuation from Hungnam, Korea, December 26, 1950. This too was an all Black Unit.

70TH TRANSPORTATION TRUCK BATTALION

The all Black 70th Transportation Truck Battalion was very active in Korea. Pfc. Charles F. Brinkly, New Haven, Connecticut, and Pvt. Edward Carey were soldiers of the Unit and at one time stationed in Pusan, Korea.

73RD ENGINEER COMBAT BATTALION (ECB)

The Corps of Engineers are tasked with crucial missions during combat operations. The 73rd ECB had several strategic missions to perform during the Korean War. The all Black Engineer Combat Battalion accomplished their assigned tasks in a most efficient and commendable manner. The Battalion constructed 500 miles of road along with 30 major bridges. The Unit also participated in the evacuation from Hungnam, Korea.

The US 10th Corps commanding general presented the 73rd ECB with an official Unit Citation. The Citation reads as follows:

"It is with great pride that I commend the 73rd Engineer Combat Battalion for achieving a memorable combat record in the 10th Corps sector which offers indelible proof on this Armored Force Day of the power of combined teamwork in defeating a numerically greater enemy. The 73rd has played a key role in the UN victories in the Korean campaign. Often it accomplished engineering miracles despite the enemy and temperatures which ranged down to 25 degrees below zero. Teamwork has saved the lives of thousands of United Nations Fighting men in this bitter campaign. Men of the 73rd Engineer Combat Battalion, a part of the United States land, sea and air service team has rendered the highest patriotic duty of which all Americans at home may be really proud."

The Sgt. Major of the 73rd GCB was Master Sgt. Billie Grant.

BLACK MILITARY PERSONNEL US AIR FORCE
FAR EAST COMMAND, KOREAN WAR, 1950 – 1953

Black officers and enlisted men were assigned to mostly integrated units in the Air Force during the Korean War. Capt. Frederick Parker, Jr., Chicago, IL was assigned in Korea as an Aircraft Maintenance Officer. Other members were 1st Lt. William Green, Staunton, VA; 1st Lt. Edward Drummond, Philadelphia, PA; 1st Lt. James Harvey, Mountain, PA; 1st Lt. Harold Hillery, New York City, NY, Communications Officer. 1st Lt. Frank Lee, Los Angeles, CA, Aircraft Engineering and Maintenance Officer; 1st Lt. Leroy Roberts, Anderson, SC; Major George Webb, Washington, DC, Administrative Officer, Guam, 19th Wing. 1st Lt. William Lewis, Charleston West VA, 20th US Air Force; Capt. Eldridge Williams, Kansas City, KS, Special Services Officer; 20th US Air Force; 1st Lt. Ulysses Toatley, Washington, DC, 31st Reconnaissance, Okinawa; 2nd Lt. Sidney Johnson, Springfield, OH, Adjutant, 13th Air Force; 2nd Lt. George W. Sterling, Los Angeles, CA, Technical Supply Officer, 20th US Air Force; 1st Lt. Andrew Johnson, Jr., Greensboro, NC, Adjutant, 20th US Air Force; 1st Lt. Edward J. Williams, Columbus, GA, Operations Officer, 20th US Air Force; 1st Lt. Kenneth O. Wofford, Springfield, MO, Administrative Officer, Inspector 5th US Air Force; 1st Lt. Arthur L. Ward, Birmingham, AL, Supply Officer 20th US Air Force; Capt. James L. Hall, Painesville, OH, Sales Officer, 19th US Bomb Wing; Capt. George E. Barton, New Orleans, LA, Air Material area, Honshu, Japan, Air Installation Officer; 2nd Lt. Frederick H. Samuels, Philadelphia, PA, 5th US Air Force, Information and Education Officer; Capt. John J. Suggs, Terre Haute, IN, 5th US Air Force, Information and Education Officer; Capt. Alvin J. Downing, Jacksonville, FL, 5th US Air Force, Special Services Officer; 1st Lt. Jess W. Ainsworth, New Orleans, LA, 5th US Air Force, Supply Officer; Capt. James Hurd, Fort Riley, KS, Aircraft Maintenance Officer; and 2nd Lt. Marion Rogers, Seattle, WA, Administrative Officer.

CHAPTER 4

SELECTED VETERANS

Thousands of African Americans served during the Korean War 1950 – 1953. The majority of them served in segregated all Black Units until September, 1951. The following names and hometowns represent military personnel, war correspondents, Red Cross workers and service club personnel. Because of the integration process in Korea in 1951, several names inadvertently could possible be those of non Blacks.

Corporal Clarence Adams, Memphis, TN; Pvt. Henry Adams, Philadelphia, PA; Pfc. Taft Adams, Philadelphia, PA, 24th Infantry Regiment; Pfc. Johnnie Adkins, Varner, OK; Cpl. Paul Adkins, Varner, OK; Ms Jesse F. Abbott was present in Korea in 1951 as a Red Cross worker; Pfc. Shelby Alcorn, Chicago, IL; Pvt. Charles Allen, Marshall, TX; Pfc. Floyd Allen, New Orleans, LA; Cpl Heary Allen, Rock Hill, SC; Sgt. Robert Allen, St. Louis, MO; 1st Lt. Warren Allen, Los Angeles, CA; Pfc. Roosevelt Alexander, Miliston, MS; 1 Lt. Jess W. Ainsworth, New Orleans, LA; supply officer, 5th Air Force; Pfc. Henry Anderson, Baltimore, MD; Pfc. Herman Anderson, Baltimore, MD, 24th Infantry Regiment; and Pvt. Lyonel Anderson, Eldorado, AR. Corp. Norman Anderson, Longview, TX was assigned as an air policeman at the Far East Air Force Headquarters in Japan during the Korean War. Capt. Ralph Anderson, Washington, DC, 1st Cavalry Division, Korea; Sgt. Robert Andrews, Onset, MA; PFC Ozal G. Alton served in Korea. Pvt. Charles Armstrong, Dallas, TX; 1st Lt. Clark Arrington, Philadelphia, PA, 24th Infantry Regiment; Pvt. Cleveland Avent, Enfield, NC was assigned to a medical detachment. SFC. Jackson Avery, Plaintree, SC; Corp. Elmer Bailey, 24th Infantry Regiment from the state of PA; Pvt. Levi Bailey, Baltimore, MD, 24th Infantry Regiment, graduated from Douglas High School; Airmen Willie J. Bailey, Washington, DC, served with the 6161st Air Base Wing; Pfc. Robert James, Panama, FL; Master Sgt. James Barber, Evansville, IN; Pfc. Terry Baker, Vallejo, CA; Corp. Eddie Banks, Canton VA; Pvt. James Barnes, Biggs, OK; Pfc. Robert O. Barrow, Roxbury, MA, 24th Infantry Regiment was a Bantam weight and flyweight boxing champion. Barrow was a cousin of the former World Heavy Weight Boxing Champion Joe Louis. Pfc. George Barrett, Institute, West VA; Pfc. George T. Bass, Baltimore, MD; Sgt. Floyd Battle, New York City, NY, 24th Infantry Regiment.

2nd Lt. Olga Beamon, US Army Nurse Corp., Richmond, VA was assigned to the General Hospital, Tokyo, Japan during the Korean War. Pfc. Edward Bean, Annapolis, MD; Pfc. Colin Bell, Los Angeles, CA; Pfc. Willie J. Belcher, Hampton, VA; Pfc. Arthur Bellman, Rutherford, NJ; Pfc. Wilbert Benford, Opelika, AL; LTC. Kenneth H. Berthoud, New York City, NY, US Marine Corps was the second Black to receive a regular commission in the Marine Corps. He entered the Marine Corps as a candidate for a commission, and was designated a 2nd Lt. in the reserves on 13 December 1952. On 13 July 1953 he became a regular officer. Berthoud served as an officer in the 3rd Marine Division in Japan. In 1973 he was assigned to HQ Marine Corps, Washington, DC.

Pvt. Jesse Berry, Marion City, CA served in Korea as a Sanitation Officer Inspector. Berry visited mess halls, barbershops, observing health violations. Corp. William Berry, South Kinloch, MO; Corp. Chase Best, New York City, NY; Corp. Charles Bibbs, Detroit, MI served as a medical technician during the Korean War and Capt. Bradley Biggs, former Black paratrooper in WW II served in Korea as a member of the 24th Regimental Combat Team. Corp. Al Billingsley, native of Mississippi; Corp. Billy Billingsley, Birmingham, AL; Sgt. David Beck, Birmingham,

AL; 1st Lt. Gordon H. Black, Chicago, IL was attached to the 24th Infantry Regiment and served as an Adjutant, 2nd Battalion; Pvt. Howard Blount, Monroe, NC; Corp. Robert Lee Blizzard, Newport News, VA; Pvt. Willie J. Blount, Snow Hill, VA; Pfc. Roy Blackwell, St. Louis, MO; Corp. Elvin Blackley, Portsmouth, VA; SFC. Laurence Blackman, Logan, West VA; Corp. Richell Blow, New York City, NY; Sgt. Thornton Blizzard, Newport News, VA; Corp. Leroy Bolden, Washington, DC; Corp. Arthur Booker, Houston, TX served as a radio operator in the US Air Force. Corp. Gordon Boone, Jr. Baltimore, MD served in Korea with a Task Force as a machine gunner; Pvt. Oscar Boyd Kentucky, 24th Infantry Regiment; Sgt. Earle Bourne, Lusby, MD; Pfc. James G. Boyd, 24th Infantry Regiment, St Louis, MO; Pvt. Percy Boyd, Mocan NC; Corp. Cornelius Boykin, Arlington, VA, was promoted to Sgt. Major E-9 later in his military career; Cpl. James Branch, Portsmouth, VA; Cpl. Ewing Brandon, Memphis, TN; Pfc. Clyde Bratton, Washington, DC; Pvt. Willie Brazil, Baltimore, MD; Col. Herbert L. Brewer, Marine Corps was commissioned in the V-12 program in 1948, and he was the highest ranking Black Marine Officer on active duty during the Korean War. Pfc. George H. Brickhouse, Norfolk, VA; Cpl. Frank Brimm, St Louis, MO; Cpl. John Brooks, Washington, DC; Lt. Joseph T. Brooks, Veteran of WW II served during the Korean War as a Cryptographic Specialist aboard the Navy battle ship Missouri. Col. Nelson Brocks, Washington, DC, served during the Korean War as Chief of Communication for the Philadelphia command; Sgt. Alvin Brown, Junction City, KS; Pvt. Daniel Brown, Meridian, MS; Capt. Everett Brown, San Antonio, TX; Lt. General Earl Brown, New York City, NY and Englewood, NJ flew F – 86's during the Korean War. Sgt. George Brown, Washington, DC; Cpl. James J. Brown, Jr., Durham, NC; Pvt. Jennings Brown, Fairmont, NC; Cpl. L. C. Brown, San Angelo, TX; Pfc. Joel Brown, Norfolk, VA; Pfc. Linkin Brown, Junction City, KS; Pvt. Luther Brown, Baltimore, MD; William Bland, served in Korea with a transportation truck co. National Guard, Pfc. Mack Brown, Indianapolis, IN; Cpl. Richard Brown, Baltimore, MD; Cpl. Robert Brown, Chicago, IL; Lt. William E. Brown, flew missions during the Korean War in the F – 86 Sabre Jets. He was from Englewood, NY. Cpl. George Bruckett, Philadelphia, PA; Pvt. William Buchanan, Jackson, MS; Sgt. Laura A. Bullock, Columbus, OH was assigned to the US Army Hospital in Camp Yokohama, Japan as an administrative Specialist. Cpl. Joseph Brown, New Orleans, LA; Pfc. Edward Burton, Asheville, NC; Capt. George E. Burton, New Orleans, LA was assigned to the Japanese Air Ministry as an installation officer while in Korea for the Far East Air Force. Pvt. Leroy Campbell, Dumas, AK; Pfc. Veronies Campbell, Memphis, TN; Major William Campbell, Tuskegee, AL; Cpl. Bernard Carberry, Baltimore, MD; Lt. Antonio Carr, Cincinnati, OH served with the 1st Cavalry Division while in Korea. Sgt. George Carroll, Alexandria, VA was assigned to a quartermaster Bakery Company. Master Sgt. Charles Carter, Baltimore, MD; Lt. Junior Grade Earl Carter, New York City, NY was the only Black Naval Flier in the US Navy according the a Black weekly newspaper in August of 1952. During the Korean War, he flew the Panther Jet, operating from the Task Force 77 Carrier US Bon Homme Richard off the coast of Korea. Lt. Carter participated in a raid on Pyongyang, Korea. 1st Lt. Jed E. Carter, Berkeley, CA, 14th Infantry Regiment (former 24th Infantry Regiment officer); Sgt. Laurence Carter, US Air Force, Brooklyn, NY; Sgt. Ninevah Carter, St. Louis, MO; Pfc. Carl Chambers, Baltimore, MD; Pfc. Johnson Chambliss, Chicago, IL; Pfc. Vernon L. Campbell, Memphis, TN; SD/2 Floyd Chapman, Bennettsville, SC was in the US Navy and served in Korea aboard the Battleship USS Missouri which was in action in Korean Waters in 1951. SFC. Dewey Chappelle, Norfolk, VA, 24th Infantry Regiment, I and R Platoon; Sgt. Charles Charlton, Baltimore, MD; 1st Lt. Eugene Cheatham, Montclair, NJ served during the Korean War as an assistant group Intelligence Officer in the US Air Force. His Unit was responsible for flying supplies to Korea in addition he flew the C-47 airplanes. Ferdinand Carlise Cherry, Washington, DC; Technical Sgt. George Cheaney, Columbus, OH was assigned to the 5th Air Force Sabre Jet Fighter Interceptor Wing, Korea; Howard Christian, Newport News, VA; Arthur Clark, Warren, AK; Sgt. Frederick Clarke, Long Island, NY; Pfc. Arthur Clay, Wilson, NC; Charles Coles, Atlanta, GA, 24th Infantry Regiment. Cpl. Earl Coles, Washington,

DC served during the Korean War in the 7th Infantry Division's Military Police Company; PFC. George Cole, Company H, 24th Infantry Regiment, Korea; Cpl.Alfred Coleman, Detroit, MI; PFC

Everett Coleman, Richmond, VA; Pfc. Richard Compt, Mebane, NC; Sgt John Congo, Baltimore, MD; Pfc. David Conover, Newark, NJ; Pfc. Timothy Cooley, Americas, GA; Pfc. Ralph Collins, Darlington, SC; Major Samuel Coleman, Jamaica, NY served in Korea as the Chief of the Movements and Statistical Division in the Quarter Master Depot, Taegu, Korea. He supervised the routing of materials to the front line. William Corum, Philadelphia, PA; Cpl. Isaac Coates, Washington, DC; Pfc. David Copeland, Norfolk, VA; Pvt. Henry Cotton, Birmingham, AL; Master Sgt. Clarence Covington, St. Louis, MO; Pfc. Edward Covington, Memphis, TN; Pfc. James Cox, New Castle, PA the 24th Infantry Regiment; Cpl. Sherbert Cox, Company G, 24th Infantry Regiment, Scidell, LA, was a rifleman who was credited with killing the last enemy before the 24th Infantry Regiment was retired.

LTC Woodrow Crockett, US Air Force served in Korea as Deputy Commander, 2nd all weather Fighter Squadron, F-86 – Unit, Operations Officer of 26th Air Division, Headquarter and Test pilot at Edwards Air Force Base, CA. Crockett was assigned to the National Guard Bureau HQ, Washington, DC. He is a graduate of the Air Force Command and Staff College, Maxwell Air Force Base and also served as Wing Instructor Officer at Maxwell AFB. LTC Crockett also received the Tuskegee Airmen Noel Parrish Award.

Pvt. Norman P. Cromwell, Baltimore, MD, 24th Infantry Regiment is a graduate of Booker T. Washington High School. Capt. Geneva Culpepper, Wadley, AL served during the Korean War with the Japanese Logistical Command, Osaka Hospital. She also served during WWII.

Cpl. Olander Flemming, Cumberland, VA; Pfc. Emmanuel Curry, Baltimore, MD; Pfc. William Curry, Binghampton, NY served with the 35th Fighter Group. Sgt. Laurence Curtis, US Air Force; Warrant Officer Hillard Daniels served in Korea in 1952, Norfolk, VA; PFC Freeman Davis, Youngstown, OH, 24th Infantry Regiment; Sgt. George W. Davis, TX; Pvt. Herbert Davis, Forney, TX; Sgt. James Davis, SC; Lt. Judd Davis, US Marine Corps, Fu Quay, SC was commissioned in the V-12 program as a reserve officer in 1946 and was recalled to active status in the Korean War. In 1952 he was discharged for physical reasons. PFC Cecil Davidson, Pittsburgh, PA; Matthew Dawson, Jr. Columbus, GA served during the Korean War as a Medical Technician. US Naval Reserve, Alan P. Dean, Elmford, NY served aboard a ship in the Korean Waters during the War as a Photographic Ship Officer. Col. John H. Deveaux, Jacksonville, FL, 24th Infantry Regiment served as an Aide to Bishop John Gregg, African Methodist Episcopal Church (AME). In 1938 Deveaux was pastor of the Bethel AME Church, Williamsport, PA. He married Delia Mae Phillips of Xenea, OH and became the parents of three children. Pvt. E. B. Denson, Dallas, TX; Cpl. James L. Diggs, Durham, NC; Pfc. Booker Dingle, Newtown, PA; M/Sgt. Al Derrell, Washington, DC, 9th Infantry Regiment; Pvt. Kenwood Dissie, Detroit, MI; Sgt. Howard Dixon, Baltimore, MD; 1st. Lt. David R. Dixon, DDS, Barnwell, SC, a graduate of Howard University's School of Dentistry; Airman 2nd Class Edward Dixon, LA, was assigned to the Japan Air Defense Force, 327th Aircraft Control and Warning Group as a Radar Detachment Medical Technician in Southern Japan during the Korean War. Alice H. Dolphy, Pittsburgh, PA served at the General Army Hospital, Tokyo, Japan; Pfc. Harold Douglas, Cleveland, OH; Capt. Alvin J. Downing, Jacksonville, FL, 5th Air Force, Special Services Officer; Pfc. Charles Duckworth, Vernon, OH; 1st. Sgt. Roscoe Dudley, 77th Engineer Combat Company; Sgt. A. Dunn, Ruston, LA served in Korea with the 5th Air Force, 3rd Wing, B-26 Bombers; 1st. Lt. A. Drisdale was assigned to the 801st Medical Evacuation Squadron. He assisted combat wounded soldiers in flights from Korea to Japan. The patients were transported aboard the 374th Transportation Carrier Wing's C-54 Sky master in 1952. Lt. Edward Drummond Philadelphia,

PA, was assigned to FEAF in 1950; Capt. Charles Dryden, Nutley, NJ, US Air Force FEAF completed 50 missions over Korea. During WW II, he was assigned to the 99th Pursuit Squadron. Lt. Frank E. Earl, 24th Infantry Regiment, Charlottesville, VA; Sgt. Clarence Eckles, OK served with the Far East Air Forces in Japan. His task was the processing and shipping of material in support of United Nations troops in Korea because he was assigned to a General Supply Unit.

Sgt. James Edmondson, Columbus, OH was assigned to the Far East Air Force Command; Sgt. Calvin Edwards, Washington, DC served in Japan during the war; Cpl. Fenton M. Edwards, Baltimore, MD; Cpl. William Edwards, Conway, NC of the 24th Signal Company; Cpl. Calvin Ellis, Philadelphia, PA; Sgt. Daniel Elmore, Woodruff, SC; Lt. Horace Ester, Charlottesville, VA participated in a combat action near the Kuryong river in North Korea; Cpl. James Evans, Baltimore, MD; Ruppert Evans, Columbus, OH the 24th Infantry Regiment; Lt. Earl Frank, Charlottesville, VA the 24th Infantry Regiment; PFC Carlton B. Easley, Keysville, VA; Capt. Benjamin Fair weather, Brooklyn, NY while in Korea was an Ambulance Officer in a Field Hospital in Taegu. Cpl. Malcolm Faison, NC served with the 7th Infantry Division during the Korean War. Cpl. Farrell was a member of the 25th Infantry Division band. As a trumpeter, he was one of the three Black members of the band. Capt. James E. Fassett, Camden, NJ was a physician serving with the 5th Air Force in 1951 during the Korean War. Pvt. Nick Feeny, 24th Infantry Regiment, Brooklyn NY; Cpl. Lawrence Fields, Dallas, TX; Charles Fields, Baltimore, MD; Sgt. Robert L. Fisher, Natchez, MS served in Korea with the 5th Air Force, 3rd Wing B-26 Bomber; Leon C. Fitzgerald, US Navy served in Korea also; Cpl. Isaac Fleming, 24th Infantry Regiment, Detroit, MI; Ensign Albert J. Floyd, US Navy, Cincinnati, OH, assigned to the USS Leyte (CU-32) Aircraft Carrier, Detachment 3, VC-33 while in Korea. He attended Morehouse College, GA. Cpl. Alton C. Ford, Baton Rouge, LA; PFC Algin J. Ford, Baltimore, MD served with a Military Police Unit during the Korean War; Lt. John Ford served with the 3rd Battalion, 9th Infantry Regiment while in Korea; Pvt. Harrison Ford, Atlantic City, NJ; Cpl. John H. Ford, Buffalo, NY, assigned to the 452nd Bomber Wing during the Korean War; Pvt. James Foster, Bastrop, TX; Pvt. William Frazier, Chicago, IL, 1st Cavalry Division; Pvt. Walter Freeland, Baltimore, MD; Pvt. Bernard Freeman, Philadelphia, PA, 24th Infantry Regiment and Cpl. Wesley Fulton, Rock Hill, SC.

Capt. Hosea Gabriel, US Air Force, Port Arthur, TX served in Korea as a gunner on a reconnaissance bomber, B-29; PFC Leon Gaiten, Bessemer, AL; Pvt. Moses Garrett, Emporia, VA; Pvt. Percy Garrett, Norfolk, VA; Cpl. Columbus Gill, Chicago, IL of the 1st Cavalry Division; PFC Ozie Gibbs, Elizabeth, NC; SFC Clarence Gibson, Philadelphia, PA; Cpl. Robert Gibson, Bel Air, MD; Pvt. Donald Gilbert, El Monte, CA; Cpl. Bailey Gillespie, Bessemer City, AL was a medic during the Korean War; Harry Gist, US Navy, Chester, PA served in Korea aboard the USS Messaiac which saw action in 1951 in Korean waters; Cpl. Joe Goins, Jr., 24th Infantry Regiment, Alexandria, LA; Sgt. Harvey Gorden, Philadelphia, PA served in Korea as an Administrative Clerk; Master Sgt. Jack M. Gourdine, 24th Infantry Regiment, Chicago, IL. When the colors of the 24th Infantry Regiment were cased for the last time, Gourdine had the honors.

Pvt. Annie E. Graham, US Marine Corps was on active duty during the Korean War. She was the first Black Female Marine to enlist in Detroit, MI in 1949. Cpl Charles Graham, Baltimore, MD; Sgt. Charles Graham, New Stanton, PA, US Air Force assigned to the Motor Vehicle Squadron; PFC John J. Graham, Norfolk, VA; Cpl. Lawrence Grant, Baltimore, MD served with a integrated Tank Battalion; Lt. Sam Gravely, Jr., Richmond, VA assigned to the Battleship Iowa as the Radio Officer and Division Officer who assisted in the communication and routing of all radio traffic and messages; Sgt. Oliver Grayson, San Francisco, CA served with the 24th Infantry Regiment during the Korean War; Sgt. Curtis Green, 24th Infantry Regiment, Longview, TX a reconnaissance Sgt. who work with automatic weapons; Capt. Doxie Green, Physician,

Baltimore, MD served in Korea in 1951 as a Medical Officer in the Pusan area. He is a graduate of Meharry Medical College and completed his internship at Provident Hospital, Baltimore, MD.

Sgt. Raubie Green, 24th Infantry Regiment, Chester, PA; PFC Henry Gregory, Montgomery, AL; Sgt. Louis Green, Baltimore, MD; 1st Lt. William Greene, Staunton, VA was assigned to the Far East Air Force; Cpl. Milton Greene, Birmingham, AL; LTC James Griffin, Norfolk, VA served in Korea as a Chaplain in the Engineer Aviation Unit in 1951. Staff Sgt. Abraham Gross, St. Louis, MO was a radio operator with the 18th Bombardment Group during the War.

Capt. James L. Hall, Painesville, OH, Sales Officer, 19th Bomber Wing Far East Air Force; Sgt. Herbert Hall, Lake Charles, LA; PFC Joseph L. Hadley, Philadelphia, PA, flew combat missions with the 19th Bombardment Group attached to the FEAF Bomb command (provisional) during the Korean war. 1st Lt. Owen E. Hague, St. Louis, MO was a Finance Officer with the 20th Air Force, FEAF; PFC Joseph Hamilton, Washington, DC; Cpl. Everett Harper, Dallas, TX; Cpl. Charles Hamilton, Camden, NJ; PFC James R. Harris, Oakland, CA; Rachell Harris, Detroit, MI; William J. Harris, New York City, NY served as a Medic during the Korean War; PFC Curtis Hart, Washington, DC; PFC Clifton R. Hardy, Hertford, NC; Pvt. Jessie Hargrove, Camden, AR; PFC Julius P. Harrell, Norfolk, VA; Major John W. Handy, Brooklyn, NY served in Korea as a Chaplain in the 24th Infantry Regiment; Cpl. Elanton Hall, Oakdale, LA

Colonel John Harris, Medical Corp, 2nd Infantry Division Korea as a Sanitation Officer. Harris is a graduate of Meharry Medical College, completed his internship at Lincoln Hospital, Durham, NC, served in WW II in the Asiatic and European Theatre of Operations. He also served as Venereal Diseases Control Officer for the Philippine Ryukus Command. While serving in Korea he assisted in giving medical care and advice to Korean War orphans infected with diseases. PFC Arthur Harrison, New York City, NY; Pvt. Arthur Hayes, Marion, VA served in Nugunga, Okinawa during the Korean War. Cpl. Emanuel Headen, 24th Infantry Regiment, Castle Hayne, NC; Charles F. Hearn, St. Louis, MO; Pvt. Luther Henry, New York City, NY.

2nd Lt. H. Hart, Evanston, IL, was assigned to an Infantry Battalion in Korea. He was wounded in combat and received the Purple Heart Medal. He wrote a letter to a newspaper, *Daily Northwestern Newspaper,* expressing his views on racial prejudice being decreased in the military. He wrote the following:

> "It doesn't make any difference if you are White, red, Black, Green to the men over here. No record is kept on color. When we receive a draft of men they are assigned by name and experience only. There are no rush lights out here asking your race before you are accepted. We leave that to the mature fraternity men back home. There's no way we find out a man's color until we see him and by that time he's already in a foxhole and an integral part of his team. Our three Negro Corpsmen continually risk their lives to aid wounded men. We have no idea how many lives they have saved."

PFC Edgar J. Herman, Baltimore, MD; 1st Lt. David Hicks, Houston, TX served in Korea with the 5th Air Force, 3rd Wing, B-26 Bombers; Cpl. Harry Hicks, Baltimore, MD; James L. Hicks, Baltimore, MD was one of the first Black War Correspondents during the Korean War; Capt. Wesley Hicks, Dr. of Dental Surgery, DDS, graduate of Meharry Medical College and served in Korea; Cpl. William Hicks, Marianna, AR, 24th Infantry Regiment; Capt. Harold Hillery, Harlem, NY a pilot and Forward Ground Controller in the 24th Infantry Division. He was stationed near Taejon, Korea. It was reported that he was one of the aides to Major General Dean. Fortunately, he was able to escape from the North Koreans. PFC Edgar Hinton; SFC David Hinson, Bartow, FL, 24th Infantry Regiment; and Sgt. Jesse Hill, Chicago, IL also of the 24th Infantry Regiment.

Lt. Edward Norman Hodges, Detroit, MI served in Korea as a Public Information Officer, USAF at an air base in Pusan, Korea 1951. He is a graduate of the University of MI.

War Correspondent Albert S. Hinton was the Associate Editor of the Norfolk Journal and Guide Newspaper as well as the National Negro Publishers Association Pool War Correspondent. The 26 missing and presumed lost in the crash of a military plane off the Japanese coast in May, 1950, he was one. Three other war correspondents were on the plane enroute to the battlefront in Korea. The plane went down South of Oshima, Island and there was only one survivor. The other correspondents aboard the plane were James O. Supple, Chicago Sun Times; Maximillan Philonmo, Agencie Francais and Stephen Simmons, Hilton Press and London Picture Post.

Hinton was born in Portsmouth, VA, graduated from Elizabeth State College, NC, and studied at Howard University, Washington, DC. He joined the staff of the Journal and Guide as a reporters' city editor. He was married to Dovie Collins of Norfolk, VA and they were the parents of four children Albert Jr., Lelia, Carl and Gale. His siblings were Mrs. Daisy Oliver, Mrs. Flora Brown, Mrs. Mildred Gray, Mrs. Emma Bell, Mrs. Dorothy Hinton and Leonard Hinton.

Technical Sgt. Milburn Hodson, 3rd Air Rescue Squadron, Johnson Air Base, Japan. He was from Tuscon, AZ. Lt. James Hogan, Medical Corps, US Army, 1st Cavalry Division. Hogan was a member of the 38th Parallel Medical Society of Korea. He was from Means, FL. Staff Sgt. Horace Holland, Newport News, VA served in Korea with the 6147th Tactical Control Squadron, USAF; Cpl. Arthur J. Honore, Baton Rouge, LA, 5th Air Force Fighter 49th Bomber Wing, USAF; Master Sgt. David Howard, 24th Infantry Regiment, Cleveland, OH served as a Motor Sergeant in Korea; Sgt. William J. Howard, Denver, CO, USAF served with the 6127th Air Terminal Group, 3rd Bomber Wing, B-261; Pvt. John P. Howe, Grapeville, PA was assigned to the FEAF Airbase 6161st Wing, Japan; Sgt. George Hudson, Chicago, IL, was assigned to the Air Terminal Group during the Korean War. Sgt. Edgar R. Huff enlisted in the training at the Montford Point Camp, became a drill instructor at the Point and was the first Black to complete 30 years of regular service in the Marine Corps. His career included service in the Korean War and Vietnam War. He served as a Gunnery Sgt in Weapons Company, 2nd Battalion, 1st Marine during the Korean War also on the East Central front. At one time he was the only Black man in his Company; PFC John Humphrey, Pittsburgh, PA served in Korea with a Quarter Master Battalion; Cpl. Thomas Humphrey, Columbus, OH; PFC Walter Hyman, Florence, AL, 24th Infantry Regiment; PFC Willie Isaac, Eutaw, AL, 3rd US Infantry Division; PFC James E. Irving, Washington, DC; Cpl. Andrew Jackson, Chicago, IL, was stationed near YongDong Po, Korea in August, 1951; Carol J. Jackson, Chicago, IL; Cpl. Charles Jackson, Martin, TX; PFC Donald Jackson, Baltimore, MD; Cpl. Levi Jackson, Philadelphia, PA, 24th Infantry Division; PFC Timothy Jackson, Kilgore, TX; PFC William Jackson, Jr., Brooklyn, NY, K Company, 31st Regimental Combat Team, 7th Infantry Division.

General Daniel Chappie James, Jr., Pensacola, FL was the first Black Four Star General USAF. During the Korean War he flew 101 combat missions in F-51 and F-80 airplanes. He also served with the 13th Air Force in the Philippines; Sgt. Robert Janifer, Pottstown, PA, 24th Infantry Regiment, Sgt. Clarence Jeffrey, Newport News, VA, 24th Infantry Regiment; Lt. Constance Jenkins, Philadelphia, PA served as an Army Nurse with the Air base hospital in Japan; Lt. Jasper Jackson, Durham, NC, 24th Infantry Regiment; William K. Jenkins, Navel ROTC graduate, IL, Polytechnic Institute, a veteran of WWII was commissioned an Ensign and assigned to inactive status. During the Korean War, 1st Lt. Louise Jenkins, ASAF was assigned to the 801st Air Evacuation Squadron; Sgt. Julius Jiggetts Pittsburgh, PA; Pvt. Louis D. Johns Wausau, FL; Pvt.

Alfred Johnson; 1st Lt. Andrew Johnson, Greensboro, NC served as an Adjutant, 20th Air Force, FEAF during the Korean War; Bernard H. Johnson, Norfolk, VA; Calvin W. Johnson, Baltimore, MD; Capt. Ruth Faulkner Johnson, US Air Force, Nurse Corps, Chicago, IL served during the Korean War at the Far East Command hospital, Tokyo, Japan; PFC Henry Johnson, Hopkinsville, Kentucky; PFC Leroy Johnson, Philadelphia, PA; Sgt. Junior Johnson, Marion, SC, 24th Infantry Regiment; PFC Marvin Johnson, Baltimore, MD; Technical Sgt. M. Johnson, US Air Force, Columbus, OH, 5th Air Force Fighter Interceptor Wing; Cpl. Robert Johnson, Jr., Richmond, VA; 2nd Lt. Sydney Johnson, Springfield, OH, Adjutant 13th Air Force, FEAF; Cpl. Davis Jones; Cpl. Edward L. Jones, Indianapolis, IN; PFC Harry Jones, Lynchburg, VA; Airman 1st Class James C. Jones, US Air Force, Norfolk, VA. He served with the 4th Fighter Interceptor Wing F-86 Jet Base Korea. Jones attended Booker T. Washington High School.

Sgt. John L. Jones Madisonville, OH was assigned to an Air Force Combat Unit in Korea; Staff Sgt. Louis Jones, Portsmouth, VA served during the Korean War as a Jet Aircraft Mechanic, US Air Force All Weather Squadron, 35th Fighter Interceptor Aerial Defense Unit, Wing, Japan; Cpl. Robert Jones, Washington, DC; Cpl. George W. Jordan, Eastville, VA; Airman Denner Judd, US Air Force was a member of a B-26 crew during the Korean War; PFC John Judge Bessemer, AL; Cpl. Dennis Isaac, Sumter, SC; Cpl. James Keeton, Ft. Worth, TX, F Company, 24th Infantry Regiment; Johnnie Kennerly, Washington, DC; Cpl. Irving King, Washington, DC; James C. King, Detroit, MI served in Korea as a telephone Operator, US Air Force Airways Communication Services that provided weather information for Korea; Capt. Robert King, New York City, NY was a communication Officer with the Far East Bomber Command during the Korean War; Pvt. Ross King, Chicago, IL; Lt. George W. Kirkland served in Korea with a Quarter Master Baking Company; Sgt. John W. Knight, Suffolk, VA served in Korea as a cook with the 5th Air Force, 4th Fighter Interceptor Wing; PFC Clarence Kearney, Warrenton, NC; Pvt. Frank Lavor, Milwaukee, WI, 24th Infantry Regiment served in Korea as a Medical Technician; PFC William Lawrence, Henderson, TX, 24th Infantry Regiment; Cpl. William Lawes, Philadelphia, PA was assigned as a Baker in a Quarter Master Baking Company; Cpl. L. B. Lay, Chicago, IL, F Company, 24th Infantry Regiment; PFC David Lee, St. Louis, MO; Lt. Frank Lee, Los Angeles, CA, FEAF was assigned as an Aircraft and Maintenance Officer.

Lee Earl Oliver, former Mayor of Brookville, OK, Pottawatome County served during the Korean War and is the recipient of the Purple Heart Medal. Pvt. John Lee, Washington, DC; Lt. Paul D. Lehman, Los Angeles, CA, 19th Bombardment Group and served as a Bombardier Radar Navigator on an airplane; Lt. Charles Lenon, Kansas served with the 77th Engineer Combat Company; Sgt. Leo Lesser, Indianapolis, IN; Cpl. David C. Lester, Louisville, KY; Cpl. Philip Lett, Pensacola, FL; Cpl. A. Lewis, Oakland, CA 5th Air Force. Cpl. Clinton Lewis, Milwaukee, WI was a radio operator while in Korea; 1st Lt. William H. Lewis, Charleston, W. VA, 20th Air Force, FEAF; Pvt. Willie Lightfoot, 24th Infantry Regiment, Niagara Falls, NY; Pvt. J. Lilley, Hobbsville, NC served with a medical hospital unit in Korea; Cpl. Wendell Lindberry, Lawrenceville, VA US Air Force; Tech. Sgt. William Linson, La Fayette, AL was assigned as a Communication Chief, 3rd Bombardment Wing, Kunsan, Korea and Iwakuni, AFB Japan. PFC James H. Little, Norfolk, VA; Pvt. Oscar Little, Jersey City, NY; LTC Harry F. Lofton, Washington, DC served briefly as Commander of the 3rd Battalion, 24th Infantry Regiment and in addition was a veteran of WW II. Pvt. James Long, Pocomoke, MD served in Korea as an automatic rifleman with the 25th Infantry Division; Nathaniel Long, Baltimore, MD; Pvt. Jack Love, 24th Infantry Regiment, Gallatin, MS was a medical technician; Lt. Juanita Long served in Korea near Pusan in 1951, where she conducted classes for Korean nurses. She was from Boston, MA. PFC Robert Lee Lowery served in Korea and was assigned to a Marine Unit. He also won a lightweight title in a boxing tournament; Pvt. Levin Lucas, Washington, DC; Sgt. John Lyle,

Baltimore, MD, 24th Infantry Regiment; Sgt. Archie Lynn, Chicago, IL; Sgt. Walter H. Mason, Company H, 24th Infantry Regiment.

Capt. Thomas Mac Calla, US Marine Corps, was a member of the second Battalion, 5th Marines 81st Mortar, 1st Marine Division, born in Bridgeport, CT July 2, 1929. As the son of Dr. Reuben A. Mac Calla, DDS and Esther Conway Mac Calla, he is a graduate of Fairfield University. In 1964 he was awarded a Doctorate Degree in Education by the University of CA at Los Angeles. Mac Calla married Jacqueline E. Campbell and they are the parents of three children. Thomas Mac Calla enlisted in the US Marine Corp in 1952 and was assigned to Quantico, VA where he completed the Officer's Candidate course and was assigned to Korea. He also attended the 14th Special basic training course. It is believed that Lt. Mac Calla was the first Black Marine Officer assigned to receive a command position as a Platoon Commander. He was also the first Black Officer to be assigned to a General Staff, First Marine Division as a Historical Officer with the responsibility of writing and compiling the Division's Prisoner of War (POW) exchanges. Mac Calla wrote the official diary and assembled the pictorial exchange of the US Marines War exchange of prisoners during the period July – August, 1953. He was discharged from the active Marines and became a Marine reserve officer with the rank of Captain.

Mac Calla worked briefly as an employee with the Connecticut Welfare Agency and later he taught school in the Santa Monica High School. He also worked at Santa Monica City College as a College Professor, Chairman of the English Department, and Administrator. In 1957 he was selected to participate in the production of an Academy Award Documentary Film called "A Force and Readiness".

PFC John Mac Grow, Kilgore, TX served in Korea in 1950; SFC Carlos Mackey, Baltimore, MD; MSgt. Harold F. Macklin, Baltimore, MD; Pvt. Leonard W. Macklin, Chicago, IL; Pvt. Howard G. Mason, Chicago, IL; Airman 2nd Class (A 2/c) Joe H. Martin, Martinsville, VA served in Korea with the 51st Fighter Interceptor Wing as a heavy vehicle operator; Colonel John Martin, Washington, DC, served during the Korean War as a public Information Officer in the US Army Command Headquarters in Japan. He was also a Military Assistant in the office of the Assistant Secretary for Manpower and Reserve, Department of Defense, Pentagon, Washington, DC. Col. Martin was appointed Director of Selective Service, Washington, DC.

Cpl. Joseph J. Martin, Norfolk, VA served with the 24th Infantry Regiment during the Korean War; Ralph Matthews was a War correspondent for the Baltimore Afro American, as well as the Norfolk Journal and Guide Newspapers in Korea. He was also present for the news coverage of the founding of the United Nations at San Francisco, CA; Sgt. Walter H. Mason, Company H, 24th Infantry Regiment; Lt. Lawrence Martin, Eden, MD assigned to the General Hospital, Tokyo, Japan during the Korean War. LTC Hurdle Maxwell, US Marine Corp enlisted in the Marines and attended State Teachers College. He was Commissioned a reserve 2nd Lt. in March 1953 and a regular Officer in September the same year. Maxwell was on active duty during the Korean War and was promoted to LTC in 1969. He was the first Black Officer to command an Infantry Battalion, 6th Marines and retired in 1971.

MSgt. Thomas McCullough, Greenville, SC served in Korea with the 24th Infantry Regiment; Major Armour McDaniel, Martinsville, VA was assigned to the 315th Air Defense Headquarter; 2nd Lt. Charles E McGee a veteran of WW II, was assigned to the 67th Fighter Bomber Squadron during the Korean War. He flew the P-51 missions; PFC Monroe McGhee, Chicago, IL; PFC John C. Mac Grow, Kilgore, TX; MSgt. Harold McLeod, 24th Infantry Regiment, Washington, DC; Pvt. David McMullen, Atlanta, GA served with the 1st. Cavalry Division in Korea; Sgt.

Howard Mc Murren, Elizabeth, NC; Lt. Clifton McVey, San Antonio, TX; Capt. Nathaniel Mc Wee, Buzzard Bay, MA, the 24th Infantry Regiment.

MEDICAL DOCTORS

There were medical doctors who served during the Korean War either in the United States, Japan or Korea. Some of them were:

Dr. Alvin Jerome Thompson, a graduate of Howard University College of Medicine, 1946. His specialty is gastroenterology and served as Chief Medical services at Ramsey Air Force Base Hospital.

Dr. James Allison Miller, graduate of Washington, DC public schools, Lovejoy Elementary, Garnett Paterson Jr. H. S. and Dunbar H.S. He is a 1948 graduate of Howard University College of Medicine and completed his internship at Katie Bitting Reynolds hospital in Raleigh, NC. During the Korean War he was assigned as a Commander of a hospital that treated mainly paratroopers. After the war, Miller was an assistant Chief of Orthopedics, Valley Forge Hospital, Phoenixville, PA. When the late President Dwight Eisenhower was a patient at Walter Reed Army Medical Center in the 1950's, one of the physicians attending him was Dr. Miller. He also served in Vietnam. Dr. Miller retired from the US Army with the Silver Star Medal, Bronze Star Medal, V for Valor, Purple Heart with Oak Leaf Cluster, and three US Presidential Citations as well as a Presidential Citation from the Korean Government. As a civilian, he became Chief of Orthopedics at the Sunset Permanente Hospital in Los Angeles, CA, an Associate Clinical Professor at Marin Luther King General Hospital and Charles Drew Hospital Graduate Medical School, 1974 – 1976. He also served as assistant Professor at the University of CA.

Captain Howard W. Kenny, M.D. received his BS degree from Bates College and MD degree from Meharry Medical College. During the Korean War he served as a Captain in the US Army Medical Corps.

Col. John F. Harris, Medical Corps, graduate of Howard University with a BS degree and Mc Harry Medical College for the MD degree. He received a MS degree in Public Health at the University of Michigan. Harris served in WW II and the Vietnam War. During the Korean War, he was a Regimental Surgeon, 2nd Infantry Division. He was the recipient of the Silver Star and Legion of Merit Medals.

Dr. Kenneth W. Clement, US Air Force, Medical Corps born in Vashti, Pittsylvania County, VA and reared in Cleveland OH. Clement graduated from Oberlin College and Howard University, College of Medicine, 1945. During the Korean War, Dr. Clement served as a Flight Surgeon for US Air Force Medical Corps, 1951-1953. He also served as the Chief Professional Services, Lockbourne Air Force Base Hospital.

LTC Lawrence Greene, Medical Corps, Brookfield, OH was a veteran of WW II. During the Korean War Greene was assigned to the 382nd General Hospital as Chief, Out Patient Service.

Aris T. Allen was born December 17, 1910 in San Antonio, TX and graduated from Howard University, College of Medicine, 1944. He studied at the Universities of Buffalo, Harvard, New Mexico and New York. During the Korean War Allen served as a Flight Surgeon in US Air

Force Medical Corps, 1953-1955. Upon retirement he had a medical practice in Annapolis, MD and was also a member of the Maryland State Legislature.

Arthur L. Johnson, Jr., US Air Force was a graduate of Howard University, College of Medicine class of 1943. During the Korean War, Johnson was a US Air Force medical doctor assigned to the Alaskan Command.

Captain Clyde W. Phillips, US Air Force Medical Corps, is a graduate of Howard University, College of Medicine, 1946. During the Korean War he was assigned Chief of Surgery, 6110th US Air Force Base Hospital, Nagoya, Japan.

Dr. Howard A. Boyd, US Army is a graduate of Howard University College of Medicine, class of 1946. He was stationed with the 2nd Infantry Division in Korea and his specialty was internal medicine.

Dr. Albert Lee Gaskins, US Navy, Philadelphia, PA, received his BS degree and MD degree from Howard University in 1943 and 1948. During the Korean War he had an assignment with the US Navy.

Captain Rudolph Miller, US Marine Corps, a graduate of Howard University, College of Medicine, 1947. During the Korean War he served in Japan as a Captain in the US Marine Medical Corps.

Dr. Emerson Coleman Walden, Cambridge, MD, US Air Force was born on October 7, 1923. Walden is a graduate of the Howard University College of Medicine, 1947. He is past President of the National Medical Association. During the Korean War Walden was the Chief of the Surgical Section, US Air Force Hospital at Mitchell Air Force Base, Long Island, NY 1951-1953.

ADDITIONAL SELECTED VETERANS

Pfc. John D. Miller, 24th Infantry Regiment, served in Korea; Cpl. Philip A. Miatt, Richmond IN, 5th US Air Force, 48th Fortress Bomber Wing. He was assigned to the Finance section while in Korea; Major Donald Miller, New York City, NY, served as a Battalion Sgt. Major during the Korean War; 1951-1952. In 1956, he was a distinguished graduate of the US Army's Infantry Officers Candidate School and was commissioned a 2nd Lieutenant. Miller received a BS degree from the University of MD and retired in 1969. In 1971, he served as a Deputy Assistant Secretary of Defense for Equal Opportunity.

Sgt. Horace Miller, Norfolk, VA served in a Combat Engineer Battalion during the Korean War; SFG Russell Miller, Baltimore, MD; PFC Richard K. Miller, Memphis, TN; PFC Earl Minn, Jr., Chicago, IL, 24th Infantry Regiment; Pvt. Robert Mitchell, St. Louis, MO; PFC Belton Mobley, Philadelphia, PA, served in Korea and Japan with a AAA Squadron as an Electrical Power man Technician; PFC William Moffett, Michigan served in Korea, 1951; Sgt. Herbert Montgomery, Homestead, FL, 24th Infantry Regiment; Pvt. Robert Mountain, Washington, DC served as a Medical Technician in Korea. Cpl Charles B. Moore, New York City, NY; PFC Edward Moore, 24th Infantry Regiment, Los Angeles, CA, was the recipient of the Combat Infantry Badge; Cpl. John D. Moore, Gary IN served in Korea; Pvt. Marcus Moore, New Orleans, LA, served in Korea with the 49th Fighter Bomber Wing as an Armorer. He was responsible for the loading of rockets into F-80 Jet Shooting Star Airplanes at an Air Force Base in Korea.

Cpl Robert Moore, Pittsburgh, PA, US Air Force, assigned as a Munitions Specialist for the 6161st Air Bomber Wing in Japan; PFC Stanly Moore, Baltimore, MD, served in Korea as a Medical Technician; PFC Thomas C. Morgan, VA; Lt. Clarence Mosely, Roselle, NJ, 24th Infantry Regiment; PFC James Mosley, New York City, NY; PFC Thomas Motley, St. Louis, MO, US Army 1st. Cavalry Division; PFC Alexander Myers, Jr., Washington, DC; Sgt. H. Nelson, St. Louis, MO; Cpl. Robert R. Nelson, Chicago, IL; Lt. Wilbert J. Newsome, Houston, TX, former member of the 24th Infantry Regiment. However, as of November, 1951, he was assigned to an integrated Unit in Korea and his platoon had only three Black members. Lt. Royal Nickens, Philadelphia, PA; Cpl. Oscar Nixon New York City, NY, a member of the 8th Army Military Police Battalion in Korea; PFC William J. Owens, Company F, 24th Infantry Regiment, Korea.

Sgt Harry Page, Dillon, SC served in Korea in 1951; SD/3 Matthew Paige, US Navy, Winchester, VA served in Korea aboard the USS Missouri which saw action in the Korean waters. Capt. John Palmer, US Air Force Medical Corps, Yipsalanti, MI, served during the Korean War as a surgeon with the 121st Evacuation Hospital, Seoul, Korea; Cpl. Julius Parham, US Marine Corps was a member of the framed Marine Black Sheep Fighter Squadron, Far East Air Command. He was a native of New York City, NY; PFC Roland Parham served in Korea was from Waverly, VA; Capt. Frederick Parker, US Air Force, Chicago, IL, assigned to the Far East Air Force Command as an Aircraft Maintenance Officer; Lt. Elgen Parkins, Oakes, ND; Cpl. John Parker, Detroit, MI, 35th Infantry Regiment; PFC Samuel Paschael, Roanoke, VA; Sgt. Lawrence Patterson, Chicago, IL, 24th Infantry Regiment; Cpl. Elmer Payne, Marblehead, MA assigned to the Armed Forces Radio Network in Korea, 1951.

Pvt. Payton W. Hayes, Norfolk, VA, US Army, 7th Infantry Division, 17th Infantry Regiment. Assigned in Korea as a Machine Gunner and was the recipient of a Combat Infantry man's Badge; Lt. Hazael Peoples served in Korea with the 77th Engineer Combat Company; Cpl. William Peoples, Columbia, SC was assigned to a Quarter Master Baking Company; PFC Roosevelt Perin, Lawrenceville, VA served in Korea with the 35th Infantry Regiment.

Lt. General Frank E. Petersen, US Marine Corps received his commission and flying status (wings) in October, 1952 at the Naval Air Station, Pensacola, FL. He served during the Korean War in 1953 and completed 64 combat missions. Petersen earned the Distinguished Flying Cross and six air Medals. He retired in 1988; PFC Arnold Peters, Bronx, NY served in Korea; Corp. Ernest W. Pickett, Berwyn, OK; PFC David Pigford, Magnolia, NC; Cpl. John L. Pierce, San Francisco, CA 24th Infantry Regiment; Pvt. James Pikes, Chicago, IL; PFC Edward Pierson, Indianapolis, IN; PFC Ellis Pitt, Edgecombe, NC, served in Korea; Lt. Edgar Potts, Cleveland OH, served during the Korean War with the 1st Cavalry Division. PFC Joe W. Potts, Fresno, CA; PFC Paul W. Pope, Chicago, IL; PFC Tomnas Potter, VA, served in Korea with the 17th Infantry Regiment, 7th Infantry Division in 1952; 2nd Lt. Silas Pratt, Newsberry, SC, received his ROTC training at South Carolina State College, Orangeburg, SC. He served in Korea as a Platoon Leader, I Company, 3rd Battalion, 35th Infantry Regiment. Master Sgt. Earl P. Prince, Nashville, TN; PFC George Pullin, Jr. Philadelphia, PA, 24th Infantry Regiment; SFC Anthony Pugh, Charlotte Courthouse, VA served in Korea with an Engineer Aviation Battalion as a Heavy Equipment Operator; PFC William Quaterman, Fairmont, West VA.

Lt. Dayton Ragland, US Air Force, Kansas City, MO, assigned to the 4th Fighter Interceptor Wing where he flew the F-86 Sabres plane at Air bases in Taegu and Suwon, Korea. Lt Ragland participated in a surprise attack on the communist air field at Uiju, Korea. There were 12 Migs parked on the runway and with the assistance of his fellow pilots, two Migs were destroyed and some were badly damaged. SFC Joseph Randall, Phoenix, AZ served in Korea in 1952; PFC

Morris Randall, Phoenix, AZ; Cpl. William Raney, Baltimore, MD; Master Sgt. Walton Ratliff, Wilson, VA 3rd Battalion, 24th Infantry Regiment; Pvt. Howard Ray, East St. Louis, IL; Capt. Moses Ray, US Air Force, Washington, DC served as a Dental Surgeon with the 4th Fighter Wing in 1951. Ray is a graduate of Howard University and had a dental practice in Tarboro, NC; Major Lee Rayford, US Air Force was the Commander of the Kimpo Air Base in Korea, 1951; Cpl. Milton Reed, US Army, San Francisco, CA, assigned to the 25th Infantry Division Band during the Korean War; PFC James Reed, Baltimore, MD; Pvt. Andrew Reeves, Chicago, IL; PFC Merle Reynolds, St. Joseph, MI was a Medical Technician during the Korean War; Airman Albert W. D. Rice, US Air Force, Nashville, TN was assigned to the 49th Fighter Bomber Wing, 5th Air Force. Rice's duty assignment was to patch up flak holes on the F-80 Jet Planes; Sgt Clarence Reynolds, Chicago, IL was assigned to the 212th Military Police Company; Lt. Ellis Richardson, US Air Force, Tuskegee, AL was a Routing Officer for the 6127th Air Terminal Group, Korea. Richardson is a graduate of Tuskegee University.

Alvin R. Ricks, US Navy, Norfolk, VA, was assigned to the light cruiser, USS Juneau which played a prominent role in the Korean Conflict.; 1st Lt. Claudia Richardson, US Air Force was on active duty during the Korean War; SFC Jack M. Richardson, US Army, Corpus Christi, TX served in Korea as a member of the 24th Infantry Regiment's Intelligence and Reconnaissance Platoon; PFC Richard Rivers, Memphis, TN served in Korea during 1951; Sgt. James Roberts, Philadelphia, PA; 1st Lt. Leroy Roberts, US Air Force, Anderson, SC, was assigned to the Far East Air Force during the Conflict; Sgt. William Roberts, 24th Infantry Regiment, Norfolk, VA; PFC Freddie L. Robertson, Company C, 27th Infantry Regiment, Blackstone, VA. Robertson served in Korea as a rifleman.

PFC William Robertson, Chicago, IL was assigned to the 49th Fighter Bomber Wing during the Korean War; Sgt. Dean Robinson, a veteran of WW II served in Korea in 1950 and calls home Leland, MS; PFC Leroy Rodgers, Warren, OH, served in Korea.

GM/3C Phil Rogers, S/D 3/C William Walker and S/D 3/C Louis Washington were crew members aboard the US Navy's USS Lind. The Lind spent nine months as part of the United Nations' blockade force during the Korean War.

2nd Lt. Marion Rogers, US Air Force, Seattle, Washington was assigned as an Administrative Inspector of the Far East Air Force during the Conflict; Seaman James Royal, US Navy, Brooklyn, NY; PFC Nathaniel Royal, US Marine Corps, NY; Cpl. Albert Samuel of Winston Salem, NC served in Korea in 1951; Frederick H. Samuels, US Air Force, Philadelphia, PA served with the 5th Air Force, Far East Air Force Command as an Information and Education Officer during the Korean War; Pvt. Albert Samson, 24th Infantry Regiment, Hampton, VA; PFC F. Sanders, Company I, 24th Infantry Regiment, Baltimore, MD; PFC Grover Sanders, Clayton, NC served in Korea, prior to enlistment he was a student at Shaw University, Raleigh, NC; Sgt. Clayton Savey, Annapolis, MD; Sgt. Leonard G. Sawyer, Portsmouth, VA; Roosevelt Sawyer, Newport News, VA; Master Sgt. Bernie Scott, 24th Infantry Regiment, Echman, West VA; Pvt. Harold Scott, Canon, GA; Cpl. James F. Scott, Richmond, VA; Cpl. Thomas K. Scott, 24th Infantry Regiment, Newport News, VA a graduate of Huntington H. S. and served as a Radio Technician while in Korea; Pvt. Vernon Scruggins, Richmond, VA; Capt. Thomas F. Sellers, Philadelphia, PA served with a Quartermaster Baking Company in Korea; Sgt. David Session, Alexandria, VA; Sgt. Charles Simmons, Greensboro, NC; PFC Calvin J. Simons, Chicago, IL; Sgt. Joseph Simmons, 24th Infantry Regiment Combat Team, Charleston, SC; PFC Jack Simpson, Detroit, MI; Hospital Corpsman Arthur Singleton, Houston, TX; Cpl. Thomas Shaw, US Air Force, Philadelphia, PA was a gunner on a B-29 Reconnaissance aircraft while in Korea; Cpl. Jesse Shelley, Miami, FL; Sgt. Edward T. Shelton, Chicago, IL.

PFC Harry Shirley, Madison, AL; PFC Theophilius Shirley, Indianapolis, IN, 24th Infantry Regiment; Cpl. James Short, Beach Grove, IN; PFC Leon Short, Chicago, IL

Brigadier General George M. Shuffer, Palestine, TX was born September 27, 1931 and served as the Assistant Deputy Chief of Staff for Personnel, US Army Europe and Assistant Division Commander, 3rd US Infantry Division US Army Europe. Shuffer also served heroically during the Conflict as indicated by his receiving the Silver Star Medal, Legion of Merit, Air Medal, Purple Heart, Combat Infantryman Badge and the Parachutist Badge.

Sgt. Leroy A. Shuttlesworth, Tacoma, Washington; PFC George Sloan, Aberdeen, MD; PFC John T. Sloan, Chicago, IL; Cpl Ernest Smiley, AL; Sgt Martin Smith, Baltimore, MD; Cpl. Norman Smith, Baltimore, MD; Sgt. Thomas J. Smith, US Air Force, Miami, FL, served with the 5th US Air Force Command in Japan during the Korean War; Sgt. William Smith, Baltimore, MD; PFC William R. Snowden, Baltimore, MD; PFC Curtis Solomon, Monticello, GA.

Hospital man 3rd C Frank Sparks, Jr., US Navy, Norfolk, VA served in Korea with the 1st Marine Division and participated in the assault landing at Inchon and the liberation of Seoul, Korea. He was at the withdrawal from the Chosin Reservoir. Sparks is a graduate of Booker T. Washington H. S. Norfolk, VA. During his tour of duty he earned the Bronze Star Medal and the Korean Service Ribbon with three Stars. Cpl. Joe F. Speaks, 24th Infantry Regiment, Jacksonville, MS; Pvt. Oscar Spearman, Washington, DC; Sgt. Vernon Spence, Baltimore, MD was assigned to the 616th Air Base Wing, Tokyo Japan. He serviced and maintained B-29 Bombers which were conducting daily combat strikes against North Korean targets. Sgt. Joe Spivey, Toledo, OH served with a grave registration Unit; Cpl. Willie Staples, Tuscaloosa, AL; Airman 3rd Class M. Stanford, Jr., Norfolk, VA; Sgt. Edward Starks, Baltimore, MD; PFC Richard Stephens Norcross, GA; Cpl. Robert L. Stephenson, Portsmouth, VA served with the 64th Heavy Tank Battalion during the Korean War. He also was a graduate of Norcom H S.

2nd Lt. George W. Sterling, US Air Force Los Angeles, CA was assigned as a technical Supply Officer, 20th Air Force, Far East Air Force Command during the Conflict; PFC Samuel Stephen, Akron, OH; Richard Stevens, Cleveland, OH; Cpl. Robert Stevenson, New Orleans, LA

Cpl. Cessie D. Stewart, Petersburg, VA while in Korea was the recipient of the Commendation Medal; Sgt. Charles Stewart, Baton Rough, LA; Sgt. William Stewart, Newsport, VA; Cpl. Bardett Stills, Shreveport, LA; Cpl. Garfield Stone, US Air Force, Richmond, VA assigned as an Armorer responsible for loading the 50 caliber machine gun on the F-84 Jets during the Korean Conflict; Capt. Lillian Stone, US Air Force, Philadelphia, PA served as a nurse at the US Air Force Base Hospital, Nagoya, Japan; MSG David Stover, TN; Cpl. Leroy Strong, New York City, NY served as a surgical technician in Korea. Capt. John J. Suggs, Far East Air Force, Terre Haute, IN; PFC John W. Sutton, Company C, 24th Infantry, Pricedale, PA; Sgt. Linwood Sutton, Hartford, NC. Cpl. Marvin Taft, Baltimore, MD; Sgt. Thaddeus Taft, Los Angeles, CA served as an Armorer in the 8th Bomber Squadron during the War; Pvt. Clarence Tanaker, Alexandria, LA also served in Korea.

SFC James Taliaferro Baltimore, MD; PFC Oscar Taliaferro, Amburg, VA; Cpl. Marvin Tapp, Durham, NC; PFC Luther R. Taylor, Crockett, TX was awarded the Commendation Medal; Cpl. Nathaniel Taylor, Jersey City, NJ; Capt. Ordie Taylor was assigned to 24th Infantry Regiment prior to integration. In 1951 November he was reassigned to Headquarter, 25th Infantry Division. He lived in New Jersey. Cpl. Richard Taylor, Company H 24th Infantry Regiment; Major Ulysses Taylor assigned Maintenance Officer, 49th Fighter Bomber Wing during the Korean War; PFC Claudius Taylor, Golston, NC; PFC Baron Lee Tennelle, Jasper, AL; PFC Curtis Thomas, Los

Angeles, CA; Sgt. H. W. Thomas, Washington, DC; SD/3 Wade Theus served aboard the US Navy USS Missouri Battleship that was in action in Korean waters. The Dreadnaught steamed approximately 41,000 miles in the combat zone and fired on targets in the vicinity of Chongjin in 1951. PFC Philip Thomas, 24th Infantry Regiment; Cpl. Clinton Thomas served with the 1st Marine Division; Pvt. James Thomas, Philadelphia, PA; Sgt. Albert S. Thompson, Company E, 9th US Infantry Regiment, Philadelphia, PA served as a Medical Technician; Pvt. James D. Thompson, Baltimore, MD; PFC Jesse Thomas, Warren, AR; Pvt. Silas Thompson, Youngstown, OH, 35th Infantry Regiment; PFC Arthur Thorn, Lewis, SC; Cpl. Carl S. Throiner, Fordyce, TX; Pvt. Robert Tillman, Gloucester, VA; Lt. Ulysses Toatley, Washington, DC stationed in Okinawa during the Korean War; Cpl. Floyd Townsend, Milford, Delaware served with the 32nd US Infantry Regiment, 7th US Infantry Division in the Honor Guard. PFC Sammie Troy, San Francisco, CA; Cpl. Andrew Turner, Annapolis, MD; PFC Bobby Tyson, Kentucky; Cpl. Lionel Valentine, New Orleans, LA served with the 25th US Infantry Division, 1951; PFC James Vaughn, Staunton, VA; PFC Walter Venable, Pamplin, VA; Cpl. J. Verner, Wisconsin; PFC Ray Vincenti, Hagerstown, MD.

Cpl. William Wade, Bristol, VA; PFC Thaddeus Waiters, Charleston, SC served during the Korean Was as a US Air Force Policeman. Capt. Roger S. Walden, US Army, a veteran of WW II served during the Korean War with the 24th Infantry Regiment. From Detroit, MI, he was assigned Company F, 2nd Battalion; Capt. Horace Walker, Kansas City, KS, led a patrol in Korea near the area of Wonju and returned with some enemy Prisoners of War; Cpl. James Walker, 24th Infantry Regiment, Newark, NJ; PFC Moses Walker, 24th Infantry Regiment served near Yechon, Korea, and lived in Chester, PA; PFC James W. Wallace, Washington, DC; Sgt. Willard Wallace, Texarkana, TX; Pvt. Moses Walker, Chester, PA; Master Sgt. Andrew Walton served with the 77th Engineer Combat Company while in Korea

Sgt. Lois Wanzo, Marietta, OH served in Yokohama, Japan and was assigned a Chief Clerk, Safety Branch, Central Command Headquarters; Pvt. Albert Ward, Portsmouth, VA; 1st Lt. Arthur L. Ward, US Air Force, Birmingham, AL served during the Korean War as a Supply Officer, 20th Air Force, Far East Air Force Command; PFC Leonard Warden, 24th Infantry Regiment, G Company; Cpl. Wilmer Warr, US Army, Detroit, MI served as a member of the 25th Infantry Division band; Cpl Bonnie Warren, Dallas, TX ; PFC John D. Warren, Jamesburg, NJ; Cpl. John W. Washington, Norfolk, VA; Sgt. Levi Washington, Company H, 24th Infantry Regiment; Pvt. Raymond Washington, Chicago, IL; Capt. Sullus Washington, Chaplain was stationed in Gifu, Japan in 1951 lived in Gary, IN; PFC Thomas Washington, Fredericksburg, VA served with a Quartermaster Battalion during the Korean War.

Ms Shirley M. Walton was present in Korea in 1951 as a Red Cross Worker; Cpl. Harry Watley, St. Thomas, Virgin Island; PFC Edward I. Watson, Roverfield, VA; Major George W. Webb, US Air Force, Washington, DC was assigned as an Administrative Officer, 19th Wing, Guam, Far East Air Force Command during the Korean War; Sgt. George Wellison, assigned Headquarters Company, 25th US Infantry Division; Capt. Rosalie H. Wiggins was assigned to the General Hospital, Tokyo, Japan; PFC James Whening, Rockhill, SC; Frank Whisonant, a WW II veteran, 370th Infantry was a war Correspondent for the Pittsburgh Courier Newspaper; Sgt Archie White, Norfolk, VA, assignment the 2nd Armored Division; Ms Gyree White was present in Korea in 1951 as a Red Cross Worker; SFC John O. White, Des Moines IA; Capt. Charles F. Whitten, Medical Corps, Wilmington, DE was a Staff Surgeon at Camp GiFu in 1951. He is a graduate of Meharry Medical College; PFC Clarence Whitmore, 24th Infantry Regiment served near Sangju, Korea; PFC Clarence Whitemore, St Louis, MO; Sgt. Eldred Wilkerson, Baltimore, MD; Pvt. Jerry Wilkerson, Reidville, NC served with the 19th Combat Engineers in 1951; Cpl. William Wickes, CA; Staff Sgt. Hiram Wilkins, St. Louis, MO a veteran of WW II and a draftsman assigned to 939th Engineer Aviation Group, 5th Air Force Command; SFC Clarence Wilson, Petersburg, FL; Staff Sgt. Lowell Wills, US Air Force, Detroit, MI assigned to 822nd Engineer Aviation Battalion Company A, 417th Engineer Aviation Brigade, during Korean War; Pvt. Archie Williams, Wichita, KS; Dr. Fred Williams, Medical Corps, Phoenix, AZ assigned as a physician at Tokyo General Hospital; Capt. Eldridge Williams, Kansas City, KS served as a Special Services Officer, 20th US Air Force, Far East Air Force Command.

Major Wilson is a veteran of WW II, 99th Pursuit Fighter Squadron, 332nd Fighter Group. During the Korean War, Wilson was assigned as Finance Officer, 3rd Bomber Wing where he flew 25 combat intruder missions and later was assigned as Assistant Professor of Air Science and Tactics for the US Air Force's ROTC program at NC Agricultural and Technical University at Greensboro, NC. Sgt. Herman L. Winans, 24th Infantry Regiment, Chicago, IL; Cpl. Eugene Winchester, Atlantic City, NJ in the 7th Infantry Division, 32nd Buccaneer Infantry Regiment, the Honor Guard Unit; Pvt. Robert Wineheny, Wichita, KS; Cpl Jacob E. Winfield, Littleton, VA, veteran of WW II served with the US Air Force during the Korean War and assigned to the Strategic Air Command, 91st Strategic Reconnaissance Squadron near Tokyo, Japan; Kenneth O. Wofford, Springfield, MO was assigned as Administrative Inspector, 5th US Air Force, Far East Air Force Command; Sgt. Thomas Wood, Junction City, KS.

1st Lt. Edward Williams Columbus, GA assigned as Operations Officer, 20th Air Force, Far East Air Force Command; PFC Robert L. Williams, Columbus, GA, 24th Infantry Regiment; Sgt. Wilburn Williams, Greenwood, MS served with the 930th Engineering Aviation Unit; Cpl. Wilkes Williams, part of 1st Marine Division in Korea, 1950; PFC Willie Williams, Clairton, PA; Capt. William Williams an Executive Officer of a Battalion, 24th Infantry Regiment lived in Washington, DC;

Command Sgt. Major John E. Wise, US Army was a part of the 3rd US Infantry Division and the recipient of three Bronze Stars, Combat Infantryman's Badge, Army Commendation Medal, Purple Heart and Silver Star Medals; PFC Leon Wilson, Wilmington, NC was a member of the 55th ETB, Korea; Pvt. Leroy Wilson, Lake Charles, LA; PFC Ozzie Wilson, Norfolk, VA and a member 24th Infantry Regiment; Major Theodore A. Wilson, Roanoke, VA, US Air Force served in Japan during the Korean War and flew some combat missions over Korea. Cpl. Bennie Woodard, Norfolk, VA assigned as a Company Clerk, 17th Infantry Regiment, 1951; Major Jacob Woods, Ann Arbor, MI was assigned to an Ammunition Storage Point; Staff Sgt. James A. Wooten, Pinetops, NC; PFC Jack Wright served in Korea as a member of Company G, 5th Marine Regiment; Staff Sgt. James Wright, Jr., Rockford, Ct. US Air Force assignment Far East Air Force Command; Sgt. Perry Wright, Deep Creek, VA; PFC Lee Wyman, Dallas, TX; SFC Ulysses Yarber, St. Louis, MO; Pvt. Huey Young, Modesto, CA; Pvt. John Young, Omaha, NE; Pvt. Alphonse Zampier, Jr., St. Louis, MO was 18 years old when reported missing in action, 1950. He was the son of Gladys and Alphonse Zampier, Sr., St. Louis, MO and cousin of Anton Bailey who lives in Denver, CO.

CHAPTER 5

REPORTED MILITARY WOUNDED IN ACTION

Military men and women who are exposed to combat conditions are subject to being inflicted with wounds from various warfare ammunition, grenades, mortars and rockets. Those who receive the battlefield wounds are eligible for the award of the Purple Heart Medal. During the Korean War, 1950-1951, a considerable number of African Americans received combat wounds in action. Some of those courageous military personnel were:

PFC. Homer Allen, St. Louis, MO was reported wounded in action in July, 1951; PFC Alexander M. Alton, Norfolk, VA wounded in action July, 1951; Cpl. Benjamin Amos, San Francisco, CA, US Army, 25th Infantry Division wounded in action, 1950 and recuperated at Tokyo General Hospital was the recipient of the Purple Heart and Bronze Star; Pvt. James L. Alexander, Chicago, IL wounded in 1951; PFC William H. Alexander, Chicago, IL wounded in action; Cpl. Robert W. Arrington, Washington, DC reported wounded in action; Lt. Clark Arrington, Philadelphia, PA was assigned to Company F, 24th Infantry Regiment and reported wounded in action; PFC Thomas E. Arrington, Washington, DC wounded in action in Korea.

Sgt. George Banks, St Louis, MO wounded in action; Pvt. John Beaver, St. Louis, MO wounded in action; PFC Colin Bell wounded in action 1950. Wounded in the neck, Bell recuperated at an American Red Cross Hospital in Korea. PFC Fred Bennett, Jr. Washington, DC wounded in action; Master Sgt. George Berry, St. Louis, MO wounded in action July, 1951; Capt. Bradley Biggs, Newark, NJ wounded in action and treated at Tokyo General Hospital; PFC Steven Bogan, Daytona Beach, FL wounded by rifle fire July 28, 1950; PFC Rapier Bond, Chicago, IL, 19 years old, wounded in action; PFC Albert E. Boone, 17 years old wounded in action July, 1950 lived in St. Louis, MO; PFC Wendell E. Borge, wounded in action, lived in Norfolk, VA; Cpl. Bowser, 24th Infantry Regiment was wounded in action near Yongdong, Korea, August 13, 1950. He received the Purple Heart Medal. PFC Vernon F. Boyd, Newport News, VA 24th Infantry Regiment wounded in action in 1950; Cpl. Ewing Brandon, Memphis, TN wounded in action; Sgt. Clyde Bratton, Washington, DC reported wounded in action; Steward 1st Class Morris H. Brooks, Cleveland, OH wounded in action aboard the destroyer Mansfield when the destroyer struck a mine. PFC Lee Brown, Washington, DC, 24th Infantry Regiment was reported wounded in action, August 8, 1950 and he received the Purple Heart Medal. PFC Joel Brown from Virginia wounded in action August 11, 1950; Cpl. Leo B. Brown, Washington, DC wounded in action and received treatment at Portsmouth Naval Hospital, VA; PFC Robert L. Brown, Chicago, IL wounded in action; Sgt. Edward Bumbray, Alexandria, VA, 25th Infantry Division wounded in action and received the Purple Heart Medal; Cpl. Charles Bryant, Baltimore, MD wounded in action; Pvt. Elwood Burnette, Washington, DC wounded in action; Pvt. Thomas R. Byrd, Norfolk, VA wounded in action in 1951.

Master Sgt. Leonard Callahan, Pittsburgh, PA, Company B, 24th Infantry Regiment was wounded in action; PFC Allen Camp, Statesville, NC wounded in action in 1951; PFC Charles Cannon, Los Angeles, CA wounded in action; Cpl. Bernard Carberry, Baltimore, MD was wounded in action; PFC Booker T. Chambers, St. Louis, MO was wounded in action; PFC Johnson Chambliss, Chicago, IL was wounded in action; 1st Lt. Carlisle Ferdinand Cherry, Washington, DC wounded in action in 1950. He is the son of the physician, Dr. Albert H. Cherry, Washington, DC. Cpl. James Clark, 77th Engineer Battalion was wounded in action near Mansan, Korea, August 6, 1950 and received the Purple Heart Medal. PFC Alex C. Clay, Memphis, TN was reported missing in action March 3, 1951 and he was 19 years old. Pvt. John E. Collins, St. Louis,

MO reported missing in action July, 1951; Cpl. John Cox, St. Louis, MO reported wounded in action; PFC Norman Cromwell, 24th Infantry Regiment, WW II veteran was reported wounded in the left arm; Cpl. Emmanuel Curry, B Battery, 159th Field Artillery Battalion was wounded in action and lived in Maryland. PFC Maurice L. Curry, Chicago, IL reported wounded in action; PFC Fred Curtis, Jr., 18 years old reported wounded in action July, 1950; PFC Fred D. Curtis reported wounded in action and lived in St. Louis, MO.

PFC William Daniels, Los Angeles, CA wounded in action; Pvt. James L. De berry, Portsmouth, VA wounded in action and was also a WWII veteran; PFC Harvey Dickerson, 18 years old, Washington, DC, Company L, 9th US Infantry Regiment, 2nd Infantry Division wounded in action; Sgt. Howard Dixon, Baltimore, MD; It was reported that his feet were frost bitten; PFC Paul R. Dowdy, Golston, NC was reported wounded in action in 1952; Cpl. James A. Edwards, Louisville, KY, US Marine Corps wounded in action August, 1952; PFC James E. Edmondson, Nashville, TN wounded in action; PFC William Y. Eichelberger, Greenville, SC wounded in action in 1951; PFC Norman E. Ellis, 24th Infantry Regiment, Cleveland, OH was wounded in action; PFC James W. Evans, St. Louis, MO reported wounded in action; PFC William Frazier, Baltimore, MD reported wounded in action; PFC Bernis Fennell, 20 years old, Suffolk, VA wounded in action; Pvt. Lester Finch, Chicago, IL wounded in action; Cpl. Herbert Fordham, Brooklyn, NY wounded in action; Cpl. Jesse L. Fulton reported wounded in action and lived in Baltimore, MD.

SFC Frank P. Freeman, Monett, MO, veteran WW II and served in Korea with the 2nd Infantry Division. Reported wounded at Yongdon, Korea and received treatment at the 155th Station Hospital, Korea. Freeman received the Purple Heart Medal. Cpl. Percy Garret, Hertford, NC reported wounded; Cpl. Nathaniel Gilbert, New York City, NY served with the 2nd US Infantry Division. He was reported wounded in the PoHang ambush and recuperated at St. Albans Hospital; Cpl. Kenneth Marcell Givens, 22 years old, South Norfolk, VA reported wounded in action; Cpl. Frances A. Gordon, Chicago, IL was wounded in action ; Sgt. Louis Green, Baltimore, MD reported wounded in action; PFC George Griffin, Chicago, IL wounded in action; PFC William Hall, Norfolk, VA was wounded in action, he was a member of the 24th Infantry Regiment; PFC Harold Hardin, Memphis, TN wounded in action in May 1951. Pvt. Jerry T. Harden, Baltimore, MD, 38th Infantry Regiment was reported wounded in action; Pvt. George Harris, Portsmouth, VA wounded in action; Sgt. James Harper, 21 years old, Washington, DC was wounded in action; PFC Francis Hawkins, Baltimore, MD was wounded in action; PFC Edward Henderson, Cleveland, OH was wounded in action; PFC Allen R. Hickman, AL, was wounded in action; Pvt. Rudolph Highsmith Halifax, NC was wounded in action and received the Purple Heart Medal.

Sgt. Samuel Hodges, Cleveland, OH wounded in action on Hill 160 in Korea; 3rd Class Melvin Hogan, US Navy, Worcester, MA was wounded in action in 1950 and treated at the forward aid station, Inchon, Korea; PFC Jesse J. Holloway, Rocky Mount, NC wounded in action November 26, 1950; PFC Earl Holmes, 19 years old, Baltimore, MD wounded in action; PFC John Marion Howard III, Los Angeles, CA reported wounded in action; PFC Major C. Holloway, Jr. Chicago, IL reported wounded in action; PFC Theodore B. Hudson, Headquarters and Service Company, 7th Marine Regiment, 1st Marine Division reported to have recovered from frost bitten feet at the Great Lakes Naval Base Hospital; Cpl Herbert Hughes, St. Louis, MO wounded in action; PFC Robert D. Humbord, Iowa was wounded in action. He was a member of the 24th Infantry Regiment; PFC Chester W. Hunter, Washington, DC was reported to have suffered from frost bitten feet. PFC Preston Lee Hutton, Chicago, IL was wounded in action; PFC James Irving, Washington, DC wounded in action in Korea; PFC Johnny Jackson, St. Louis, MO wounded in action; Cpl. Levi Jackson, St. Louis, MO was wounded in action, was assigned to the 24th

Infantry Regiment and the US Army's Heavy weight Boxing Champion. Jackson was wounded August 13, 1950 trying to assist several wounded Infantrymen out of an area that was under enemy fire. He was a medical technician. Cpl. John James was wounded in action and lived in Baltimore, MD; PFC James Earl Jeffries, Memphis, TN was reported wounded in action May, 1951; PFC Harold A. Jenkins was wounded in action; Pvt. Alfred Johnson, Chicago, IL, 24th Infantry Regiment reported wounded in action; PFC Albert E. Johnson 24th Infantry Regiment, a veteran of WW II wounded in action in 1950. He lived in Washington, DC; Cpl Andrew Johnson, St. Louis, MO reported wounded in action; Pvt. Thomas Jennings, Norfolk, VA reported wounded in action; Cpl. Leonard Johnson, Richmond, VA reported wounded in action in 1951.

SFC Ray Johnson, Augusta, GA was reported wounded in action in Korea; Sgt. Roy Johnson, New York City, NY wounded in action; PFC Leroy Jones, Baltimore, MD was wounded in action in 1950. He was assigned to the 24th Infantry Regiment; Sgt. Cloyd B. Jordan, Washington, DC was reported wounded in action in November, 1951; Sgt. Walter Joseph, St. Louis, MO was wounded in action; PFC Arthur Kelly, 19 years old, St. Louis< MO wounded in action in July, 1951. PFC Dupree Kelly, Spartanburg, SC, 15th Infantry Regiment, 3rd Infantry Division was reported wounded in action; Pvt. Johnny Lanier, Washington, DC reported wounded in action; Pvt. Ross King, Chicago, IL was wounded in action; PFC Ellison R. Lee, Baltimore, MD 24th Infantry Regiment was wounded in action in 1951; PFC Francis Leonard, 19 years old, Washington, DC was wounded in action; Cpl. James A. Lockinour, Chicago, IL was reported wounded in action; Pvt. Levin J. Lucas, Norfolk, VA was wounded in action in 1951; Cpl. Richard E. Lundy, Philadelphia, PA was wounded in action, his injuries consisted of a broken leg, and a shot in the jaw. Norval Lacy, Washington, DC wounded in action; PFC Walter Mackey, Baltimore, MD was reported wounded in action; Pvt. Leonard Macklin, 18 years old, Washington, DC was reported wounded in action; Pvt. James E. Martin, 17 years old, San Andreas, CA was wounded in action. He received a wound in the leg, was treated at the 155th Station Hospital, Korea. He was a member of the Regimental Combat Team and was awarded the Purple Heart Medal. PFC Lloyd J. Martin, 20 years old, Chicago, IL was wounded in action; Pvt. Howard G. Mason, Chicago, IL was reported wounded in action; SFC Raymond Matthews, Baltimore, MD was wounded in action and his recuperation was in a hospital in Japan. Sgt. George W. McClease, Norfolk, VA was reported wounded in action in 1950. He was assigned to a Signal Corps Unit and was shot down from a communication pole suffering a fracture of the spine. He attended Booker T. Washington HS in Norfolk, VA. PFC Monroe McGhee, Chicago, IL was wounded in action; PFC Henry McGruder, Columbus, GA, 565th Military Police Battalion was wounded in action and received the Purple Heart and Bronze Star Medals.

Sgt. Wilson McKindra, St. Louis, MO was reported wounded in action; PFC Henry E. McLaurin, Washington, DC, 25th Infantry Division, was wounded in action in 1950; Sgt. Nathaniel McCall, Leesburg, FL, 24th Infantry Regiment, veteran of WW II was reported wounded in action in 1950.

Cpl. Walter R. Meekins, Norfolk, VA was reported wounded in action in April, 1951. He received a wound in the right leg and recuperated at the 8th Station Hospital in Japan. Col. Clarence A. Miller, Jr., Chatfield, TX was born July 21, 1931 He was assigned to the 23rd Infantry Regiment, 2nd Infantry Division and reported wounded in action while in Korea. Miller was a graduate of Praire View A. & M University, TX and Indiana University. His awards were the Legion of Merit, Purple Heart and Meritorious Service Medals. Later he served as Deputy Director for Instruction, Defense Race Relations School, Patrick Air Force Base, FL, Senior Army Air Defense Advisor, US Military Training Mission, Saudi Arabia and Professor of Military Science, Indiana, University.

Cpl. Wilbert Mills, Norfolk, VA, 31st Infantry Regiment, US 7th Infantry Division was assigned automatic rifleman. Mills was reported wounded in action and received the Purple Heart Medal. Cpl. Thomas Mobley, Alexandria, VA, veteran of WW II was wounded in action in 1950. PFC Arthur Moore, Norfolk, VA was wounded in action in 1951. Cpl. William Moore, Checotah, OK, 24th Infantry Regiment was reported wounded in action; PFC James Morrow, 24th Infantry Regiment, Company G was reported wounded in action from an enemy mortar round.

PFC John Nickens, Jr., Arlington, West Virginia was reported wounded in action; 1st Lt. Henry C. Norcom, Norfolk, VA was wounded in action and received the Purple Heart Medal; Lt. R. C. Norcom, Portsmouth, VA was wounded in action on May 28, 1951. Norcom was a 1948 Honor graduate, ROTC, Hampton University; PFC Arthur L. Patterson, Memphis, TN was wounded in action; Cpl. Legus Patton, Oklahoma City, OK, attended Langston University, OK and was reported wounded in action near Pohang, Korea, September 17, 1950. His injury was in the chest area.

Cpl. Willie Lee Perry, 24th Infantry Regiment, St. Louis MO was wounded in action; PFC James Pikes, Jr. Chicago, IL was wounded in action; Master Sgt. Charles Pitts, Jr., Washington, DC wounded in action; PFC Warren Plowden, Baltimore, MD was wounded in action and received the Purple Heart Medal. PFC Paul Pope, Chicago, IL was reported wounded in action; Sgt. Samuel Porter, Cleveland, OH, wounded in action; PFC Earl Powell, Chicago, IL wounded in action and treated at Tokyo Japan American Hospital in 1950; Cpl. Willie E. Price, Littleton, NC, an Automatic Rifleman, 24th Infantry Regiment was wounded in action; Lt. Oscar Pusey, New York City, NY wounded in action and recuperated at Walter Reed Army Medical Hospital, Washington, DC; Pvt. Leon Rainey, Chicago, IL, Company F, 38th Infantry Regiment was reported wounded in action; PFC Cornelius Reed, Chicago, IL was wounded in action; Pvt. Andrew H. Reeves, Chicago, IL was wounded in action; PFC Arthur L. Richardson, St. Louis, MO reported wounded in action July, 1951.

Pvt. Vincent Richardson, reported wounded in action and treated at the US Tripler Military Hospital, Hawaii; PFC Richard Rivers, Memphis, TN reported wounded in action and he was 19 years old; PFC William M. Roberts, Norfolk, VA wounded in action; PFC Paul E. Robertson, New Windsor, MD wounded in action and treated at the 155th Station Hospital, Korea. He received the Purple Heart Medal; PFC Earl Rowell, Chicago, IL was wounded in action; PFC Isiah Robinson, Buford, SC, 24th Infantry Regiment was reported wounded in action near Hassan, Korea in August, 1950. He also received the Purple Heart Medal. Pvt. Joseph J. Reeder was wounded in action and lived in Baltimore, MD; PFC Benjamin L. Ross, St. Louis, MO was reported wounded in Korea; PFC Clifton J. Roulhac, Norfolk, VA was wounded in action in 1951; Cpl. William Russell, New Jersey, reported wounded in action, was assigned to the 42nd Transportation Truck Company.

Cpl. Leslie Scott, Norfolk, VA was wounded in action; PFC James Scarbor, 18 years old was reported wounded in action in November, 1950. He attended Booker T. Washington HS in Virginia; PFC Benjamin Selden, Newport News, VA reported wounded in action; PFC Leon Short, Chicago, IL was wounded in action; Pvt. Calvin Simons, Chicago, IL reported wounded in action; PFC Robert H. Sloan, 20 years old, St. Louis, MO reported wounded in action; PFC Melvin O. Slaughter, Norfolk, VA was wounded in action in 1952. He was a former student at Booker T. Washington HS; Pvt. Leroy Smith, Sharon Hill, PA reported wounded in action; Cpl. Raymond C. Smith, St. Louis, MO reported wounded in action; Cpl. William C. Smith, Baltimore, MD was reported wounded in Korea, 1951. Sgt. Joseph D. Speller, Norfolk, VA reported wounded in action and recuperated at the Army Hospital in Tokyo, Japan. PFC Harold Spriggs, Baltimore, MD, a WW II veteran was reported wounded in action in Korea. Master Sgt.

Hayward Starling, SC, 25th Infantry Division was wounded in action. His injury was in the wrist bone.

SFC Olden C. Stevenson, Baltimore, MD was reported wounded in action; PFC Linwood Stewart was wounded in action and received the Purple Heart Medal. He lived in Norfolk, VA; PFC Ahren Stokes, Waynesboro, OH was reported wounded in action; Pvt. Edward Tarleton, Topeka, KS was reported wounded in action and treated at Tokyo General Hospital Japan; PFC Carl Tate, 2nd Division was treated for frost bite at the Army Hospital, Battle Creek, MI; Pvt. Ray Taylor, 25th Infantry Division, Arkansas was reported wounded in action and received the Purple Heart Medal. Cpl. Herbert Thomas, St. Louis, MO was reported wounded in action; PFC Robert Thompson, Washington, DC reported wounded in action; Sgt. Otis Towns, Dermont, AK, 2nd Infantry Division was reported wounded in action.

The total reported Korean War wounded in action Statistics of June 1, 2000 was 92,134 wounded.

CHAPTER 6

PRISONERS OF WAR (POW'S)

Several sources of statistical data has been released over the years which indicate that approximately 7,190 Americans were Prisoners of War. Some 3,000 Americans died and 4,000 returned home from the Chinese Camps and from several North Korean Peoples Army Camps. The North Korean administered Camps were Kangdong, North Korea, Camp 9, Bean, Paks Palace, and Camp 12 located near Suwon, Korea. The Chinese Camps were Camp one, Branch one, Chongsong, Korea; Camp two, Branch two, Pinchon-ni, Korea; Officers Camp, Branch three, Changni, Korea; Officers and Air crew Camp, Camp three, Branch one, Changsong, Korea; Branch one, Enlisted men and other ranks; Branch 2, Songsa-Dong, Korea was established August 1952 for new prisoners. Camp 4, Kuuptong, Korea was for sergeants, Camp 5, Pyoktong, Korea for enlisted men and other ranks after October, 1951. There were some camps called The "Caves" located on the south bank of Yalu River near Pyoktong, Korea. The Caves were Prisoners of War Camp 12. The Caves were shelters built by the North Koreans which were 15 feet wide, large holes with trees over the top and logs built right over the hill top. Sometimes soldiers would be placed in the Caves until they died, some were able to survive. The permanent facilities at Camp 12 consisted of the Prisoner of War's quarters, toilet facilities, dining room, store rooms, kitchens, guard quarters and administration buildings. There were also facilities at the Camp for a Central Peace Committee, commandant quarters, and a school house. There were very few POWs escaping from the camps and those who tried were recaptured.

Operation Little Switch occurred between April 20 and May 3, 1953. Approximately 149 sick and wounded Prisoners of War were returned by the Chinese and North Koreans to the United Nations lines. Some POW Camps began to change their policies and gave some POW's clothing, underwear and food. The Chinese tried to convince American soldiers to renounce their citizenship and voluntarily remain behind and go to China. They wanted some POW's to establish Progressive Communist Clubs in America and attempt to infiltrate the Federal Government.

Camp Bean had 900 Prisoners of War and the majority of them were Americans. There were some British, Canadians, Australians, and Turkish prisoners. The Camp served as a collection point. The conditions at the Camps did vary. Some camps had prisoners who displayed a bully personality. They would use vulgar language and intimidate prisoners. There were instances where prisoners would steal from each other and take advantage of the weak and wounded ones.

Prisoners suffered from exhaustion, malnutrition, pneumonia, dysentery, pellagra, beriberi and they were exposed to contaminated water. Some POW's arrived in the camps with compound fractures, bullet wounds of the legs and arms and frost bite. The lack of adequate medical care caused some men never to be treated. Many camps had crowded rooms and little heat in the buildings. The prisoners' diet mainly consisted of bean balls made from millet, soybeans with no seasoning and boiled sorghum. Some POW's would smoke cigarettes made out of paper. It was reported by some former prisoners that some POW's discovered wild marijuana plants while on a wood search detail .and would later smoke it. The prisoners' mail was also censored.

The Chinese used a method of control in the camps that consisted of companies of 125 men each. The prisoners wore uniforms that consisted of a black shirt, trouser, and a cap. The Chinese called the prisoner's students. The Prisoners of War were required at times to read literature such as the life of Karl Marx. There were daily mandatory lectures on the subject of "China and the

United Nations, Wall Street USA, Big Business and the decline of Capitalism and the subject of Communism". Some camps had newspapers that were used in camp discussions.
The POW's experienced several death marches. They were required to march over difficult terrain on foot, sometimes without their combat boots. The seriously wounded were carried on ox carts, and the wounded ones who could walk were forced to march over rugged mountains. There were many deaths that occurred due to the lack of food and water resulting in malnutrition.

During a death march to Pyongyang, Korea in October, 1950, some 296 men survived out of a total of 400 men. Later the men were transported on railroad flat cars leaving the area of Taejon and Hadong, Korea.

African Americans were representative of the many prisoners of war during the Korean War, who were confined in detention or prison camps by the Communist North Koreans and the Chinese. There were members from the all Black 503rd Field Artillery Battalion who were captured as Prisoners of War. The 503rd suffered a great loss of men and equipment along with the troops of the 2nd Infantry Division, who were positioned along the Chongchon river area valley near Kunuri`, Korea. There were reports that the Chinese subjected some Black POW's to racism in the prisoner of war camps. At times the Chinese camp authorities would segregate the Black prisoners from the White prisoners. The Chinese tried to persuade some Black POW's to speak in a negative manner about the United States. The Chinese were curious and concerned when the Black prisoners would unite and sing. Some Black prisoners tried to conduct religious services and pray together in secret. Cpl. Alphonso Johnson would lead some religious services. George McGowan, Robert Sheperd, Cpl. Melvin Taylor, Pvt. Richard Drennan, Cpl. John Green, Cpl. Richard Davis, Cpl. Ellas Preece, Stanley Furnish and Cpl. Lawrence McShan were members of a singing group.

A heroic event occurred when members of a Black Tank Battalion (possibly the 64th battalion) were instrumental in the rescue of some non-African American prisoners of war near Namwon, Korea. There were 86 men to include some Mexican American or Hispanics (prior to the integration of the military in 1953, the Native Americans and Hispanics were able to serve in White units and they were classified as Whites).

A former Black prisoner of war stated that when the Black POW's were released from the Chinese POW Camps and transferred to the US Authority, they experienced racial discrimination. Some former Black POW's were segregated on the USS Nelson Walker, the ship that transported them back to the United States. The Black POW's believed that the US Military demonstrated minimal concern and assistance for the ex-Black prisoner of war's physical conditions.

During the Korean War many Black military personnel suffered frost bite especially in the lower extremities, principally the feet. It is interesting how some medical experts in 1951 would develop hypotheses and medical inferences about Blacks' exposure to frost bite. A newspaper article dated February 24, 1951 discussed the frost bite medical problems. These problems were directed toward the African American troops especially those who suffered from frozen feet in combat conditions and as prisoners of war in the prison camps. The article stated that the visible diagnostic symptoms of frost bite were difficult to observe in Black patients because of their dark pigment. Some of the major symptomatic characteristics of frozen feet or frost bite that were discussed in an article of the Armed Forces Medical Journal were "First degree frost bite, numbness, swelling, erythema (redness) of the involved part, second degree vesication (blistering or peeling) of the skin's thickness. Third degree, entire thickness of the skin, sometimes present deeper into the tissues area of the toes, heels, and tips of the fingers. Fourth degree extends the thickness of the skin. Sometimes the bone results in the amputation of an extremity or part." I pose the question, were these alleged medical opinions in the 1950's questionable because a biological and genetic fact is that African Americans are of a diverse geneotype than many ethnic groups and definitely represent a rainbow color resplendent of varying degrees of melanin deposits. This is just another nutritional reasoning or "food for thought".

Some of those brave and courageous African Americans who were Prisoners of War during the years 1950-1953 were as follows: Cpl. Clifford Allen, Los Angeles, CA was listed as a POW in 1952; Pvt. George Atkins, Cincinnati, OH, reported a POW in January 1952; Cpl. R. L. Banks reported a POW, from Cambridge, MD; Pfc. Julius Barber, Atlanta, GA was listed a POW in 1952; Cpl. Joseph Barnes, New Orleans, LA was listed as a POW in 1952; Cpl. Richard Barnes, Houston, TX was reported a POW in 1952; Pvt. Lucian Arceneaux, New Orleans, LA was listed a POW in January, 1952; Pvt. Page Baylor, Washington, DC reported a POW in Korea; Cpl. Albert Billips, was a member of a chemical decontamination unit during the Korean War. He sustained some wounds and was a POW for 20 days; MSgt. Joe Black, Columbus, GA was listed a POW in 1952; PFC C. Bolton, Memphis, TN was listed a POW in 1952; J. W. Bowers, St. Louis, MO was listed a POW; Cpl. Ewing Brandon, Memphis, TN reported a POW in 1952; PFC Robert Brooks, Reidville, NC was reported a POW in Korea; PFC Robert Boyd, Pittsburgh, PA reported a POW; Cpl. Harold Brown, New York City, NY listed as a POW in January, 1952; Cpl. James Brown, Durham, NC listed a POW in 1952; Cpl. Charles Bryant, Jr. Cincinnati, OH listed a POW in Korea in 1952; PFC James T. Bryant, Norfolk, VA listed a POW in 1952; PFC Billy J. Buchanan, Atlanta, GA was listed a POW in January, 1952; Cpl. Joseph Burns, New Orleans, LA was also listed a POW in 1952.

PFC Booker T. Campbell, Memphis, TN listed a POW in January, 1952; PFC Veroneece Campbell, Memphis, TN was listed a POW in January, 1952; PFC Walter Chambers, Harrisburg, PA listed as a POW in January, 1952; Cpl. Edward Melvin Carrington, New York City, NY listed a POW in January, 1952; Sgt. Ninevah A. Carter, St. Louis, MO was listed a POW in January, 1952; Cpl. Willie Cheatman, Baltimore, MD reported a POW; Cpl. James F. Chillis, Cleveland, OH listed a POW in January, 1952; Sgt. Robert J. Coffee, Chicago, IL listed as a POW in January, 1952; PFC Everett Coleman, Richmond, VA was listed a POW in January, 1952; PFC D. H. Colvin, 25th Infantry Division, Chicago, IL listed a POW in January, 1952; Cpl. Benjamin Conley, Columbus OH listed a POW in January, 1952; PFC Charles Cook, Trenton, NJ reported a POW at POW Camp 5, Pyokdong, Korea; MSgt. Wallace Copeland, Chicago, IL listed as a POW January, 1952; PFC Thomas Crawford, Memphis, TN listed a POW in January, 1952; PFC Charles Coston, Portsmouth, VA listed as a POW in January, 1952; MSgt. Clarence Covington, St. Louis, MO listed as a POW in January, 1952; PFC Edward Covington, Memphis, TN listed a POW in January, 1952; Cpl. William Cox, Gary, IN was a POW in POW Camp 5, Pyokdong, Korea; Sgt. Robert Dotson, Chicago, IL reported a POW in Korea January, 1952; Floyd Rothwell, Battery A, 503rd Field Artillery Battalion, Chicago, IL reported a POW in January, 1952; also Cpl. Frank Fox, East St. Louis, IL reported a POW in February, 1951.

Pvt. Donald Gilbert, Elmore, CA was reported a POW; Sgt. Vonica Gilipse, Chicago, IL listed a POW in January, 1952; SFC John F. Goodman, Brewton, AL was reported a POW; Sgt. Elmer J. Grady, Seattle, WA was reported a POW; Thomas Grant, Orangeburg, SC reported a POW in 1952; Cpl. James W. Green, Chicago, IL listed as a POW in January, 1952; PFC Edgbert W. Hall, Pittsburgh, PA listed as a POW; Pvt. William Hall, Indianapolis, IN was a POW in Camp 5, Pyokdong, Korea; Cpl. Thomas Hampton, 2nd US Infantry Division, Chicago, IL listed as a POW in January, 1952; Major John C. Harlan, Baltimore, MD listed a POW, was a former Assistant Professor of Military Science, Morgan State University, Baltimore, MD; Herbert W. Harris, Norfolk, VA listed as a POW in January, 1952; Cpl. Smith Harris reported a POW and was from

New York City, NY; Cpl. Charles, F. Hearn, St. Louis, MO listed as a POW; Sgt. Charles Lida, Baltimore, MD; Pvt. William Lewis, Jr., Cleveland, OH listed a POW January, 1952; Lt. Alvin A Anderson, Los Angeles, CA also listed a POW January, 1952.

Lt. Edward H. Lyles, Cleveland, OH listed as a POW, January, 1952; Sgt. Horace Maddox, Atlanta, GA was listed a POW in January, 1952; Pvt. James Martin, Andrea, CA reported a POW; Cpl. Amos McClure, St. Louis, MO listed a POW in January, 1952; Pvt. Emmett, McDavid, Memphis, TN reported a POW in 1952; PFC Lionel Meyers, Broadnax, VA was reported a POW; PFC Richard K. Miller, Memphis, TN listed as a POW in January, 1952; Sgt. Donald L. Minter, Chicago, IL listed a POW January, 1952; Pvt. Harold Neal, Greensboro, NC was reported a POW; Sgt. John H. Nelson, St. Louis, MO reported a POW in January, 1952; Cpl. Robert R. Nelson, Chicago, IL reported a POW; Pvt. Thomas Nicholson, Norfolk, VA reported a POW in January, 1952; PFC Edgar J. Hinton, St. Louis, MO listed as a POW in January, 1952; Cpl. Herbert Hodge, Chicago, IL reported a POW in January, 1952; PFC James Holder, Chicago, IL reported a POW in January, 1952; Cpl. Ellis Jackson, Birmingham, AL listed as a POW in January, 1952; Cpl. William Jackson was reported a POW from Washington, DC; Pvt. Frank James, Memphis, TN reported a POW in January, 1952; Cpl. Frank Jeter, Norfolk, VA listed a POW in January, 1952; Richard Jett, Richmond, VA reported a POW; Pvt. Alfonso Johnson, Cleveland, OH listed as a POW in January, 1952; Cpl. Robert Johnson, Jr. Richmond, VA was listed a POW in January, 1952; Pvt. Frank Jones, Memphis, TN was listed a POW in January, 1952; Cpl. Abraham Kearns, Wichita, KS was reported a POW at Camp 5, Pyokdong, Korea; David Kimbrough, Memphis, TN reported a POW in January, 1952; Norman C. Powers, Jr. Portsmouth, VA was listed a POW in January, 1952; Pvt. Louis Pryde, St. Louis, MO listed as a POW in January, 1952; Lt. Dayton W. Ragland, Kansas City, MO reported a POW in 1952;Pvt. Paul Robertson, New Windsor, MD reported a POW; Cpl. Leon C. Ross, Springfield, MO, 25th Infantry Division, Regimental Combat Team reported a POW; Cpl. Calvin Royal, Brooklyn, NY reported a POW; Cpl. Roosevelt Sankey, Montgomery, AL was listed a POW in January, 1952; Pvt. Vernon Scroggins, Richmond, VA was reported a POW; PFC Amos Scott, Portsmouth, VA listed as a POW in January, 1952; Cpl. James Scott, Richmond, VA was listed a POW in January, 1952; Pvt. Albert L. Smith, St. Louis, MO listed as a POW in January, 1952; Tyrone Simmons, Washington, DC reported a POW; Cpl. Elijah Smith, Columbus, OH was listed a POW in January, 1952; Cpl. John Spivey, Washington, DC reported a POW; William Milford Stanley, 24th Infantry Regiment, WW II veteran, Montclair, NJ was also a POW.

PFC Henry Stevens, Chicago, IL was listed a POW; PFC Leroy Sykes, Savannah, GA listed a POW in January, 1952; Cpl. Rodney Thomas, Portsmouth, VA listed as a POW in January, 1952; Cpl. Donald Tyce, New York City, NY was reported a POW and it was stated he was released in January, 1952; PFC Louis Warford, Kingsport, TN reported a POW however it was stated that he was later released; Major Frank Walker, Columbus, OH listed a POW in January, 1952; Cpl. Vernon Warren, St. Louis MO was also listed as a POW in January, 1952.

Cpl. Wilbert M. Warring was one of the first groups of repatriated American Prisoners of War. Warring was wounded by Mortar fire and five days later he was a POW. He sustained wounds in the leg, thigh, arm and face. Later he was transferred to a Chinese hospital at Cherwan, Korea. Warring stated that he received two operations and his wounds were dressed every three days and fed a diet of rice. Some of the Chinese nurses were male and Americans as well as other United Nations troops were treated at the hospital. When he was given paper to write, censored letters, they were told to indicate they were doing fine. The Chinese doctors and nurses gave some prisoners a party prior to their leaving the hospital. They had Chinese wine and a Korean Band played while a Korean girl was singing Danny Boy. Warring said two of the Chinese doctors had been educated in San Francisco. Pvt. Walter Webster, Massachusetts, was a POW; Pvt. Don M.

Wheldon, Oregon City, OR was a POW; Albert L. Wilkerson, Houston, TX listed as a POW in January, 1952; Sgt. Roosevelt Williams, Chicago, IL listed as a POW in January, 1952; Sgt. Bernard Wilson, Memphis, TN listed as a POW in January, 1952; Pvt. Melvin J. Woodhouse, Norfolk, VA listed as a POW in January, 1952; Pvt. C. L. Wright, Memphis, TX listed as a POW in January, 1952

When the Korean War ended and the United States Prisoners of War were repatriated, twenty-one American soldiers decided to defect to China in 1954.

The Prisoners of War Defectors

On July 27, 1953, an armistice was signed ending the Korean War. Later some 3,700-4,000 POW's were transferred to the United Nations' camps during Operation Big Switch at Freedom Village, Panmunjon, Korea. All of the US former Military POW's wanted immediate repatriation as well as a return to the United Nations authorities. However, there were 21 Americans who made a decision not to be repatriated and wanted to live in Communist China. The defectors were called "Turncoats and Traitors.

The majority of the defectors were captured during the winter of 1950-1951. They represented the states of Maryland, Michigan, Pennsylvania, Rhode Island, Ohio, Mississippi, Louisiana, Florida, Oklahoma, Tennessee, Arkansas, Illinois, Texas and Minnesota. The defectors were from the 1st Cavalry Division, 2nd Infantry Division, 7th Infantry Division, 24th Infantry Division and the 25th Infantry Division all of whom spend at least three years in the prison camps when the cease fire was declared. The Chinese Communists had time and the opportunity to work on the POW's emotions, personal problems and ideologies.

The Chinese determined who should be given the opportunity to defect to China. The 21 defectors who did not desire repatriation were detained for approximately three months in a neutral isolated area near Pan mun jon, Korea. They were under the supervision of a United Nations Indian General Officer, General T. S. Thimaya. The US Military authorities allowed the defectors to explain why they should not return to the United States. Prior to the defectors leaving the neutral zone camps, the Chinese authorities gave them a banquet and they were told that they would receive an education, employment and a wife if desired. The defectors marched carrying propaganda banners with slogans at a press conference before their departure from the UN neutral camp.

On January 24, 1954 the defectors, wearing civilian clothes, boarded trucks for a two day trip to Kaesong, Korea. The daily newspaper and weekly magazines carried articles about the 21 defectors and attempted to provide some interesting facts about their lives and possible reasons for their decisions to accept non-repatriation and start a new life in Communist China. Some of their friends and relatives provided some information for the news personnel. Some of the hometowns they were from are Detroit, MI, Vandergrift, PA, Providence, RI, Santa Barbara, CA, Akron, OH, Plumerville, AR, East Carondelet, IL, Jacksonville, FL, Corsicana, TX, and New York City.

Some of the defectors that went to China attended the Peoples and Wuhan Universities and were enrolled in preparatory courses such as world history, history of China, Chinese ☐ichael social development and Chinese language. The men who attended one university lived in a dormitory with several rooms and a dining hall. Their recreation was playing basketball, "bing bong" (ping pong) and attended weekend dances.

Three years after the 21 defectors arrived in China, 14 defectors had departed China for the US. It is believed that one defector died in China. Three defectors went to Europe and three defectors remained in China and later returned to the United States. Once returning to the US, they were apprehended by the military police; however, the US Supreme Court had ruled that the US Army had no jurisdiction over former servicemen for crimes committed while they had been in uniform. The men were released according to the report.

Several national magazines, in the 1950's, published research articles on the social and family backgrounds of the defectors and their profiles. Some significant highlights of the profiles were:

"In most instances the defectors were from small towns in the rural areas. Approximately 17 did not complete high school. Two attended college and one defector was reported to be a graduate of the Baltimore City College. Some defectors had minimal formal education and there were some who were not employed prior to enlisting in the military. The majority of the defectors attended church as youngsters. Four were Roman Catholics, one Greek Catholic, and sixteen were Protestants. Twenty defectors were regular army volunteers, only one was a draftee and some were career non-commissioned officers (NCO's). In addition, five were WW II veterans and two were the recipients of the Bronze Star Medal. There were three defectors who experienced juvenile problems as truants and no self discipline. A few had been exposed to drug abuse and criminality. It was stated that 12 had been accused of informing the Chinese authorities about some of their fellow prisoners of war. Some defectors were not aware of the communist philosophy and the United Nations' mission in the Korean War."

There were three African American soldiers among the 21 defectors and they were Cpl. Clarence Adams, Cpl. La Rance Sullivan and PFC William C. White.

Corporal Clarence Adams

Cpl. Clarence Adams was born January 4, 1929 in Memphis, TN. He was the son of Mrs. Gladys Peoples. A reliable source stated that his father was deceased and he had a stepfather. Clarence was the oldest of five children. It was reported that the family lived in a predominantly white neighborhood in a tenant house on the land of a former Civil War Mansion, (the Coward place). They were the only known Black family in the area. Adams played with the White youngsters; however, he attended segregated schools. It was also revealed that Clarence was a nice disciplined young man and attended Sunday school and Bible classes at the Metropolitan Baptist Church in Memphis. At one time Adams worked in a Baptist hospital and his mother worked as a laundry checker.

Clarence attended Booker T. Washington HS, but it was said that he left school during his third year to enlist in the Army at 18 year of age, September, 1947. He was assigned to the 24th Infantry Division in Korea in 1950. Adams was reported missing in December, 1950 and was a POW in the Communist Camps for three years. It was stated that he wrote his mother in 1950 and said "If I do not get back you will know I have done my best". He also wrote the minister of the Metropolitan Baptist Church, Reverend S. M. Queen, and asked him to pray for him.

Cpl. Adams was raised in the south and possibly was confronted with the legal segregation and discrimination that existed throughout the southern states to include Memphis, TN. It was believed that Adams was vociferous in his opposition to segregation, racism and probably was not as complacent as many southern Blacks were during the era of segregation. Unfortunately after he left the south, he would experience segregation in the United States Army.

Adams made a personal decision in 1953 amidst the continual segregation and discrimination in America to accept non-repatriation and live in the Communist state of China. Sources have stated that Adams lived in China for approximately 12 years and was the recipient of three offers the Chinese promised him at Pan mun jom, Korea in 1953-1954. He was successful in mastering the Chinese language and received a graduate degree from a Chinese University. He also married a Chinese woman and they are the parents of two children.

When Cpl. Clarence Adams returned to the US in 1966 to his hometown of Memphis, TN, he was requested to testify before the House Committee on Un-American Activities, (HUAC). The Committee attempted to charge Adams with treason; however the Committee decided to drop the charge against him. Clarence Adams died in December, 1999 at 70 years of age.

Corporal La Rance Sullivan

Corporal La Rance Sullivan, Jr. was born February, 1931 in Denver, CO. He is the son of LaRance Sullivan, Sr. and Anita Sullivan-Palmore. His father was a furniture warehouseman and the family lived in Santa Barbara, CA as well as Omaha, NE. Sullivan's parents divorced and he had a stepfather. La Rance was a quiet and nice youngster who was not considered a leader but a follower. He liked reading, music, hiking hunting and spear fishing. Sullivan was a member of the Boys Club and was a National Champion. He had an average IQ and completed three years of high school.

Sullivan enlisted in the US Army February 25, 1948 and was assigned to the 2nd Infantry Division in Korea. In 1950 he was reported missing in action; but later his parents learned that he was a prisoner of war and in December, 1951, they received his personal belongings. Sullivan's parents went to California in September, 1953 to meet a ship transporting some POW's returning from Korea. They believed that La Rance might be returning home. Unfortunately, they learned that their son had accepted non-repatriation and decided to go to Communist China to live. When his father learned that he was a POW defector, he said, "His son was never subjected to harsh treatment or segregation. He never lived in the south."

Private first class (PFC) William C. White

PFC William C. White was born May 9, 1930 in Plumerville, AR, a small town, 600 residents and 50 miles from Little Rock, AR. Mrs. Mattie Lee Gorman was his mother and Walter Gorman, his stepfather. His mother worked in a garment factory in Morrilton, AR. William's nick name was "WC." Some of his neighbors described him as a nice youngster. He was raised by his grandparents on a rural farm. White attended a four room segregated school on the outskirts of Plumerville and he had an average IQ; however, he did not graduate from high school.

At the age of 17, William enlisted in the US Army March 17, 1948. During the Korean War he was assigned to the 2nd US Infantry Division. He was captured as a prisoner of war in December, 1950. PFC White accepted non-repatriation and went to China; however, he later returned to the United States.

CHAPTER 7

MISSING IN ACTION

There were some African American Military personnel during the Korean who were reported as missing in action. They were as follows:

SFC Raymond J. Adams, St. Louis, MO reported missing in 1951; Sgt. Earl Banks, Memphis, TN reported missing in action; Pvt. Page Baylor, Washington, DC reported missing in action; Pvt. William M. Benn, Chicago, IL was reported missing in action, July, 1951; Pvt. Benny Berry, St. Louis, MO was reported missing in action; Cpl. Floyd Bey, Chicago, IL was reported missing in action; PFC James Borum, Washington, DC was reported missing in action; PFC Edwin Earl Brown, St. Louis, MO reported missing in action in 1951; Cpl. George Brown, Jr. reported missing in action; PFC William Brown, 24th Infantry Regiment, Washington, DC reported missing in action; PFC Henry Buckner, Vallejo, CA reported missing in action in April, 1951;Cpl. Rudy Buckner, Vallejo, CA, Company B, 74th Engineer Combat Unit reported missing in action

PFC Don H. Colvin, Chicago, IL reported missing in action; PFC Vernon Lee Campbell, Memphis, TN reported missing in action; Pvt. Claude Clark, South Norfolk was reported missing in action; PFC Patrick Cornelius, Chicago, IL reported missing in action; Sgt. Melvin Cotton, Chicago, IL reported missing in action; MSgt. Clarence Covington, St. Louis, MO was reported missing in action; Pvt. Maurice Curry, Chicago, IL, was reported missing in action; Pvt. Curtis L. Daniels, St. Louis, MO reported missing in action; Sgt. Leroy Davis, Chicago, IL reported missing in action; PFC Lee A. Dewey, Chicago, IL reported missing in action; Sgt. Lawrence E. Flack reported missing in action in Korea, 1950; Cpl. Fox, St. Louis, MO was reported missing in action; Sgt. Oswald Freeman, New York City, NY reported missing in action. He had received the Bronze Star Medal; Sgt. Vunice Lee Glisple, Chicago, IL was reported missing in action.

Sgt. Elmore Goodwin, South Hill, VA, WW II veteran was reported missing in action in Korea in October, 1950; Sgt. Alonzo Grier, Norfolk, VA, 25th Infantry Division was reported missing in action; Pvt. Danny Handley, St. Louis, MO reported missing in action; Pvt. Raymond Handy, Washington, DC reported missing in action; PFC Artheris M. Harris, St. Louis, MO reported missing in action; PFC Joe W. Howard, Washington, DC was reported missing in action in 1951 and Pvt. Elijah Hursey, Washington, DC reported missing in action in 1951.

Cpl. Bernard J. Jackson, Chicago, IL, reported missing in action in Korea in 1951; Pvt. Elmer Jenkins, Chicago, IL was reported missing in action; PFC Clarence Johnson, Los Angeles, CA reported missing in action; Cpl. Norman R. Johnson, Chicago, IL was reported missing in action in Korea, 1951; Cpl. Calvin Jones, Norfolk, VA was reported missing in action in Korea, June, 1951; PFC Samuel Kelker, Chicago, IL reported missing in action in Korea, 1951; PFC Lindsey Lockett, Richmond, VA was reported missing in action; PFC James Albert Lockinour, Chicago, IL reported missing in action; PFC Robert McCain, reported missing in action in September 1950. He lived in Baltimore. Sgt. Paul G. Martin, Chicago, IL reported missing in action, 1951; Cpl. Amos McClure, St. Louis, MO was reported missing in action in 1951; 2nd Lt. Edmond McCullough, Miami, FL was reported missing in action, February, 1951; PFC Alexander Midgett, St. Louis, MO reported missing in action, 1951; Sgt. Donald L. Minter, Chicago, IL was reported missing in action in 1951; Pvt. Hercules Moore, St. Louis, MO reported missing in action in 1951; PFC James Moore, St. Louis, MO reported missing in action; Cpl. John D. Moore, Jr., Gary, IN was also reported missing in action in Korea.

Sgt. Albert Morgan, Chicago, IL was reported missing in action in Korea, 1950; Pvt. Edison Owens, Chicago, IL reported missing in action in 1951; MSgt. Robert Parks, Washington, DC was reported missing in action; PFC Baltimore Payne, Chicago, IL reported missing in action; Cpl. Kermit Prather, Washington, DC was reported missing in action; Cpl. Willie Rowe, Hampton, VA reported missing in action in Korea, July, 1950; PFC Leonard Scott, St Louis, MO was reported missing in action in 1951; PFC Ferdinand Sedgewick, Chase, MD was reported missing in action in 1951; PFC A. L. Sharpe, Portsmouth, VA was reported missing in action; PFC James Simpson, St. Louis, MO reported missing in action; PFC Vernon Scroggins, Richmond, VA was reported missing in action; PFC Ulysses Sherman Yarber, St. Louis, MO was also reported missing in action.

PFC Earl W. Taylor, St. Louis, MO was reported missing in action in Korea; PFC Karl W. Taylor, St. Louis, MO reported missing in action; Cpl. Rodney Thomas, Portsmouth, VA reported missing in action, 1952; Pvt. James Thomas, Jr., St. Louis, MO was reported missing in action; Cpl. Theodore Thornton, St. Louis, MO was reported missing in action; Cpl. Reuben Thurman, Jr., Norfolk, VA was reported missing in action in Korea in June, 1951; Cpl. Samuel Warren, Norfolk, VA reported missing in action in Korea; Cpl. Vernon Warren, St. Louis, MO was also reported missing in action

Lt. George West, Jr., Baltimore, MD was reported missing in action in Korea, June, 1951. West was a graduate of Morgan State University; Sgt. Robert Williams, Portsmouth, VA reported missing in action; MSgt. Melvin J. Woodhouse, Norfolk, VA reported missing in action; Pvt. Joseph Clifton Windon, St. Louis, MO was reported missing in action in 1951; PFC C. C. Wright, Memphis, TN, reported missing in action in February, 1951; and Cpl. Robert Lee Wyatt, Baltimore, MD also reported missing in action in Korea.

CHAPTER 8

REPORTED KILLED IN ACTION

PFC Thessalonia Adams, St. Louis, MO was reported killed in action; PFC William Patrick Amaker, High Point, NC was reported killed in action; PFC Joseph Anthony Norfolk, VA reported killed in action; Cpl. Elbert Arrington, Washington, DC was reported killed in action; Joseph P. Avery, St. Louis, MO was reported Killed in action.

2nd Lt. Travis Banks, Greenville, NC, 1st Cavalry Division was reported killed in action. It was stated that he was a graduate of North Carolina A and T College, Greensboro, NC; Joseph T. Bass, Carlisle, PA was reported killed in action on September 9, 1950. Pvt. Douglass Baxter was reported killed in action. He was from Baltimore, MD. Lawrence Bell, Memphis, TN was reported killed in action. He was assigned to Company E, 7th Infantry Regiment, 3rd Infantry Division. Cpl. Percy Bennett, Chicago, IL was reported to have served as a prisoner of war for 11 days and was wounded prior to his capture. PFC Walter Booker, Portsmouth, VA was reported killed in action. Sgt Nicodemus Brewer, Warrenton, NC was reported killed in action.

1st Lt. Jesse B. Bolling, Enfield, NC, was reported killed in action. He was a tank Platoon leader and had been decorated twice for bravery. Bolling was wounded in action three times, was a veteran of WW II and a distinguished military graduate of Virginia State College, Petersburg, VA Jesse was a member of the Alpha Phi Alpha Fraternity and in 1951 an annual award was established for an outstanding cadet at the college, the "Jesse B. Bolling Award." Pvt. Phillip James Baughans, Newport News, VA was reported killed in action. He was a graduate of Huntington H S. Lt. Eugene Briggs, US Air Force, Trenton, NJ was reported killed in action. He was a veteran of WW II. Technical Sgt. Walter Broadus reported killed in action. He was from Washington, DC; Lt. William Butts, Chicago, IL reported killed in action; PFC Clayton Byrd, 24th Infantry Regiment was reported killed in action. Sidney G. Cabell, Lynchburg, VA reported killed in action, September, 1950. He was a graduate of the Campbell County Training School, Rustburg, VA. PFC Archie Carman, Jr., Nashville, TN was reported killed in action, August, 1950; SFC Winston Carr, Newport News, VA was wounded twice in battle and reported killed in action in March, 1951. Carr was a 1948 graduate of Huntington high school.

PFC Robert H. Cheeks, Washington, DC reported killed in action, July, 1951; Lt. Curtis W. Christopher, 1st Cavalry Division, Jacksonville, FL was reported killed in action by enemy machine gun fire while on a patrol. It was stated that at the time of his death, he was the only Black officer assigned to his company. Christopher was a Reserve Officers Training Corps (ROTC) graduate of Howard University, Washington, DC. Alex Clay, Memphis, TN was reported killed in action due to the wounds he received in combat, March 3, 1951. Pvt. William Collins, St. Louis, MO was reported killed in action; Pvt. James A. Dilver, Baltimore, MD reported killed in action, December 18, 1950; Sgt. Hosea L. Evans, Chicago, IL was reported killed in action; Milton Foster from Russellville, AR and the son of Mr. and Mrs. Clyde Foster was reported killed in action. Pvt. Ernest Hale was reported killed in action, August 10, 1950. He was a member of the 24th Infantry Regiment. Hale enlisted in the Army in 1948 and it was stated that he was from Tulsa, OK. MSgt. Randolph Hale, Portsmouth, VA reported killed in action from the wounds he received in battle. Cpl. Alfred Gregory, Wealthia, VA was reported killed in action May 23, 1951.

Cpl. Clifton Howell, Greensboro, NC, Medical Unit, 17th Infantry Regiment reported killed in action October 18, 1952. He was a graduate of North Carolina A & T College, Greensboro, NC. Pvt. Dennie Irving, Chicago, IL was reported killed in action, July 1951; Cpl. Woodson Ivy, Cleveland OH, 24th Infantry Regiment was reported killed in action. PFC Ned Hinnant, 24th Infantry Regiment, Fairmont Heights, MD was reported killed in action. Sgt. James Johnson, Norfolk, VA reported killed in action in Korea, September 18, 1951. Cpl. John Johnson, 24th Infantry Regiment, Oxon Hill, MD was reported killed in action. Johnson graduated from Shaw Junior high school and Phelps Vocational high school, Washington, DC; Pvt. Charles Jones, Bowers Hill, VA was reported killed in action, August, 1951; Cpl. David Jones, 2nd Infantry Division, Norfolk, VA reported killed in action. Sgt. Clarence C. Kearney was reported killed in action, June 1951. He was from Warrenton, NC. Kearney was a graduate of John R. Hawkins high school. Sgt. Herman H. Little, 24th Infantry Regiment reported killed in action. He was from Norfolk VA; PFC Herbert Logan, Dillwyn, VA was reported killed in action, April, 1951.

PFC Herbert Ulysses Mack, Charleston, SC was reported killed in action, September 22, 1951 and he was awarded the Purple Heart Medal posthumously. PFC William Maddox, St. Louis, MO reported killed in action in February, 1951; Albert J. Martin, 24th Infantry Regiment, New Orleans, LA was reported killed in action; Douglas McCaine, Baltimore, MD reported killed in action; Pvt. Herbert McClendon, Campbell, OH was reported killed in action; PFC Robert L. McCormick was reported killed in action. He was from Baltimore, MD. Pvt. Delmar Theodore McDaniel, Portsmouth, VA reported killed in action on October, 1951. PFC James A Milton, Norfolk, VA reported killed in action; Pvt. John D. Murphy, Chicago, IL was reported killed in action; Cpl. Willie E. Price, Halifax County, Littleton, NC was reported killed in action. He was a member of the 24th Infantry Regiment and a veteran of WW II. PFC Thomas Reed, Phoenix, AZ was reported killed in action and his family was denied permission to bury him in the veteran's section of the Greenwood Memorial Park Cemetery for six weeks because their son wasnot a White American. Previously Negro veterans were buried in this section, but their families were required to submit three notarized letters from veteran organizations. This requirement was established by the cemetery owners, Arizona's Lodge of Free and Acceptance Masons. This was not a requirement for White soldiers. Reed's father refused to submit the required paperwork; and after six weeks of controversy, the Cemetery's Board of Trustees decided to waive its rules and permit Thomas Reed's remains to be buried in the veteran's section of Greenwood Memorial Park. Pvt. Leo Othis Robinson, St. Louis, MO was reported killed in action in August, 1951; Pvt. Johnnie B. Rhodes reported killed in action was from Lebanon, TN; Cpl. Wade E. Ruthledge,25th Infantry Division, New York City, NY was killed in action and received the Bronze Star Medal posthumously. Pvt. Pilton Scoon, Elizabeth City, NC was reported killed in action; PFC Floyd Shepard, Tulsa, OK was reported killed in action; PFC Orville L. Simpson, Chicago, IL was reported killed in action; PFC Gerald Smith, 24th Infantry Regiment, Chicago, IL was reported killed in action; Pvt. Roy L. Smith, Norfolk, VA reported killed in action; Cpl. James Steward, Norfolk, VA was reported killed in action; Joseph L. Ward, East St. Louis reported killed in action in April, 1951. PFC Charles L. Washington, Jr., St. Louis, MO was reported killed in action; Cpl. Leslie White, Wealthia, VA was reported killed in action in May, 1951. Maurice Williams, Washington, DC reported killed in action in April, 1951 and PFC Morris Woodson, Louisville, KY was also reported killed in action.

HEROIC ACTS OF COURAGE

African Americans have responded to the call to arms to defend America the beautiful during numerous conflicts. Blacks' fidelity, bravery and courage have been largely over looked in America's published histories. They had to overcome many obstacles while fighting under handicaps and unequal conditions. This chapter recounts the heroic acts of courage the Black service personnel exhibited during the Korean War. These acts are further proof of their abilities on the battlefield.

Some of their prestigious and distinctive awards are the Medal of Honor, Distinguished Service Cross, Silver Star, Legion of Merit Medals, Bronze Star, Purple Heart Medals and the combat Infantryman's Badge (CIB).

CHAPTER 9

HEROIC ACTS OF COURAGE

Calvin R. Allen, 24th Infantry Regiment, Roseland, VA received the Combat Infantryman Badge. 1st Lt. Warren Allen, Second Ranger Company, 7th US Infantry Division, Fayetteville, NC was awarded the Silver Star Medal for gallantry in action against the enemy. Sgt. James H. Alston, Littleton, NC was awarded the Silver Star Medal for his gallantry when he manned his machine gun and assisted 14 wounded soldiers to safety before leaving his position. Cpl. Benjamin Amos, Los Angeles, CA was awarded the Purple Heart and Bronze Star Medals. He was wounded and recuperated in Tokyo General Hospital. Amos was a member of the 25th Infantry Division. Cpl. Eric Anderson, of East Orange, NJ, Company I, Heavy Mortar Company, 24th Infantry Regiment received the Bronze Star Medal. Sgt. Frederick Anderson, 24th Infantry Regiment, Philadelphia, PA was awarded the Distinguished Service Medal; MSgt. Fred Anderson, Company A, 24th Infantry Regiment received the Bronze Star Medal. He was from Georgetown, SC. Pvt. James Anderson, 24th Infantry Regiment, Ft. Worth, TX received the Distinguished Service Cross. Sgt. Charles Austin, Ada, OK received the Combat Infantryman Badge; Cpl. Paul Ayers, Cape Charles, VA was awarded the Bronze Star Medal. He was a gunner in a Chemical Mortar Battalion, X Corps; PFC C. Bagey, 24th Infantry Regiment, Clarkwell, TX received the Combat Infantryman Badge; Cpl. S. E. Baker, 24th Infantry Regiment, Dermont, AR received the Combat Infantryman Badge; Sgt. Emanuel Balleg, Louisville, KY, 24th Infantry Regiment received the Bronze Star Medal; Booker Bailey, 24th Infantry Regiment, Waterboro, SC received the Combat Infantryman Badge. Sgt. Wendell Barge, Norfolk, VA received the Bronze Star Medal for heroic action. He suffered some wounds and also received the Purple Heart Medal.

Sgt. Jerome Barnwell, 77th Engineer Combat Company, Wichita, KS was awarded the Silver Star Medal posthumously. The citation stated that "On August 6, 1950 near Haman, Korea Barnwell's platoon was ambushed while advancing across a hillside and were pinned down risking intense fire. Sgt. Barnwell advanced alone toward an enemy machine gun but before reaching it, he was mortally wounded." Cpl. Willie J. Baty, Mexio, TX was awarded the Distinguished Service Cross; Pvt. Willie J. Belcher, Hampton, VA was awarded the Silver Star Medal for heroism near Haman, Korea, September 1950. He assisted in saving the battalion area. Cpl. Will Bell, 24th Infantry Regiment, Detroit, MI received the Distinguished Service Cross

2nd Lt. William Benefield, 74th Engineer Combat Company, 25th Infantry Division, Alexandria, VA was killed in action while attempting to clear a minefield single handedly at Sanju, Korea under enemy fire. Benefield was awarded the Distinguished Service Cross posthumously. The Medal was pinned on his two year old son at a ceremony. PFC Phillip J. Beverly, Company K, 31st Infantry Regiment, received the Purple Heart Medal for wounds received in action; Cpl. Charles K. Bibbs, 24th Infantry Regiment Company B, Detroit, MI received the Combat Infantryman Badge; 1st Lt. William N. Bivens, Headquarters Company, 3rd Battalion, 24th Infantry Regiment was awarded the Bronze Star for heroic achievement; Sgt. Willis Blakley, Company E, 24th Infantry Regiment, Brooksville, FL was the recipient of the Bronze Star Medal for heroic achievement; PFC Melvin Body, Elmira, NY was awarded the Silver Star Medal; Pvt. Shelly Barnes, St. Louis, MO was awarded the Bronze Star Medal. He was a member of the 3rd Battalion, 24th Infantry Regiment. Sgt. Samuel Bowen received the Bronze Star Medal for heroism. PFC Albert Briscoe, Baltimore, MD was awarded the Bronze Star Medal; Cpl. Ewing Brandon, Company L, 24th Infantry Regiment received the Bronze Star Medal. Horace G. Brooks, 24th Infantry, Regiment, Chattanooga, TN received the Combat Infantryman Badge. Sgt. Jewell Brooks, Alexandria, VA received the Bronze Star Medal posthumously. He was a demolition expert. Pipefitter 2nd Class George Broom, US Navy, Greenville, MS received the

Bronze Star Medal for outstanding performance while serving aboard the destroyer USS Collett. Cpl. Cassell Brown, 9th Regiment, 2nd US Infantry Division, Portsmouth, VA received the Bronze Star Medal and Combat Infantryman Badge. It was stated that he suffered severe frostbite while serving in Korea.

Ensign Jesse L. Brown, US Navy was born October 13, 1920 in Hattiesburg, MS. He was the first known African American to earn Naval Aviators wings. On December 4, 1950, while serving with the Fighter Squadron 32 aboard the Corsair Carrier USS Leyte, Brown participated in a four plane Sortie. Their mission was to search for targets around a reservoir. His plane was hit by enemy anti-aircraft fire. He radioed that he had lost oil pressure and was turning southward near a clearing on a mountain side and would try a belly landing in the snow. Lt. Brown came in for a landing but the engine hit something in the snow which tore a part of the plane causing it to come to a halt. The plane's forward fuselage was jammed upward at a sharp angle pinning Brown's leg under the hydraulic panel. Lt. (JG) Thomas Hudner, US Navy saw Brown slide back the canopy and wave. Brown struggled to free himself but smoke began to blow back over the cockpit. Hudner circled the area in his plane at low altitude and landed flop down about 200 yards upwind. He was able to learn that Lt. Brown received injuries from the rough landing of his plane and was conscious but in pain. Hudner radioed for help and tried to free Brown. A helicopter arrived 45 minutes later, but Jesse Brown had died of internal injuries. Lt. Hudner received the Medal of Honor for his attempts to rescue Brown.

Lt. Brown was awarded posthumously the Distinguished Flying Cross and the Air Medal. In 1973, a naval warship, Knox Class Destroyer was commissioned at Boston Harbor into the US Navy as the DE-1089 USS Jesse Brown. This warship was the first known naval warship to be named for a Black naval aviator.

SFC Willie Bryant, Detroit, MI, 24th Infantry Regiment was awarded the Bronze Star Medal; PFC Luther Brown, Pawley Island, SC was awarded the Bronze Star Medal. MSgt. William L. Bryant, 24th Infantry Regiment, Sand Francisco, CA was awarded the Silver Star Medal for heroism. PFC Robert C. Carpenter, 24th Infantry Regiment, Columbus, OH received the Combat Infantryman Badge. SFC John H. Carter, 24th Infantry Regiment, New York City, NY received the Combat Infantryman Badge. Cpl. Dewey Chappell, Norfolk, VA received the Combat Infantryman Badge. Pvt. John Clark, 24th Infantry Regiment received the Combat Infantryman Badge; Cpl. Leroy Clark, 24th Infantry Regiment, Fordyce, AR was awarded the Bronze Star Medal.

Sgt. Cornelius H. Charlton, Company C, 24th Infantry Regiment, 25th US Infantry Division was born in East Gulf, West VA and entered the Army in New York City, NY. Charlton distinguished himself on June 2, 1951 by acts of heroism for which he was awarded the Medal of Honor. His citation read as follows:

> "Sgt. Cornelius H. Charlton RA 12265495, Infantry US Army, a member of Company C, 24th Infantry Regiment, 25th Infantry Division distinguished himself by conspicuous gallantry and intrepidity above and beyond the call of duty in action against the enemy near Chi pori, Korea on 2 June 1951. His platoon was attacking heavily defended positive positions on commanding ground when the leader was wounded and evacuated. Sgt. Charlton assumed command, rallied the men and spear headed the assault against the hill. Personally eliminating two hostile positions and killing six of the enemy with his rifle fire and grenades. He continued up the slope until the Unit suffered heavy casualties and became pinned down. Regrouping the men he led them forward only to be hurled back again by a shower of grenades. Despite a severe chest wound, Sgt. Charlton refused

medical attention and led a third daring charge which carried to the crest of the ridge. Observing that the remaining emplacement which had retarded the advance was situated in the reverse slope, he charged it alone, was again hit by a grenade but rallied the position with a devastating fire which eliminated and routed the defenders. The wounds received during Charlton's daring exploits resulted in death; but his indomitable courage, superb leadership and gallant sacrifice reflect the highest credit upon himself, the Infantry and the Military service."

PFC Edward Clearborn, Company A, 34th Infantry Regiment was one of the soldiers who assaulted a ridgeline and confronted the enemy in a hand to hand fight. Some 25 men were killed or wounded and some withdrew to safety. Clearborn faced the enemy until he had no more ammunition and sacrificed his life. PFC Clearborn was awarded the Distinguished Service Cross posthumously. Memorial services were conducted for him at the Metropolitan Baptist Church, the Rev. S. A. Owen, Pastor, Memphis, TN.

Pvt. Joseph Clemmons, 24th Infantry Regiment, Florence, SC received the Combat Infantryman Badge; 1st Lt. Arthur Collins, Washington, DC was awarded the Silver Star for gallantry in action near Masan, Korea and he also received the Purple Heart Medal. Cpl. Robert L. Cook, Inglewood, CA received the Bronze Star Medal; Charles R. Cooper, 3rd Infantry Division, SC received the Silver Star Medal posthumously for his heroic actions near Uijong bu, Korea. The medal was presented to his parents, Mr. and Mrs. Thomas W. Cooper. 1st Lt. Ernest J. Craigwell, US Air Force, Brooklyn, NY flew wing man for the 5th US Air Force famed "Flying Parsons" in the Korean War, and was awarded the Distinguished Flying Cross for his heroism on duty. Henry G. Cramer, 24th Infantry Regiment, Newburgh, NY received the Silver Star Medal for his bravery. Oliver P. Cravin, 24th Infantry Regiment, Palestine, TX received the Combat Infantryman Badge; Cpl. Lewis Credle, 24th Infantry Regiment, Norfolk, VA received the Combat Infantryman Badge; PFC Julian E. Cromartie, 24th Infantry Regiment, Washington, DC was awarded the Bronze Star Medal; PFC Isaac Davis, 24th Infantry Regiment, Niles, TX received Combat Infantry Badge; Cpl. Lindsay D'Armond, Columbus, OH received the Soldiers Medal for extraordinary heroism at Kimpo Air Force Base, Korea. Steward 3rd Class William H. Davis, US Navy was awarded the Submarine Combat Pin while serving aboard the USS Pickerel during the Korean War. Cpl Earl Dill, 24th Infantry Regiment, Chicago, IL received the Combat Infantryman Badge; Pvt. Rudolph Dinwiddie, Taft, OK received the Combat Infantryman Badge; Sgt. Edward Douglass, 24th Infantry Regiment, Louisiana, MO received the Combat Infantryman Badge; Sgt. Wylie Dotson, 24th Infantry Regiment, Philadelphia, PA received the Combat Infantryman Badge and Overton Duckworth, 21st Infantry Regiment, Collins, MS received the Combat Infantryman Badge.

SFC Arthur C. Dudley, Company B, 19th Infantry Regiment, Florida received the Distinguished Service Cross for heroism at Changnyong, Korea. It was stated that he killed 50 North Koreans during a three day battle. He also unjammed a machine gun for a comrade while under heavy fire. Ray Donley, 24th Infantry Regiment, Coffeyville, KS received the Combat Infantryman Badge; Cpl. Walter Duncan 24th Infantry Regiment, CA was awarded the Bronze Star; 1st Lt. Roy H. Duggan, Hampton, GA was awarded the Bronze Star Medal; Early Rutherford, Jr., Company B 24th Infantry Regiment, St. Louis, MO was awarded the Bronze Star Medal. PFC Alphonso Edwards, 24th Infantry Regiment, Oklahoma City, OK was the recipient of the Purple Heart Medal. He was a graduate of Douglas HS. PFC Carl Edwards, Philadelphia, PA received the Combat Infantryman Badge; Cpl. Calvin Ellis, Philadelphia, PA received the Combat Infantryman Badge. Major Joseph Elsberry, US Air Force, 18th Fighter Bomber Wing, Oklahoma City, OK served as a communications officer. He was the recipient of the Distinguished Flying Cross, and he was also a fighter pilot during WW II. His parents resided in Pauls Valley, OK.

PFC Amos Emerson, 24th Infantry Regiment received Combat Infantryman Badge. He was from Texas. Sgt. James D. Evans, 24th Infantry Regiment, Newton, MI received the Combat Infantryman Badge; and Cpl. Lawrence Fields, San Antonio, TX, 24th Infantry Regiment was awarded the Bronze Star Medal. Sgt. Horrie Flowers, Jr., Headquarters and Headquarters Company, 3rd Battalion, 24th Infantry Regiment was awarded the Silver Star Medal posthumously. His citation reads as follows:

> "On November 30, 1950 near Kunuri hostile elements had infiltrated the Battalion area where preparations were being made to move vital supplies and equipment. Sgt Flowers organized a small group to combat the enemy and then directed the removal of ammunition and trucks. Although fatally wounded the Sgt. refused evacuation until all trucks had been withdrawn and the enemy force was eliminated."

MSgt. Spencer Forside, St. Louis, MO was awarded the Silver Star Medal for action in Korea. He displayed a heroic act when he confronted the enemy's machine gun fire and small arms fire. Cpl. Henry Foster, Middlesex, VA served in Korea and received the Bronze Star Medal; PFC William Foster, 24th Infantry Regiment received the Combat Infantryman Badge. He was from Louisburg, NC. SFC Frank Freeman, Monett, MO was awarded the Purple Heart Medal for wounds received in combat action at Yongdong-po, Korea. Sgt. Malcolm Fulcher, 24th Infantry Regiment, Brooklyn, NY received the Combat Infantryman Badge.

Leon S. Gainer, Jr., Detroit, MI, 24th Infantry Regiment received the Combat Infantryman Badge; Cpl. Tinnie Gardner, Bridgeport, CT received the Combat Infantryman Badge. He was assigned to the 24th Infantry Regiment. Sgt. Leander Geddes, 24th Infantry Regiment, Jacksonville, FL was awarded the Distinguished Service Cross; PFC Lewis C. Gibson, 24th Infantry Regiment, Lubbock, TX received the Combat Infantryman Badge; Pressley Giles, 3rd Infantry Battalion, 24th Infantry Regiment, Yoakum, TX was awarded the Bronze Star Medal; Lawrence Glover, Baltimore, MD was awarded the Silver Star Medal for gallantry in action near Ku Nu-ri. In addition, he also received the Purple Heart Medal. Willie Goff, 24th Infantry Regiment, Roane, TX received the Combat Infantryman Badge. PFC John Goode, Mobile, AL received the Distinguished Service Cross posthumously for heroism in Korea. He was assigned to the 9th Infantry Regiment, 2nd US Infantry Division. Goode displayed extraordinary heroism against the enemy near Yongsan, Korea on the Naktong river line. He was killed in action on September 17, 1950.

Sgt. Zacharis Gooding, Macon, GA, 24th Infantry Regiment was awarded the Bronze Star Medal. US Navy Chief Steward William B. Goodman, San Francisco, CA was awarded the Distinguished Service Cross. He served as a tail gunner on a Navy Bomber and made some 35 missions over Korea. SFC Jack Gourdine, 24th Infantry Regiment, Chicago, IL received the Combat Infantryman Badge; Cpl. Walter Graham, 24th Infantry Regiment, Birmingham, AL; Freddie Gransberry, 24th Infantry Regiment, Youngstown, OH received the Combat Infantryman Badge; PFC Earl Grant was awarded the Bronze Star Medal for Meritorious Achievement. He was from Whiteboro, NJ. Sgt. Hiram C. Grant, Jr., son of Mr. and Mrs. Hiram C. Grant, Akron, OH received the Bronze Star Medal for Meritorious service. PFC Joseph C. Grant, Baltimore, MD received the Combat Infantryman Badge. Cpl. Robert E. Graves, 24th Infantry Regiment, Fontane, CA received the Combat Infantryman Badge. Major George Gray, US Air Force, West VA was killed in action while flying a combat mission. He was awarded the Distinguished Flying Cross for his valor. SFC James Gray, 24th Infantry Regiment, Norfolk, VA received the Bronze Star Medal; Cpl. Curtis Green, Company D, 24th Infantry Regiment, Longview, TX was awarded the Bronze Star Medal; Pvt. James Greene, 24th Infantry Regiment, Detroit, MI was awarded the Distinguished Service Cross; and Leon A. Green, Moria, NY was awarded the Silver Star Medal for gallantry in action near the Kum river. Brigadier General Edward Greer, Gary West VA served in Korea. He was awarded the Silver Star, Legion of Merit and Bronze Star Medals. He was born on March 8, 1924 and was a graduate of West Virginia State University and George Washington University. Pvt. Charley Gussie, 24th Infantry Regiment, Lena Station, LA received the Combat Infantryman Badge; Pvt. Charles B. Gregg, 24th Infantry Regiment, St. Louis, MO received the Combat Infantryman Badge.

PFC Joseph L. Hadley, 2nd Infantry Division, Washington, DC received the Purple Heart Medal; Cpl. James C. Hairston, Martinsville, VA received the Combat Infantryman Badge. James B. Harris, Oakland, CA was assigned to the 3rd Battalion, 24th Infantry Regiment was awarded the Bronze Star Medal. Sgt. Rachael Harris, 24th Infantry Regiment, Detroit, MI received the Combat Infantryman Badge. 1st Lt. James Harvey, US Air Force, Far East Air Force, Mountain Top, PA was awarded an Air Medal for Meritorious Achievement while participating in aerial flights against the enemy. Harvey was an F-80 pilot credited with 33 missions and he also served as an Intelligence Officer. During WW II he was assigned to the 332nd Fighter Wing. George Hayes, 24th Infantry Regiment, Cleveland, OH received the Combat Infantryman Badge. James W. Henderson, 24th Infantry Regiment, Jackson, MS received the Combat Infantryman Badge; PFC William J. Herdon, 24th Infantry Regiment, Greensville, SC; Sgt. John O. Herring, 3rd Battalion, 24th Infantry Regiment was awarded the Bronze Star Medal; PFC Hickman, Alabama, 24th Infantry Regiment received the Combat Infantryman Badge; Pvt. James Hicks, 24th Infantry Regiment, St. Louis, MO received the Combat Infantryman Badge; PFC Oscar Hill, 24th Infantry Regiment, Dallas, TX received the Combat Infantryman Badge; Cpl. McBert Higginbotham, New York City, NY was awarded the Bronze Star Medal; Cpl. Albert Hill, 24th Infantry Regiment, Providence, RI received the Combat Infantryman Badge; PFC John L. Hicks, 24th Infantry Regiment, Brooklyn, NY received the Combat Infantryman Badge; Cpl. Robert L. Holeman, Memphis, TN received the Purple Heart Medal and a Presidential Unit Citation; Sgt. Major Eldern Holley was a recipient of the Bronze Star Medal. He previously served in WW II, the Vietnam War and was the recipient of two Commendation Medals. Master Sgt. Levy V. Hollis, TX was awarded the Distinguished Service Cross for heroism; Oliver W. Holmes, 24th Infantry Regiment was the recipient of the Combat Infantryman Badge; PFC Tatum, 24th Infantry Regiment, of Oklahoma received the Combat Infantryman Badge; PFC John Hull, Brooklyn, NY, 24th Infantry Regiment received the Combat Infantryman Badge; SFC Mayo Howard, 24th Infantry Regiment, Tallahassee, FL received the Combat Infantryman Badge; and Cpl. Roosevelt Hughes, Vallejo, CA, 24th Infantry Regiment received the Bronze Star Medal. Cpl. Robert D. Humburd, 24th Infantry Regiment, from Iowa was wounded in action during the Korean War. He received the Purple Heart Medal; 1st Lt. Marshall Hurley, 159th Field Artillery Battalion, Washington, DC was awarded the Bronze Star Medal.

1st Lt. Clarence Jackson, 5th Infantry Regiment, 1st Cavalry Division Platoon Leader, was awarded the Silver Star Medal for outstanding heroism and gallantry under fire. Jackson was from Pittsburgh, TX and was a graduate of Prairie View A & M College, in Prairie View, TX.; Cpl. Emery L. Jackson, 24th Infantry Regiment, St. Louis, MO was awarded the Distinguished Service Cross; Cpl. Levi Jackson, Jr., Cayce, SC was awarded the Distinguished Service Cross; PFC Herbert Jackson, 24th Infantry Regiment, Syracuse, NY received the Combat Infantryman Badge; PFC Lonnie Jackson, 24th Infantry Regiment received the Combat Infantryman Badge. He was from Texas. Cpl. John James, 24th Infantry Regiment, Baltimore, MD was awarded the Silver Star Medal for heroism in combat. PFC Charles Jamison, 24th Infantry Regiment, Topeka, KS received the Combat Infantryman Badge; Sgt. Robert Janifer, Pottstown, PA received the Combat Infantryman Badge; Pvt. Monroe Jenkins, Pratt, KS, 24th Infantry Regiment received the Combat Infantryman Badge; Charles A. Johnson, Evansville, IN received the Silver Star and the Bronze

Star Medals while serving during the Korean War. Sgt. Cornelius Johnson, Petersburg, PA received the Silver Star Medal; Edgar Johnson, 24th Infantry Regiment, Detroit, MI was awarded the Silver Star Medal for heroism in Combat; PFC Leroy Johnson, Jr., 24th Infantry Regiment Fostoria, OH received the Combat Infantryman Badge and was also awarded the Silver Star Medal; Sgt. Prince Johnson, 24th Infantry Regiment, Savannah, GA received the Combat Infantryman Badge; PFC Robert E. Johnson, Allentown, PA was awarded the Bronze Star Medal; PFC Aaron Jones, Memphis, TN was awarded the Silver Star Medal for heroism. Jones's Browning automatic weapon and some hand grenades were instrumental in his capturing some rifles and an abandoned machine gun to confront the enemy. PFC Jones was the only Black soldier in his nine man squad that had a mission to seize a hill held by Chinese troops who were hurling grenades. PFC Albert Jones, 24th Infantry Regiment received the Combat Infantryman Badge. He was from New Orleans, LA. Arthur Jones, 24th Infantry Regiment received the Combat Infantryman Badge and he was from Ossining, NY. PFC Eddie Jones, 24th Infantry Regiment, Lake City, SC received the Combat Infantryman Badge; Edward L. Jones, Indianapolis, IN received the Soldiers Medal for heroism by responding to a fire call at the Pusan, Korea Port where a railroad car contained explosives. MSgt. Henry Jones, 24th Infantry Regiment, Birmingham, AL was awarded the Silver Star Medal.

SFC John H. Jones, 65th Heavy Tank Company, 3rd US Infantry Division, was awarded the Silver Star Medal for gallantry in action at Wonchon-ni, Korea on January 30, 1951. His Company was assaulting an enemy roadblock of 27 supporting troops. Sgt. Jones was a Tank Commander and as such, moved his tank to a forward position some 100 yards beyond a wooded bend in the road. This position neutralized enemy fire that was coming from the north and west. Sgt. Jones and four infantry men were faced with enemy fire from two positions during their advance. One soldier was killed instantly and the enemy allowed the other three infantry men to attempt to recover the body and weapon of their comrade. Suddenly the enemy troops started to fire their machine guns, rifles and a mortar. Jones immediately turned his tank to the west and ordered his crew to fire on the enemy for fortification. In complete disregard for his life, Sgt. Jones exposed himself to the enemy and started to fire his machine gun. Jones' machine gun was hit several times, the ammunition box was destroyed and a part of the tanks turret was damaged by bullets. Jones continued to secure his position until the three infantry men withdrew to a safe position with the body and weapon of the mortally wounded soldier.

PFC Robert Jones, 24th Infantry Regiment, Los Angeles, CA received the Combat Infantryman Badge; MSgt. Robert E. Jones, 24th Infantry Regiment, Boston, MA received the Combat Infantryman Badge; SFC Sam Jones, Chattanooga, TN was awarded the Bronze Star Medal; Clyde B. Jordan, Washington, DC was awarded the Bronze Star Medal for heroism; and 2nd Lt. Kenneth Ingram, Oklahoma City, OK received the Silver Star Medal. Sgt. James King, Chicago, IL was awarded the Bronze Star Medal; Lt. William Knox, Washington, DC was awarded the Bronze Star Medal; Sgt. Myer B. Kyer, Alameda, CA received the Combat Infantryman Badge; and Pvt. Richard King, 24th Infantry Regiment, Waugh, AL received the Combat Infantryman Badge.

PFC Wilfred Lamar, 24th Infantry Regiment, Vacharic, LA received the Combat Infantryman Badge; PFC Jesse Lane, 24th Infantry Regiment, Chicago, IL received the Combat Infantryman Badge; PFC Joseph La Prince, 24th Infantry Regiment, Charleston, SC received the Combat Infantryman Badge; Sgt. Walter Larkins, 24th Infantry Regiment, Vicksburg, MS received the Combat Infantryman Badge; Sgt. William Lawrence, 3rd Battalion, 24th Infantry Regiment, Baltimore, MD was awarded the Bronze Star Medal; Wyman J. Lee, 24th Infantry Regiment, New York City, NY was awarded the Silver Star and the Bronze Star Medals. Lt. Chester Lenon, 77th Combat Engineer Company, 25th Infantry Division, Independence, KS was awarded the

Distinguished Service Cross for gallantry. PFC James Lonon, 24th Infantry Regiment, Kinston, NY received the Combat Infantryman Badge; P. E. Lewis, 24th Infantry Regiment, New Castle, DE received the Combat Infantryman Badge. Sgt. George Long, 24th Infantry Regiment, Bessmer, AL received the Combat Infantryman Badge; SFG George Love, 24th Infantry Regiment, Gurdon, AR was awarded the Bronze Star Medal.

Pvt. George Lowery, Jr., 24th Infantry Regiment, Washington, DC was awarded the Combat Infantryman Badge during Korean War. Lowery died on September 25, 2002 and is survived by his wife, Shirley Lowery, a brother, Eddie C. Lowery and a sister, Sylvia L. Rogers.

PFC James Lucas, 24th Infantry Regiment, Ft. Worth, TX received the Combat Infantryman Badge; PFC Louis Lyons, Henderson, TX also received the Combat Infantryman Badge.

PFC Herbert Ulysses Mack, Charleston, SC was awarded the Purple Heart Medal posthumously. He was survived by his parents, Mr. and Mrs. William Mack, sisters and brothers. PFC Mack was buried in Emanuel Cemetery with full military honors. PFC Henry Marrow, 24th Infantry Regiment, Halifax, NC was awarded the Distinguished Service Cross for heroism; Sgt. Charles E. Massie, Battery A 503rd Field Artillery Battalion, 2nd Infantry Division was awarded the Silver Star Medal for gallantry in action. He was from Ohio; and his citation stated that near the town of Somin-dong, Korea his Unit was attacked from the rear. Massie left his protective cover and directed his 155mm Howitzer on the attacking force. Although under hostile fire, Massie released phosphorous ammunition toward the enemy forces and was able to stop the attack. Sgt. Erin B. Mathena, 3rd Battalion, 24th Infantry Regiment, Chicago, IL was awarded the Bronze Star Medal; Walter Matthew, 24th Infantry Regiment received the Combat Infantryman Badge. He was from Savannah, GA; Capt. Theodore Mc Clain, Boston, MA was Commander of a Tank Unit in Korea and received the Bronze Star Medal. Edward D. McDavid, St Paul, MN, 24th Infantry Regiment was awarded the Silver Star Medal; Major Charles F. McGee, Chicago, IL of the US Air Force received the Distinguished Flying Cross for extraordinary achievement and heroism in action in Korea. PFC Claude McGarrity, Tucson, AZ of the 24th Infantry Regiment received the Distinguished Service Cross Medal; Cpl. Robert Mc Cray of Company H, 24th Infantry Regiment, Akron, OH was a forward observer, 81 mm Mortar Section; and was awarded the Bronze Star Medal for gallantry in action near Sanju, Korea. PFC Henry Mc Gruder, Columbus, GA 56th Military Police Company was wounded in action and he received the Purple Heart, the Bronze Star and the Silver Star Medals. Lt. Col. Luther McManus was awarded the Distinguished Service Cross for gallantry in action inspiring his troops with his personal fearlessness and calling them to fix bayonets as he led them in a determined charge against a hostile enemy position near Wolbong-ni, Korea. SFC William McPheeters, 24th Infantry Regiment, 25th Infantry Division served in Korea and was awarded the Bronze Star Medal during ceremonies at Kimpo Air Force Base, Korea. He was decorated by General Douglas Mac Arthur. PFC James Mellon, Norfolk, VA received the Bronze Star Medal; PFC Johnnie Meyers, 24th Infantry Regiment received the Combat Infantryman Badge and he was from Wilmington, NC; MSgt. Robert Miller, Columbus, OH was a member of the 24th Infantry Regiment and received the Combat Infantryman Badge.

PFC James Mitchell, San Francisco, CA, 24th Infantry Regiment received the Combat Infantryman Badge; Sgt. Johnnie Mitchell, Opelika, AL received the Combat Infantryman Badge; Sgt. Hubert Montgomery of the 24th Infantry Regiment, Homestead, FL received the Combat Infantryman Badge. PFC Edward Moore, 24th Infantry Regiment, Los Angeles, CA received the Combat Infantryman Badge; PFC James Moore of New Orleans, LA the 24th Infantry Regiment also received the Combat Infantryman Badge. Cpl. Thomas Moore, 24th Infantry Regiment, Memphis, TN received the Distinguished Service Cross Medal; 2nd Lt. Clinton Moorman of the 24th Infantry Regiment, Columbus, OH received the Combat Infantryman Badge.

SFC Early G. Morgan of Dayton, OH received the first Oak Leaf Cluster to the Bronze Star Medal with the letter V device for gallantry in action. Early also received the Army Commendation Ribbon with Metal Pendant for Meritorious Service and was the recipient of the Purple Heart Medal. His heroic acts were depicted when his platoon was counter – attacked by numerically superior hostile forces and withdrawal was ordered. Cpl. George Morris of the 24th Infantry Regiment, Tampa, FL received the Combat Infantryman Badge; Cpl. John C. Morrison, 24th Infantry Regiment, Pine Bluff, AR was the recipient of the Combat Infantryman Badge. Lt. Samuel W. Mosley from Farmville, VA was a member of the 7th Infantry Division and received the Silver Star Medal for gallantry in action. PFC Walter Mullin, 24th Infantry Regiment, Muskegan, MI received the Combat Infantryman Badge; Cpl. William Nann, Newport News, VA received the Combat Infantryman Badge; Julian O'Bannon, Dallas, TX received the Soldiers Medal; PFC Leon Ogwin, of the 24th Infantry Regiment, Morgan City, LA received the Distinguished Service Cross. Sgt. Lawrence Owens, East St. Louis, IL received the Combat Infantryman Badge; PFC Sidney Odom, 24th Infantry Regiment, Florida was the recipient of the Combat Infantryman Badge. Pvt. Harry Paterson, 24th Infantry Regiment, Los Angeles, CA received the Combat Infantryman Badge; PFC Robert Pemberton, 24th Infantry Regiment, New York City, NY also received the Combat Infantryman Badge.

Willie G. Pender, Atlanta GA was a member of the 24th Infantry Regiment, Headquarters and Headquarters Company. His convoy was attacked near Yonchon, Korea, November 2, 1950. Pender dismounted from his jeep and began to deliver heavy fire until his rifle was shot from his hand. While looking for a new weapon, he discovered two wounded comrades and evacuated them to safety. Pender then moved through the hostile lines and was able to contact friendly troops and return to the combat lines with reinforcements. Willie C. Pender was awarded the Silver Star Medal for heroism in action.

Cpl. Jack Persall, a member of the 3rd Infantry Battalion, 24th Infantry Regiment, Los Angeles, CA received the Bronze Star Medal. PFC Otis Phillips, Company C, 31st Infantry Regiment, 7th Infantry Division, Norfolk, VA was awarded the Silver Star Medal for heroism in action. Phillips volunteered to carry a flame thrower for his platoon to destroy an enemy position on a strategic hill. When his patrol approached their objective, they confronted hostile fire and grenades. PFC Guy Pickins, 24th Infantry Regiment, New York City, NY received the Combat Infantryman Badge; PFC David Pigford, 24th Infantry Regiment, Magnolia, NC received the Distinguished Service Cross Medal; Pvt. Paul Plowden, Jr., 24th Infantry Regiment, Sumter, SC was the recipient of the Combat Infantryman Badge; PFC Rudolph Polk, Alameda, CA was a member of the 24th Infantry Regiment and the recipient of the Combat Infantryman Badge. SFC Cassius W. Preston, Martinsville, VA was awarded the Bronze Star Medal. Lt. Col. Walter J. Preston, Atlanta, GA a member of the 159th Field Artillery Battery and the recipient of the Silver Star Medal for gallantry in action. According to Preston's citation, "His artillery Battalion was supporting the Infantry from August 4 to 14 August, 1950 against enemy attacks at Haman, Chingong-ni and West Masan, braving road mines and hostile patrols. Ltc Preston moved among the batteries, maintained communication, directed fire, and solved numerous tactical problems. When one battery faced the threat of being overrun, Preston drove through heavy fire to direct its effective defense and led the men to new positions. They were able to advance to an exposed vantage point to relay fire missions from a forward observer.

MSgt. Charles D. Pugh, 24th Infantry Regiment, Columbus, GA won the Bronze Star and Distinguished Service Cross Medals for heroism in combat. Sgt. Charles B. Rangel, New York City, NY a US Congressman served in the Army, 1948-1952. He was awarded the Purple Heart and Bronze Star Medals for valor and also the US Presidential Citation and the Korean

Presidential Citation. Rangel also received three battle Stars while serving in combat with the 2nd Infantry Division in Korea After military service, he completed high school and later graduated from New York University's school of Commerce, 1957; and he was on the Deans List. In 1960 Rangel received a law degree from St. Johns' University School of Law. He was elected to the 92nd Congress in 1970.

PFC M. Rankins, Company B, 24th Infantry Regiment, Jeffersonville, IN was awarded posthumously the Silver Star Medal for gallantry; MSgt. Walter Ratliff, 24th Infantry Regiment received the Bronze Star Medal. He was from Wilson, VA; PFC Larry Riley, 24th Infantry Regiment, Brooklyn NY was awarded the Distinguished Service Cross Medal; Sgt. Martin Rivers, 24th Infantry Regiment, New York City, NY received the Combat Infantryman Badge; Cpl. William Roberts, 24th Infantry Regiment, Norfolk, VA was awarded the Silver Star Medal for his heroic actions on August 10, 1950. Roberts' convoy was attacked by a large enemy force and he crawled through heavy fire to rescue a wounded soldier. It was necessary for him to drive his jeep through hostile fire lines and also protect the wounded soldier. Cpl. Harold Rogue, Jr., 24th Infantry Regiment, Eldorado, AR received the Combat Infantryman Badge; Cpl. Alfred Ross, 31st Infantry Regiment, Takoma Park, MD was awarded the Purple Heart Medal; Cpl. Louis Roundtree, Augusta, GA received the Purple Heart and the Silver Star Medal for bravery in action in Korea, June, 1951.

Sgt. Hilton Saunders, 24th Infantry Regiment, Compton, CA was awarded the Distinguished Service Cross Medal; Melvin H. Schools, Philadelphia, PA served during the Korean War with the 24th Infantry Regiment. He received the Combat Infantryman Badge; PFC Russell Scott, Riverdale, CA, 24th Infantry Regiment received the Combat Infantryman Badge; PFC Tommie Scott, Kingstree, SC, 24th Infantry Regiment received the Combat Infantryman Badge; SFC Vernie Scott, 24th Infantry Regiment, Eckmon, West VA received the Combat Infantryman Badge; and Lt. Thomas Sears, Norfolk, VA served in Korea as a Liaison Officer and Air Observer in an artillery battalion, 25th Infantry Division. He received the Air Medal and Distinguished Flying Cross Medal for 50 missions

Sgt. Clements Sharp, Stillmore, GA was awarded the Bronze Star Medal for Valor in Combat; Charles F. Simmons, 24th Infantry Regiment received the Combat Infantryman Badge; MSgt. Joseph Simmons, 24th Infantry Regiment received the Bronze Star Medal; Robert L. Simmons, New Orleans, LA was the recipient of the Combat Infantryman Badge; Alonzo Singleton, 24th Infantry Regiment, Miami, FL received the Combat Infantryman Badge; 1st Lt. James B. Smith, Columbus, OH received the Silver Star Medal for heroism in combat. Later he was assigned Public Information Officer at Camp Gifu, Japan, 1951. Sgt. Nicholas Smith, 24th Infantry Regiment, Baltimore, MD was awarded the Silver Star Medal for bravery in combat; Sherman W. Smith, Los Angeles, CA, 24th Infantry Regiment received the Combat Infantryman Badge; Cpl. Wortham Smith, 24th Infantry Regiment, Houston, TX was awarded the Distinguished Service Cross Medal; Joe F. Speaks, Mississippi received the Combat Infantryman Badge; and Sgt. Floyd Spencer, Wellsburg, West VA received the Bronze Star Medal. Sgt. Russell Spencer, 24th Infantry Regiment, Detroit, MI received the Combat Infantryman Badge; PFC Claude Springs, 24th Infantry Regiment, Charlotte, NC received the Combat Infantryman Badge; Charles R. Stanfield, Alexandria, LA received the Combat Infantryman Badge; Samuel Roscoe Strothers, US Navy, served aboard the USS Missouri during the Korean War. He was awarded the Bronze Star Medal for bravery; PFC Norman Stubbs, St. Louis, MO was also awarded the Bronze Star Medal. Lt. Harry Sutton, 3rd US Infantry Division received a medal for his outstanding heroism during the Korean War. Talmadge Swinney received the Combat Infantryman Medal. He was from Monroe, GA; PFC Ray Taylor, 24th Infantry Regiment, of North Little Rock, AR also received the Combat Infantryman Badge.

PFC Johnnie Terrick, 24th Infantry Regiment received the Combat Infantryman Badge. He was from Kenner, LA; Pvt. Luther Terry, 24th Infantry Regiment, Fayetteville, NC received the Combat Infantryman Badge; Pvt. Willie Terry, 24th Infantry Regiment, of Henderson, NC also received the Combat Infantryman Badge. Sgt. Jesse Teverbaugh, US Marine Corps received the Silver Star for heroism during the Marine withdrawal from the Yalu River in 1950. He was from Chicago, IL. Sgt. Albert S. Thompson, Company E., 9th Infantry Regiment served during the Korean War and was awarded the Silver Star Medal for heroic actions at Bloody Ridge mountain. Lt. John C. Thompson, Jacksonville, FL, performed heroically during the Korean War and was awarded a Medal for bravery.

PFC William Thompson, Company M, 24th Infantry Regiment, 25th US Infantry Division was born in New York City, NY and entered the military service in Bronx, NY. He displayed great bravery near Haman, Korea, when he was mortally wounded. Thompson was awarded the Medal of Honor for his courage and sacrifice. His Citation reads:

> "PFC William Thompson , Company M, 24th Infantry Regiment distinguished himself by conspicuous gallantry and intrepidity above and beyond the call of duty in action against the enemy near Haman, Korea on 6 August 1950. While the platoon was reorganizing under cover of darkness, fanatical enemy forces in overwhelming strength launched a surprise attack on the Unit. Pvt. Thompson set his machine gun in the path of the onslaught and swept the enemy with withering fire, pinning them down momentarily, thus permitting the remainder of his platoon to withdraw to a more tenable position. Although hit repeatedly by grenade fragments and small arms fire, he resisted all efforts of his comrades to induce him to withdraw. He steadfastly remained at his machine gun and continued to deliver deadly accurate fire until mortally wounded by an enemy grenade. Pvt. Thompson's dauntless courage and gallant self sacrifice reflect the highest credit on himself and uphold the esteemed tradition of military service:"

PFC Thompson was the first Black serviceman to receive the Medal of Honor since the Spanish American War, 1898. Praise was given to Thompson by General Matthew Ridgeway, Commander In Chief of the Far East Command. Ridgeway stated

> "This splendid soldier fought with distinct gallantry and fortitude for the ideals of freedom and protection of his fellow soldiers. His personal bravery and self sacrifice was far above and beyond the call of duty."

PFC Alfred Tribble, 24th Infantry Regiment, Philadelphia, PA received the Combat Infantry Badge; Sgt. Russell M. Vann, Portsmouth, VA, 2nd Infantry Division was awarded the Bronze Star Medal

1st Lt. Leroy Waites, Jefferson, TX served in Korea and was assigned to the 3rd US Infantry Division. He was awarded the Silver Star Medal for gallantry in action. His Citation stated that when his platoon was pinned down by enemy fire on June 7, 1951, while attacking a well defended enemy emplacement, 1st Lt. Waites used his reserve elements to engage the enemy in hand to hand combat and they were successful in repulsing the enemy. Edward Walker, 24th Infantry Regiment, Dublin, VA received the Combat Infantryman Badge. SFC Hardon B. Walker, Norge, VA, 24th Infantry Regiment was awarded the Bronze Star Medal. Cpl. James Walker, Newark, NJ, 24th Infantry Regiment received the Distinguished Service Cross for valor. Robert L. Walker, 24th Infantry Regiment, High Point, Korea received the Combat Infantryman

Badge; PFC Jesse Wallace, Jacksonville, TX, 24th Infantry Regiment received the Combat Infantryman Badge; Sgt. David Walwyn, 24th Infantry Regiment, New York City, NY received the Combat Infantryman Badge; 2nd Lt. William Ware, Winchester, TX was awarded the Distinguished Service Cross Medal; SFC Charles A. Warren, 24th Infantry Regiment, Trenton, NJ was awarded the Bronze Star Medal; PFC Charles Washington, was awarded the Silver Star Medal for heroism. He was from Lanham, MD. C. W. Waters, Crossbeck, TX, 3rd Infantry Battalion, 24th Infantry Regiment was awarded the Bronze Star Medal. Cpl Walter White, 24th Infantry Regiment, Stamford, CT was awarded the Distinguished Service Cross Medal; PFC David Whitehead received the Combat Infantryman Badge. He was from Richmond, IN; and PFC Percy Whitte, 24th Infantry Regiment, Detroit, MI received the Combat Infantryman Badge. Cpl. Charles Wiggins, 24th Infantry Regiment, Baltimore, MD was awarded the Distinguished Service Cross Medal; Pvt. K. Wiley, 24th Infantry Regiment, Durham, NC received the Combat Infantryman Badge; MSgt. George Williams, Petersburg, VA received the Meritorious Army Commendation Medal for meritorious service in military operations against the enemy.

James Williams, 24th Infantry Regiment, Hattiesburg, MS received the Combat Infantryman Badge; Cpl. John Winkfield, Coral Gables, FL, 24th Regiment received the Combat Infantryman Badge; and PFC Lawrence Wilson, 24th Infantry Regiment, St. Joseph, MO also received the Combat Infantryman Badge; SFC William S. Winters, Columbus, OH was awarded the Silver Star Medal for his heroic actions. As his Unit was attacking an objective in the vicinity of Haman, Korea they were subjected to intense hostile machine gun fire. Winters lead a platoon in two unsuccessful attempts before the control of the enemy fire was accomplished. Also when his platoon was counter attacked by a large superior enemy force and withdrawal was ordered, SFC Winters selected to remain with a small group to provide a covering force for the withdrawing troops. William Wingers, 24th Infantry Regiment, Pittsburgh, PA was awarded the Bronze Star Medal; 1st Lt. Ellison Wymn, Company B, 9th Infantry Regiment, 3rd Infantry Division received the Distinguished Service Cross Medal for his heroic actions during the Korean War. Pvt. John Young, 24th Infantry Regiment, Philadelphia, PA was awarded the Bronze Star Medal and PFC John Young, 24th Infantry Regiment, Lansing, MI received the Combat Infantryman Badge.

CHAPTER 10

ETHIOPIAN PROFILE

Ethiopia is located in Northeast Africa, a country whose inhabitants are representative of different ethnic social groups and physical descriptions (features). The United States has classified its inhabitants as Caucasian, Black, Hispanic, Oriental and Asian. There is no division of ethnicity with the American Black. However, in Ethiopia the people have been classified by Ethnologists, anthropologists and linguists into ethnic and racial groups based mostly on linguistics and physical descriptions. Sometimes these professionals will use the terminology "mixed" rather than state that some of the Ethiopians over centuries interbreed (miscegenation) genetically with other races mainly Arabians and Caucasians.

The Ethiopians have been classified as representative of Cushitic, a Mediterranean people, semitized Cushitic, and Nilotic Negroid peoples. Their culture is Cushitic and Semitic. It is believed that a group of Semitic people from Southern Arabia invaded Ancient Ethiopia around 1,000 B. C. to 400 B. C. and over many years developed a heterogeneous population of Blacks, Cushitic and Semites. These people mated and married and were the founders of the Axumite Kingdom. They probably were the ancestors of today's Tigrai people of Eritrea.

Geographically Ethiopia occupies approximately 457,000 square miles. The countries that border Ethiopia are Somali and Kenya, northern boarder, Sudan, western boundary, Red Sea, Djibouti, and Somali, eastern boundary. There is a northern region of the Rift Plateau where the Kingdom of Axum was located. This is the site of the present capital Addis Ababa. There is a large seaport along the Ethiopian coast of the Red Sea called Massawa.

The country of Ethiopia had been divided into twelve provinces, Eritrea and five districts. The provinces were subdivided into sub-provinces then districts.

The Ethiopian people have an interesting history of their ancestral ethnic groups. The major ethnic groups are the Amharas, Tigrais, Galla, Gurages, Agau, Falashas, Somalis Afar (Danakil) Saho, Sidamo, and the Shankellas. Genetically they could possibly be classified as Ethiopians. The Amharas and Tigrais people accepted Christianity in 400 A. D. They speak the language Geez. Both are proud of their ancestral background to the Kingdom of Axum and preservers of the Coptic religion. The Tigrais and Amhara descriptive features are "light brown to dark brown complexion, thin lips, long high bridged nose, medium sized ears, average to medium height and curly to wavy hair depending on miscegenation with other ethnic groups (Arabic or Italian).

The Gallas migrated into Ethiopia around the 16th Century and are probably of Arabic origin. The Gallas are also known as Oromo and they represent the largest ethnic group in Ethiopia. The Galla peoples have settled in various provinces and areas in Ethiopia. There are the Gallas of Kaffa, Walaga, Central Wallo, Ilubabor, Shoa, Arusi, Gamo-Gofa, Sidamo, and Harar provinces. Many Gallas are Moslems and they speak a Cushitic language. Some of the Gallas have interbreed with other ethnic groups, namely the Amharas, and Afar-Saho (Yaju Gallas).

The Gurages live in the southwestern part of Shoa province. Their religion consists of Islam and Christianity. Miscegenation between the Gurages and the Sidamo people gave the physical features consistant with Negroid features and some features similar to the Amhar-Tigrai people.

Some Gurage people were slaves of the Shoa Kingdom and spoke several dialects of a Semitic language. Their occupations have been skilled carpenters, potters and farmers.

The major social group of the Agau are the Aweya (Kumfel), Bogos, Ke'mant, Kayla, Dinder and the Quarra. They have occupied the areas of southern GoJam, Lake Tana, Begem'der province, Lasta district and the northern part of Eritrea. Their physical description is light brown with similar features of the Somalis and Gallas. The religion of the Agaus is Muslem and Christian. The Agau people are the builders of the famous Lalibela churches that were built of rocks.

The Falashas have lived in the areas of Semyen, northern part of Begemder. There are several theories as to the origin of the Falashas. They could have descended from the lineage of Menelik of Ethiopia, when 10,000 jews accompanied him back to Ethiopia after a visit to his father, King Solomon. It is also believed that the Agau were converted to Judaism by Jewish missionaries from Yemen in the 3rd or 4th century, A. D. They speak an Agau dialect, Amharic and Tigrinya and their writings are in Ge'ez. Their physical features are similar to the Amharas and Bogos of Eritrea.

The Somalis have been a nomadic people moving across the land with their animals, sheep, camels, and goats. Many of the Somalis are Moslems. They have occupied home sites in the areas of former French and British Somaliland, north western part of Kenya and provinces in Ethiopia. Somalis have settled in the Ethiopian provinces of Harage (Ogaden Awraja) and Wal Wal. The Somalis are represented in cellular groups, nations and divisions. There are two major groups, the Northern and Southern.

The northern units or groups are the Darod, Isaq and Dir. They are believed to be the descendants of an Arab group who possibly mixed with African peoples years ago. The southern group consists of those Somalis who appear to have a greater African genetic structure. The Sabs are a sub-group of the southern group. The Somalis speak Somali dialects. There have been some Somali groups located in the eastern areas of the Hararge plateau. They are the Gherri-Jarso and the Gherri-Babile a miscegenated people of Galla and Somali. The Somalis physical description is that of a tall thin people, narrow face, and light brown to dark brown complexion. Some Somalis' are similar in features to the Afar (Danakil) and the Masai of Kenya. Somalia is located in the horn of Africa. It is situated along the Gulf of Eden, and the Indian Ocean. It is bounded by Djibouti in the northwest, Ethiopia in the west, and Kenya in the southwest. Two major rivers in Somalia are the Shebelle and the Juba and the capital city is Mogadishu.

The Afar is a group that settled in the areas of the Danakil depression located near the Addis Ababa Djibouti railway, the Burt Peninsula on the north, the Red Sea on the east and the highlands of the Ethiopian plateau to the west. The Afar speak the Cushitic language.

The Saho is a semi-nomadic group who are mostly Moslems who are located in Eritrea. Their largest sub-group is the Asaorta. Some of the Saho are of Afar origin and Tigre speaking people.

There is a Cushitic group who have lived in the Ethiopian highlands and speak Tigre; a Semetic language similar to Ge'ez. A social group of the Saho is the Beni Amer, a Beja group.

The Sidamos have been classified as part of the Mediterranean race and have some Negroid traits. Their complexion is dark brown to black and the average height is 5'5". They have six major groups which are the Kaffa-Gibe, the Gimara, the Janerio, the Maji, the Bako and the Ometo. The Sidamos religion consists of Christianity and Moslem. A group of people who lived along the Sudanese – Ethiopian border are called the Shankellas. They were former slaves of some

Amharas and Tigrais. The northern Shankellas are the Kunama and the Barya. The word Barya means slave in Arabic. There was miscegenation for many centuries between the Amharas and Shankella slaves. Some other groups that live in Ethiopia are the Beni-Sciangul, Baro Salient and the Annuaks.

As early as 1875, the Italians had occupied Assab, Eritrea. The Italians later seized Massawa and established some control in Eritera. Emperor Menelik II of Ethiopia denounced a Treaty of Ucciali which the Italians attempted to use in order to establish Ethiopia as an Italian protectorate. Emperor Menelik and his courageous Ethiopian Army was victorious in defeating a "White European power" Italy at the Battle of Adowa in 1895. Unfortunately, this true fact of history, especially military history is not printed in probably most secondary and college textbooks on European and World History.

Italy did not forget her defeat at Adowa and her desire to colonize Ethiopia. Italy invaded Ethiopia on October 3, 1935 and forced Ethiopia's Emperor Haile Selassie into exile in England in May 1936. The Emperor had appealed to the League of Nations to assist him and they refused. Italy was allowed to annex Ethiopia to Eritrea. Then Eritrea, Somaliland and Ethiopia became the Italian East Africa. In 1941 with the aid of the British and other allied soldiers, Ethiopia was able to have the Italians leave the country. Emperor Haile Selassie returned to Ethiopea in 1941. After WW II, the United Nations developed a plan to have Eritrea annexed to Ethiopia. In 1962, Eritrea was made a province of the Empire again.

A few years after the annexation decision, some revolutionary movements were formed to oppose the annexation. These movements desired autonomy for their respective territories or provinces. The movements were the Ethiopian Peoples Revolutionary Democratic Front (EPRDF). It was at one time a Marxist group. The EPRDF wanted autonomy for the northern region of the country, Tigre. The Eritrean Peoples Liberation Front (EPLIF) had resisted the annexation of Eritrea to Ethiopia. They desired autonomy for Eritrea. The Ormo (Galla) Liberation Front wanted autonomy for their province. The Ormo's had been the largest Ethnic group in the southwest area of the country.

In August 1974, an Armed Forces Committee deposed Haile Selassie "Lion of Judah" after 58 years as Regent and Emperor. The Parliament was dissolved and the constitution suspended. On August 27, 1975, the world renowned, distinguished monarch, "His Majesty", Emperor Haile Selassie was reported dead in a small apartment in his former palace at the age of 83.

On February 2, 1977, Lt. Colonel Mengistu Haile Mariam was named the head of Ethiopia. Later, Mariam was confronted with the problems of Eritrea boldly desiring their independence and resistance from the Somali guerillas in the southeast region of Ogaden. When the Somali guerillas and Somali's regular armed forces threatened the city of Harar, the Soviet Union and Cuba assisted Mariam in defeating the Somalis and forcing them to return to Somali. After this incident, Mariam's regime formed a communist group to govern the country. During the period 1984 to 1991, there was tragic internal unrest in Ethiopia. The country was in a civil war between opposing rebellious liberation groups and the communist regime of Mariam.

In February, 1991 the EPRDF was victorious in their frontal attacks toward the city. They seized the capital and Mariam fled into exile. The EPLF was successful in May 1991 in assuming control of the Eastern Province. Today there is a country called Eritrea.

The above profile of the ancient historical and proud country of Ethiopia should give the reader some significant information about an African nation who the league of Nations would not come to their defense in 1936. However, Emperor Haile Selassie of Ethiopia made a decision to provide Ethiopian troops to the United Nations Command, Far East in 1951.

ETHIOPIAN KAGNEW BATTALIONS

When the Korean War commenced in July, 1950, America was still a nation of so called "Separate But Equal" and maintained legal segregation. There were also some African nations that were challenging their colonial oppressors for their independence. However, there was one independent African nation that made a decision to send their military troops to Korea to assist the United Nations Command to fight the Communist North Koreans and Chinese troops. The country was Ethiopia.

Emperor Haile Selassie selected his best trained soldiers for the Ethiopian Expeditionary Force to Korea. The troops were trained in modern weapons and warfare. The soldiers were required to study for three years in the Military Academy of the Imperial Bodyguard. They studied the Amharic language, English, French and received an overall cultural education. When the Ethiopian troops arrived in Korea, it was the first time in Ethiopia's history that the troops would leave Ethiopia to fight in another country. The Emperor selected one of his outstanding officers to form the Expeditionary Battalions. He was Brigadier General Mulugetta Bulli, Commander of the Imperial Body guard.

General Bulli was born in Sidamo province and studied Amharic and French languages in school. He was a graduate of the Lycee Haile Selassie School in Addis Ababa. When he graduated with honors, he was selected to attend the Haile Selassie Military Academy. Bulli was commissioned a captain and served as a chief instructor in the academy. During the 1936 war with Italy, he commanded a battalion. Later it was necessary that he find refuge in the country of Djibouti. The Emperor requested General Bulli to form an Army to liberate Ethiopia. When Haile Selassie was able to return to Addis Ababa, and the Ethiopian government was re-established, Bulli was responsible for the reorganization of the Imperial Guards. The General was highly praised for his participation during WWII in the liberation of Ethiopia. He organized three battalions for the Expeditionary force and they were called the "Kagnew" battalions. The word "Kagnew" referred to establishing order out of chaos and the ability to over throw the enemy. The three Kagnew battalions were designated the first, Second and Third. The Battalions, during the Korean War, had a major combat mission to conduct patrols, inflict casualties and capture enemy prisoners.

On 13 April, 1951, the First Ethiopian Kagnew Battalion departed Ethiopia for the country of Djibouti, where the battalion boarded the American Transport ship, General Macrea on 16 April, 1951 for Pusan, Korea. The president of Korea, Syngman Rhee, American Ambassador, and the Commanding General, Second Logistical Command welcomed the Ethiopian troops when they arrived in Pusan. After a 21 day voyage, the Ethiopian battalion received a six week training and orientation course prior to being attached to the 32nd Infantry Regiment, US Army 7th Infantry Division 1X Corps in Korea. The First Ethiopian battalion was assigned as the 4th battalion of the 32nd Regiment and they were stationed in the reserve area near Kapyong, Korea.

The leadership of the battalion was under the capable guidance of Lt. Col. Teshome Irgetu. He was born in Addis Ababa in 1914. Irgetu was a graduate of the Makonnen Teferi School and the Military Academy of Emperor Haile Selassie.

The Kagnew Battalion was given an assignment as a reserve unit for the 7th Infantry Division in July, 1951. The battalion was given duties to perform patrols and assist in the defense of a hill near Pangdangdon-Ni, Korea. The Kagnew battalions would demonstrate their outstanding attribute as night fighters and unique abilities to perform patrol duties most successfully.

On 14 August, 1951, Lt. Gebressus was the patrol leader with a mission to inflict casualties on the enemy and capture prisoners. The platoon separated into squads and around 1:00 a.m. 15 August, the patrol received some enemy mortar fire and they immediately prepared a defensive line to protect the hill. Mortar fire was directed toward the enemy's position causing some casualties. After four hours of fighting, the enemy withdrew. An Ethiopian soldier, Pvt. Gifar performed heroically during the combat action.

A combat patrol action occurred on 16 August, 1951 when Lt. Abele Kassahun and his men conducted an ambush mission. Kassahun's patrol proceeded to a river junction at the base of Hill 1073. The Ethiopian patrol confronted the North Koreans for three and one half hours. Lt. Abebe Kassahun was forced to withdraw with one casualty. A rear guard, Sgt. Molla assaulted an enemy position and engaged in a hand to hand encounter with the North Koreans. Molla was able to over power four enemy soldiers and his actions assisted the patrol in their withdrawal.

There was a patron action led by Captain Negatu Wandemu on August 21, 1951. After facing some hostile enemy fire, the patrol was able to overcome an enemy force. They also were prepared for a possible enemy counter attack.

Lt. Desta Gemada, the first platoon leader, was designated the Assault Unit of a combat patrol. The platoon was advancing forward and confronted enemy fire from small arms, automatic weapons and mortar. Gemada's platoon was able to obtain cover from the enemy's fire. Later the Lieutenant was able to move his platoon forward and they were able to capture one prisoner. When communications had failed, during the assault, Captain Tefera Waldetensye, liaison officer at Company I's observation post exposed himself to enemy fire and moved forward carrying instructions to the platoon. The successful platoon patrols in August, 1951 were praised by the 7th Infantry Division Commanding General, C. B. Fesenbaugh. He sent a letter dated August 19, 1951 addressed to the officers and men of the 1st Kagnew Battalion and it reads as follows:

> "I want to commend you for the enthusiasm, spirit, and cooperation displayed by each of you since your attachment to this command on July 10, 1951. Keep up the good work."

During the month of September 2952, the First Kagnew Battalion conducted some daring and courageous patrol missions. On September 12, Lema Morro was able to occupy a position on a hill and firing his machine gun toward the enemy continuously, he assisted his comrades in withdrawing to a safe area. Morro decided to remain on the hill and sacrificed his life for his fellow soldiers. A 2nd Lt. Eyob was wounded during the combat action.

Sgt. Major Teguegu Anelege showed courage in action against the enemy in the vicinity of Pangdangdo-Ni, Korea. His unit was engaged in a fight and the assault platoon was facing small arms and automatic weapons fire near a hill. As the platoon leader was directing his men to move toward a safe area, Sgt. Anelege refused to go and continued to fire toward the enemy and was responsible for stopping future counter attacks by them at that time.

On 21 September 1951 Captain Merid Gizan led his men against an enemy hill and was confronted with heavy enemy small arms and automatic fire which slowed their advance. The

Captain encouraged his men to continue to fight and eventually they were able to force the enemy to abandon the hill.

In September, while serving as a Company Commander, Captain Tefera Waldetensye led his men to attack a Hill 612 which was heavily fortified by enemy troops. The Chinese soldiers directed small arms fire and mortar against the Captain's Company. Capt. Waldetensye ordered his men to move forward in an attack against the Chinese. Although critically wounded, he continued to lead his men and fight. He remained with the men for three hours and after suffering many casualties the Ethiopians were able to move to a safe area.

Pvt. Abitte Abitewi demonstrated an act of heroism when his Unit was defending a major "terrain feature", and received considerable enemy fire from small arms, automatic weapons and grenades. Abitte volunteered to attempt to move forward through intense enemy fire and rescue two men who were missing. After he found that the two men were killed, he faced the enemy single handedly until his Company was able to renew the assault and force the enemy to withdraw. Later he was able to rejoin his Unit.

The First Kagnew Battalion was on the front lines until 26 September 1951 when the 7th Infantry Division attained a reserve status. The losses inflicted upon the enemy troops by the Ethiopian Battalion during the period 2 August 1951 to September 1951 were 587 enemies killed, 656 wounded and 10 prisoners. The Battalion was able to confiscate six machine guns, 24 sub-machine guns, and many rifles. In addition, several enemy bunkers and mortars were destroyed.

In December 1951, Ethiopian troops were involved in a combat action during the Second Battle of Mandaeri in the Punch Bowl area. The Kagnew patrol was able to cause some enemy losses, destroyed 15 machine guns, equipment and bunkers during a two day battle. On 18 December, Lt. DeJenie was killed during a combat action.

An Ethiopian patrol had a mission on 12 January, 1952 to engage enemy troops in the area of Huhanggol, Korea. As the patrol was moving toward its objective they were subjected to a heavy barrage of small arms and heavy weapons fire from a large enemy force that occupied heavily fortified positions. Three patrol members, Sgt. Wolden Michael Manno, Pvt. Kassaye Welde and Mesheta Haile performed some heroic acts. Without regard for their personal safety, they left their positions of cover and charged directly into the enemy fire; and upon reaching the enemy's trenches, they leaped into the trenches and fought. Their actions eventually caused the enemy to retreat. The Ethiopian Kagnew Battalion confronted the enemy in combat actions during operation Clamour near Mundung-Ni, Korea in February, 1952. The overall losses inflicted upon enemy forces by the Kagnew Battalion from 27 December 1951 to 14 February 1952 were 150 enemy killed and 280 wounded. The First Ethiopian Battalion served in strategic battle areas during their tour in Korea. Some of those areas were Sangyang-Ni Hill 605, Heartbridge Ridge, the Battle of Mandaeri, Punch Bowl, Operation Clamour, Huhanggol, Mundang-Ni, Kumhwa, Out post Yoke, and Chorwon, Korea.

After serving a successful and commendable tour in Korea, the First Ethiopian Kagnew Battalion departed Korea on 25 March 1952 for Ethiopia on an American Transport ship. They arrived in Ethiopia on 23 April 1952.

The Ethiopian replacement battalion, the Second Kagnew Battalion departed Ethiopia on 9 March 1952 aboard the American Transport ship Macrea. The battalion arrived in Pusan, Korea on 29 March 1952. The Commanding officer of the Ethiopian Second Kagnew Battalion was LtC. Asfaw Andargue who was a graduate of the Haile Selassie Military Academy and served in the

Imperial Bodyguard. His executive officer was Major Kebbede. On 12 April 1952, the Battalion was attached to the 32nd Infantry Regiment, 7th US Infantry Division. They were given a mission to occupy an offensive front line position and conduct patrols. The Battalion was located in a reserve area until June 1952.

On 6 June 1952, the First Company gave a platoon a night patrol mission. The patrol leader was 2nd Lt. Asefa Getahan; and they departed from the main line of resistance (MLR) with the intentions of surprising the enemy. However an enemy platoon had observed the departure of the Kagnew Patrol and allowed it to move forward. The enemy patrol opened fire with their automatic weapons. Actually, the Ethiopians were not taken by surprise because they had discovered the enemy's position; and as they approached the enemy, they attacked with hand grenades. The enemy was able to outnumber the Ethiopians in a counter attack. A hand to hand battle occurred and the Ethiopian soldiers fought with their bayonets. After a 30 minute battle the Ethiopians were forced to withdraw. There were seven Chinese enemy soldiers dead on the battlefield.

A forward observer of the Ethiopian Battalion discovered an enemy force constructing bunkers on 7 June 1952. The US troops were able to use long range weapons on the bunkers. The Kagnew Patrol was able to kill eight Chinese soldiers and cause them to evacuate their hill position.

Capt. Ballette Haile, Company Commander, directed 2nd Lt. Y. Belachew to dispatch his patrol to accomplish a mission that involved determining enemy strength, position, and capture prisoners. The objective was 3,500 yards from the MLR of the Kagnew Battalion. When the patrol reached its objective, they surprised the Chinese troops with small arms and hand grenade fire. The enemy later conducted a counter attack with hand to hand contact using bayonets. The Ethiopians were able to force the enemy to retreat. On 3 July 1952, 2nd Lt. Beniyam Bulbula was given a mission to observe enemy positions near Hill 358, some 200 yards from the United Nations Command's MLR. The patrol moved toward Hill 358 prior to midnight an enemy position on the east side of the hill had observed the patrol. Some Ethiopian soldiers were able to confront the Chinese and met a counter attack. They were able to continue to pursue the enemy and after 45 minutes of combat, the Chinese troops withdrew. There were twenty enemy soldiers killed and some were wounded.

1st Lt. Tilaye Wondimagegenehu received orders on 24 July 1952 to lead his patrol toward Hill 358. The patrol left at 10:30 p.m. As the patrol approached Hill 472 which was occupied by the enemy, they received weapons fire and the patrol continued their advance toward the objective. They were able to gain some ground before Lt. Wondimagegenehu and a sergeant were killed. The men of the patrol were able to receive some reinforcements from the Second Company commanded by Captain Melaku Bakele and First Company commanded by Captain Workneh Gebeyiou. The Commanders dispatched some squads to move toward the enemy positions and to collect their dead and wounded. The Kagnew soldiers found six Ethiopians wounded and four killed. It was reported that 25 enemy soldiers were killed and 40 wounded.

On 25 September 1952 a patrol of the 4th Kagnew Company lead by 2nd Lt. Mellesse Tessema faced the enemy in a hand grenade battle. There were ten enemy soldiers killed and 25 wounded.

1st Lt. Admasu Augneten, 2nd Company lead his patrol of 30 men on 14 October 1952 to attack Hill 250 which was occupied by enemy troops. The Kagnew patrol attacked during the night. The enemy soldiers were surprised and tried to confront the Ethiopians, but eventually they were forced to abandon the hill in a retrograde movement.

When Ethiopian soldiers of the First Company were on an ambush mission on the night of 20 October 1952, a company member displayed a heroic act. Pvt. Fekensa Gelatta observed a comrade who had become entangled in some telephone wire and was being taken prisoner by a Chinese soldier. Fekensa was able to kill the enemy soldier and rescue his fellow soldier.

In October of 1952 the Second Ethiopian Kagnew Battalion was tasked to establish a defensive line on the Kumhwa front known as the "Iron Triangle", Hill 598. The 4th Company commander, Captain Bellete Haile was given orders to defend the valley. On 23 October 1952, the Fourth Company did receive some enemy artillery and mortar fire. 2nd Lt. Gulitat Aberat was ale to lead an ambush attack with a reinforced platoon. Jeru Yayi, 2nd Company fired upon the enemy with his automatic weapon, after leaving his bunker area. 2nd Lt. Feshima Gebre Micael and Sgt. Salik performed in an outstanding manner.

On 1 November 1952 the Chinese launched an attack against the Kagnew Battalion. The enemy attacked 1st and 2nd Companies positions. Prior to the attack, Chinese artillery unit shelled their positions near the battalion's MLR from some hours. When the artillery fire ceased, an hour later the Chinese troops attacked in successive waves. Fortunately, the Kagnew soldiers were able to resist the Chinese troops with only four Ethiopians killed and nineteen wounded. The Chinese did have many losses. A patrol activity was conducted by 1st Lt. Getaneh Rebi and his platoon on 2 November 1952. Around 9 p.m. the platoon began their attack toward Hill 400. The Ethiopian soldiers leaped into the Chinese trenches and started a hand to hand battle. Lt. Rebi was wounded by an enemy bullet but he and his men continued the attack. The Chinese were taken by surprise and began to abandon the hill. The Ethiopians were successful in accomplishing their mission. There were 45 enemy soldiers killed and 75 wounded.

The Second Ethiopian Battalion departed for Ethiopia in March 1953, after performing in an outstanding manner while in Korea. The battalion was replaced by the Ethiopian Third Kagnew Battalion. On 26 March 1953, the Battalion departed Ethiopia on the American Transport ship Blatchford to Pusan, Korea. The Battalion arrived in Korea on 15 April 1953. LTC Wolde Yohannes Shitta commanded the third Kagnew Battalion and his executive officer was Major Teklu Haptemikael. Prior to the Battalion leaving Pusan, Korea, the Ethiopians soldiers, a group representative of officers and enlisted men visited the United Nations Command Cemetery and placed flowers on the graves of their deceased comrades. On 20 April 1953 the Kagnew Battalion arrived in Chorwon, Korea and was attached to the 32nd Regiment, 7th US Infantry Division.

2nd Lt. Fasika Hailemariam lead a patrol of 21 men on an ambush mission on 14 May 1953. As the patrol was moving toward their objective, they were surprised by an enemy attack. Lt. Hailemariam was able to conduct a counter attack with small arms fire and grenades. They were able to resist the enemy force. There were eight enemy soldiers killed and the Ethiopians had one wounded soldier.

During the month of May 1953, some enemy forces attacked the Ethiopian's First Company. The commander, Captain Taddese Sendeku dispatched 18 men and their leader 2nd Lt. Mamo to resist the enemy. The men hurled grenades and a battle started with the Chinese troops. US artillery provided a great assistance to the Ethiopians and they were able to cause some Chinese casualties. There were 25 enemy soldiers killed and 40 wounded. On 18 May 1953 a Chinese force tried to attack the Kagnew Battalion MLR and the Ethiopian positions on Outpost Yoke. The enemy also fired heavy artillery rounds and mortar. The Kagnew soldiers were successful in causing the enemy to withdraw using their bayonets. The mission was accomplished under the leadership of

2nd Lts. Zenebe Asfaw and Bezabih Ayele. The Chinese troops abandoned 15 machine guns and hand grenades as they suffered casualties. The Chinese troops made another attempt to occupy Outpost Yoke on 22 May 1953. Lt. Ayele had prepared his men for a possible enemy counter attack around 1:30; the Chinese Companies supported by heavy artillery and mortar fire approached the area of Outpost Yoke. The Kagnew soldiers were able to stop the enemy's advance even though some were moving forward in waves. The Ethiopians and Chinese were involved in a hand to hand fight. After several hours, the Chinese troops withdrew. There were some 80 enemy troops killed. Lt. Ayele was killed when he was trying to carry two seriously wounded men to a safe area.

Brigadier General Mulugetta Bulli commanding General of the Ethiopian Expeditionary Forces visited Korea and Japan in 1953. He arrived on 27 May 1953 and visited the United Nations Command Headquarter and was welcomed by the Commander In Chief, Far East Command, General Mark W. Clark. Bulli visited the American hospital in Tokyo, Japan and met some wounded Kagnew soldiers. Cpl. Tafara Woldemanuel and Sgt. Haile were patients at the hospital. Lts. Ayanna Aster and Kehede Berkenash were Ethiopian nurses. While visiting the UNC, Bulli decorated some American officers, Col. E. E. Farnsworth, Chief Liaison groups, UNC, and Joseph R Russ.

General Bulli arrived in Seoul, Korea on 29 May 1953 and was greeted by the commanding general, 8th US Army, Lt. General Maxwell Taylor and Ethiopian's Third Kagnew Battalion Commander, LTC Wolde Yohannis Shitta. He visited the I Corps Commanding General. On 3 June 1953, Bulli visited the Kagnew Battalion's position and talked with the troops. The General remained for three days visiting the troops.

During the battle of Porkchop Hill some Ethiopian Kagnew soldiers demonstrated their outstanding fighting abilities. They were Lt. Lemma Gebressadick, Commander, Ethiopian heavy weapons platoon; Cpl. Tiggu Waldertekee who was wounded in the arm by a grenade; Pvt. Tilahublan, Pvt. Mano Waldemarian and Cpl. Angel Seggara. An author of a book on the Korean War stated the following about the Kagnew soldiers:

> "Ethiopian patrols fighting at Pork Chop Hill established a strong base at Alligator Jaws from which they were able to ambush the enemy and capture some prisoners. Their leader was Lt. Wongele Costa."

When the Ethiopians were defending their positions on Outposts Yoke, and Uncle on 4 June 1953, the Fourth Company Commander Lt. Workinew Makkois was able to lead his men to inflict casualties on the enemy. There were 15 enemy killed, two Ethiopians killed and six wounded. On 9 June 1953, Lt. Belayneh Negatou, a patrol leader was involved in a hand to hand battle with the enemy during a counter attack.

The Ethiopian Battalions had a liaison group assigned to the United Nations Command, Far East, Tokyo, Japan. The Liaison officers that were assigned at one time were Captains T. Worknew, Tamarat Tessem, Immeru Wondee, First Lieutenants Getane Ribbi and Assefa Getahan.

It was stated that the Ethiopian Chaplains would pray and bless the troops prior to their departure for the battle lines. A book on the Korean War reported that an Ethiopian Commander was concerned about the following:

"The Ethiopian contingent was insulted when the medical reports categorized Ethiopians as Negroes. The Ethiopians insisted that they be categorized as Ethiopians. They also demanded respect for their religious beliefs that prohibited the performing of autopsies on their deceased soldiers."

There were some African American weekly newspapers that made their readers aware of the Ethiopian Kagnew Battalions' presence in the Korean War. One article cited the name of LTC Heffede Guebre.

ACTS OF COURAGE

ETHIOPIAN KAGNEW BATTALIONS

The Ethiopian officers, non-commissioned officers and enlisted men performed in a most outstanding and commendable manner in their combat missions during the Korean War.

AWARDS and COMMENDATIONS

Captain Merid Gizaw distinguished himself in the vicinity of Pan Dang Dong-Ni, Korea, 17 June 1952. He was awarded the Silver Star Medal. LTC Asfaw Andargue was awarded the Silver Star Medal; and LTC Teshome Irgetu received the Legion of Merit 10 April 1952. LTC Wolde Yohannis Shitta received the Republic of Korea Order of the Military Ulchi without Star on 2 November 1953. 2/Lt. Abebe Kassahun, Second Company was awarded the Bronze Star Medal. He distinguished himself near Pangdang dong-Ni, Korea on 16-17 August 1951 2/Lt. Gebresus Mickael, Second Company was awarded the Bronze Star Medal; Sgt. Molla Kebede, Second Company received the Bronze Star Medal and his courage was demonstrated at Pangdang Dong-Ni, Korea 15 August 1951. Pvt. Gifar Fitalla, Second Company was awarded the Bronze Star Medal and his bravery was shown at Pangdang Dong-Ni, Korea on 15 August 1951. 1st Lt. Wolde Sadic Testfaye was awarded the Bronze Star Medal and he distinguished himself in the vicinity of Pan dang dong-Ni, Korea on September 11, 1951. Pvt. Hallemarial Isheta was awarded the Bronze Star Medal and his valor was shown in the vicinity of Sam-Hyon, Korea; Pvt. Bayesa Kenate was awarded the Bronze Star Medal and he distinguished himself in the vicinity of Mandaeri, Korea. Pvt. Meshesha Haile was awarded the Bronze Star Medal for heroism in the vicinity of Huhanggol, Korea 12 January 1951. Capt. Tamarat Tesemma was awarded the Bronze Star Medal for meritorious service as the Chief Liaison Officer for Ethiopia at the UN Command, Far East for the period 17 June 1951 to November 1952. 2nd Lt. Aseffa Getahun received the Republic of Korea The Order of Military Merit Wharang with Silver Star for his courage in the vicinity of Haridong, Korea, 13 June 1952. 2nd Lt. Wolde Mamo received the Republic of Korea The Order of Military Wharang without Star and his valor was shown as a Patrol Leader. 2nd Lt. Asfaw Zenebe received the Republic of Korea The Order of Military Merit without Star also and his heroics was shown as a Patrol Leader. Pvt. Kasaye Wolde was awarded the Bronze Star Medal on 17 June 1952; 1st Lt. Tariku Berhanu was awarded the Bronze Star Medal on 15 June 1952; Capt. Nigatu Wandemu was awarded the Bronze Star Medal and Pvt. Nigga Tessama was also awarded the Bronze Star Medal. Capt. TeFera Waldetensye was awarded the Silver Star Medal.

LETTERS OF COMMENDATIONS

"Headquarters United Nations Commander In Chief to Colonel Kebbede , June 18, 1952 Appreciation of the Ethiopian Battalions to the United Nations Cause.

> Mark W. Clark
> General USA
> Commander In Chief"

"Headquarters I Corps, October 4, 1953

To: Ethiopian Kagnew Battalion

An excellent mission and combat record accomplished in a superior military manner.

> Bruce C. Clarke
> Commanding General
> Lieutenant General"

CITATION AWARDED

"Battle Honors recognition by the Commanding General, Eighth US Army, General Van Fleet, October 15, 1952

South Korea Presidential Unit Citation, Republic of Korea, President Syngman Rhee, July 17, 1953

Commanding General, 7th US Infantry Division, Major General Arthur Trudeau, awarded the Kagnew Battalion a Unit Citation, October 30, 1953."

The Ethiopian Expeditionary Force Kagnew Battalions performed in an exceptional and superb manner in fulfilling their assigned combat missions.

CHAPTER 11

THURGOOD MARSHALL and MILITARY JUSTICE

The late Associate Justice of the US Supreme Court, Thurgood Marshall was born July 2, 1908 in Baltimore, MD. He was the younger of two sons of William and Norma Marshall. His mother was a teacher and his father a yatch club steward. Marshall was the great grandson of an African slave from the Congo area of Africa.

Thurgood Marshall graduated from the Baltimore City Public Schools, Lincoln University of PA and Howard University School of Law. Marshall was a legal counsel for the NAACP, and a Trial Attorney. He played a most significant role in the Brown v. Board of Education Supreme Court decision, 17 May 1954. He argued before the Supreme Court in this famous judicial case. Thurgood was appointed the first Black Associate Justice of the US Supreme Court in 1967.

During the Korean War, some Black soldiers requested the NAACP to investigate their complaints against the Military Justice System and to provide legal assistance for those who had been court-martialed.

The NAACP decided to respond to the soldiers' request and selected their legal counsel attorney Thurgood Marshall to investigate their complaints. When Marshall applied for his passport to travel to Japan and Korea, a problem occurred. The Commanding General of the United Nations Far East Military Command, General Douglas Mac Arthur suggested to the FBI Director, Herbert Hoover, that Marshall's passport request be denied. The NAACP Executive Director, Walter White, appealed the decision. Fortunately an outstanding President, Harry S. Truman, who had demonstrated some concerns about Black Americans Civil Rights did intervene in this matter. The President gave permission for Marshall to obtain a passport to travel to Japan and Korea.

General Mac Authur wrote the NAACP Headquarters and expressed his reasons why it was not necessary for Marshall to visit the Far East Command. His cable stated

> "There is not the slightest evidence that exist here of discrimination as alleged. As I think you know in the command there is no slightest bias of its various members because of race or color or other distinguishing characteristics. Every soldier in this command is measured on a completely uniform basis with the sole criteria, his efficiency and his character. Nevertheless on receipt of your message, I at once ordered the Inspector General to make a thorough investigation of your charges and will be glad to have you forward here any evidence in your possession bearing upon the matter. If any individual trial of a soldier can obtain special counsel to defend him if he so desires, it is permissible. There would be no objection to Thurgood Marshall representing the accused and coming to this command for such purpose. You must understand, of course, that court-martials are convened by the Major Subordinate Commander and the hearings are conducted there."

Thurgood Marshall left for Tokyo, Japan on January 11, 1951 to visit the United Nations Command, Far East, Headquarters General Douglas Mac Arthur. The military was very cooperative in assisting Marshall to conduct his investigation of the Black soldiers' complaints. He was able to visit the military stockade or prison in Tokyo and was also able to interview the prisons as well as talk to Lt. Gilbert, a Black officer who was court-martialed.

Lt. Gilbert was assigned to the 24th Infantry Regiment and served during WW II assigned to the 92nd Division; and he was present in the Italian Campaign. He was discharged in 1946 and became a reserve officer. In 1947 Gilbert was called to active status and was promoted to 1st Lt. While serving with the 24th Regiment during the Korean War, he refused to obey a lawful order issued by his superior during a combat operation. It was reported that he believed that if he carried out the order he would have lead his twelve men to their death. Gilbert was court-martialed for disobeying an order and was sentenced to death. However, the Military Court of Appeals, Washington, DC reduced his sentence from death to 20 years upon review and the Board recommendations to President Truman, 1 December 1950. In 1955, Gilbert was released with a dishonorable discharge after serving 5 years. Some of the defense lawyers representing Lt. Leon Gilbert of York, PA were Attorneys Judson Rush and William Wogan, York, PA and Frank Reeves, a Washington, DC NAACP attorney. Also present at Gilbert's hearing was Congressman James F. Lind, York, PA.

Attorney Marshall questioned General Mac Arthur about the absence of Black personnel on his headquarters staff or honor guard. General Mac Arthur responded by saying "No Blacks were qualified by battlefield performance to be on his personal staff.

Marshall was accompanied to Seoul, Korea by Col. Darwin D. Martin, Inspector General, of the US Eight Army. He visited the Army Headquarters and had discussions with the military officials. He was able to interview Black and White soldiers of all ranks in the towns of Seoul, Taegu, Pusan and battlefield areas. Marshall examined military records complete court-martialed records and checked some of the soldiers' complaints. After three weeks of conducting a detailed investigation of the soldiers' complaints, Marshall was able to prepare a through report of his findings. The following accounts of court-martial cases, charges, sentences and examples of injustices were reviewed and compiled:

"Some 118 complaints were filed, 82 resulted in trials and the remaining were withdrawn or dropped. Fifty-four of the General court-martials were Black soldiers, twenty-seven were White soldiers and one was Japanese. Sixty-six of the 82 court-martial cases were investigated by White officers and 16 by Negro officers. There were 60 charges filed against Black Military personnel for violation of Article 75 (misbehavior in the presence of the enemy or cowardice)." Marshall observed in the court-martial files, complaints against White soldiers for sleeping on guard duty on the combat lines. They were not charged with any violation of Article 75, only charged with sleeping on their guard posts. They were acquitted of all charges. Even when witnesses testified that one soldier was sound asleep, the soldier still found not guilty.

Thurgood Marshall's analysis of some statistics indicated that all the commanding officers who approved the charges were White. The Inspector General's office and the trial Judge Advocate officer were 100 per cent White. He also learned that Black soldiers were being disproportionately charged with violating orders. Some White servicemen had been sentenced for misbehavior in combat, and also some Blacks. Thirty of thirty-two Blacks received a ten year sentence and two Whites were given sentences of five years or less. There was a White soldier who was relieved of duty and received a five year sentence. Later his sentence was commuted to one year.

There was a case involving four Black mess hall cooks who were on duty one night. They decided to take a jeep behind the Pusan, Korea perimeter's fighting lines, because they wanted to take a shower. Unfortunately it was too late for them to return until the next day. When they returned to their Unit, their commanding officer decided to send them to the combat front lines, where they would be facing machine guns and mortar fire. Later they were court-martialed for taking a jeep and were sentenced to ten years. Fortunately the Department of the Army Washington, DC disproved the sentence and the four soldiers were returned to their Unit.

When Marshall reviewed some court-martial charges, it was revealed that a Black had received the death sentence, 15 life sentences, 1-50 year sentence, 3-20 year sentences, 1-15 year sentence and 2-5 year sentence. No White soldiers received the death sentence, and no Whites received sentences of 5, 20, 25, 15 or 10 years. One White soldier received a 5 year sentence and one received a three year sentence. The disparities possibly raised some indications of judicial injustices in sentences toward Black military personnel during the Korean War. Thurgood stated that there had been a definite policy of sending Black troops to the front line with great publicity sometimes followed by stories of failure.

Attorney Marshall's visit to Japan and Korea and his definitive report to General Mac Arthur of a thorough investigation did arouse some military authorities to reconsider some of the court-martial cases, charges and sentences of some Black soldiers who requested the NAACP's legal assistance.

There were six Black soldiers that had their life sentences reduced to 20 years. One Black soldier had his life sentence reduced to 15 years and another to 10 years. There were two Black soldiers who had received 25 years and their sentences were reduced to 15 years. One sentence was upheld. The Army Review Board exonerated four men who had received a ten year sentence.

A Black soldier from Detroit, MI was charged under Article 75 for being absent without leave (AWOL) from his Unit. His defense was an Army record to show that he was present in a hospital suffering from frostbite at the time. However, he was still sentenced to five years. The General Legal office, Washington, DC suspended the soldier's sentence and he was returned to duty.

The NAACP's outstanding Assistant Special Legal Counsel, Attorney Jack Greenberg was successful in the defense of some Black soldiers who had been court-martialed. He argued that the court-martial appeal cases of four soldiers of the 24th Infantry Regiment before the Judge Advocate General Board of Review, Pentagon, Washington, DC, 15, December 1950. One of the cases involved a MSgt. Who was convicted and sentenced to 20 years by a military court-martial in Mason, Korea. The charge was the failure to obey an order to the combat area. The MSgt's defense was that he had suffered severe headaches and the drug or medicine that he received for his ailment was capable of causing a hypnotic condition after taking the pills and he was not aware of having been given an order.

Another case involved a PFC who was sentenced to life imprisonment for failure to obey an order given him by a warrant officer. The soldier was a prisoner at the time and would not have been able to obey the order given him by an officer not empowered to release him from his confinement. Attorney Jack Greenberg was successful in having the four 24th Infantry Regiment soldiers' sentences dismissed. The Judge Advocate General Officer rejected the "charge of cowardice" and found the men guilty of being AWOL and reduced their sentences to one year and suspended the execution of the entire sentences in each case.

When Thurgood Marshall returned to the United States, the Executive Secretary of the NAACP, Walter White sent him on a speaking tour to raise money for the NAACP and to discuss with the audiences his investigation and experiences in Japan and Korea concerning the injustice and unfair treatment of some Black soldiers. Marshall spoke to a crowd of one thousand persons at the Union Methodist Church, Boston, MA

In Washington, DC Marshall spoke to an audience of 1500 at the Bibleway Church. He stated that "the Army segregation policy is part of the Black soldiers' problem. He said the Air Force was making some progress in developing an integration policy. He also told the audience that some of the court-martials of the Black soldiers' were decided at the trial in 15-20 minutes and they did not receive a fair hearing. Marshall said the court-martial cases were either in the 24th Infantry Regiment or 503rd Field Artillery Battalion. He also learned that some of the Army's mixed Units had no court-martials. Thurgood told his audience that the blame had been placed on the 25th Infantry Division's officers in the Negro Units and General Mac Arthur was also responsible. Marshall stated that the US Air Force had Black pilots flying airplanes and that there was no excuse for the Army's segregation policy.

Thurgood Marshall had his own views about General Mac Arthur because he had stated that "Mac Arthur had the authority and responsibility for maintaining or ending racial segregation in the Far East Army Command," Marshall had observed while visiting Mac Arthur's Headquarters that there was a Headquarters' football team and not one Black player. Also there were no Blacks in the Headquarters Military Band. Marshall believed that Mac Arthur allowed discrimination in his headquarters where he was Supreme Commander of the United States and United Nations troops. It was quite obvious racism was present in high leadership positions.

The late Supreme Court Justice Thurgood Marshall has received many honors and they still are being conferred. In February 2003, he was honored with an issued postage stamp. It is unfortunate that many of Marshall's biographies do not address in more detail his outstanding career as the NAACP's legal counsel in the investigation of the segregated Black soldier's injustices in Korea. I do believe that Thurgood Marshall's trip to Japan and Korea was one of the most important experiences of his illustrious judicial career.

CHAPTER 12

INTEGRATION of U. S. MILITARY SERVICES in KOREA

The segregated policies of the US Military sometimes were justified by the military officials. On 3 April 1944 while testifying before the Congressional Armed Forces Committee, President Dwight Eisenhower, then a US Army General said,

> "In general the Negro is less well educated than his brother citizen that is White and if you make a unit integrated the Negro is going to be relegated to the minor jobs."

Four years later, a concerned President decided that the US Military services should offer equal opportunities to all personnel regardless of their skin color and ethnicity. President Harry S. Truman signed the Executive Order 9981 in 1948. The Order established the Presidents' Committee on Equality of Treatment and Opportunity in the Armed Forces. Some of the major provisions of the Executive Order were:

1. "It is essential that the (Air Force) Army Forces maintain the highest standards of democracy with equality of treatment and opportunity for those who serve in our country's defense.

2. As President of the United States by the Constitution and status of the United States and as Commander – Chief of the Armed Forces it is here by ordered as follows:

   > Equality of treatment and opportunity for all persons in the Armed Services without regard to race, color, religion or national origin. This policy shall be put in effect as rapidly as possible having due time to effectuate any necessary changes without improving morale and efficiency.

3. Create in the National Military establishment an advisory committee to be known as the Presidents' Committee on Equality of Treatment and Opportunity in the armed force services which shall be composed of members to be designated by the President.

4. The Committee authorized on behalf of the President to examine the rules and procedures and practices of the armed services in order to determine in what respect such rules, procedures and practices may be altered or improved with a view of carrying out the policy of this order. The Committee shall confer and advise the Secretary of Defense, Secretary of the Army, Navy and Air Force and make such recommendations to the President.

5. All Executive departments and government are authorized and directed to cooperate with the Committee.

6. Persons in government agencies and the military can testify before the Committee."

President Truman appointed Charles Fahy chairman of the Committee. The members were Alphonsus J. Donahoe, Lester B. Granger (Black member), Charles Luckman, Dwight Palmer, John H. Sengstacke (Black member), and William H. Stevenson.

I believe that some military leaders and service secretaries did not really support the major intentions of the President's Executive Order. It was not until 1951 that the US Military services initiated efforts to integrate the American Black soldier into units with White, Hispanic, Native Americans and Asian soldiers who were stationed in Korea during the years 1951-1953.

The following discussion will reveal some interesting highlights of the integration processes in Japan and Korea during the War:

The United States Air Force had an early start in integrating some units prior to the other services. As early as 1948, the Secretary of the Air Force, W. Stuart Symington was paving the way for changes in the official racial attitudes in the Air Force. On June 7, 1948 Mr. James C. Evans, civilian assistant to the Secretary of Defense for Manpower and Reserves addressed an official memorandum to Secretary of the Air Force, attention Mr. Eugene Zuckert, Assistant Secretary, the subject was Negro air units. Mr. Evans proposed that "The Negro Units at Lockbourne Air Force Base be decentralized reassignment of Negro airmen be made upon basis of technical speciality without regard to race.

Col. Benjamin O. Davis, Jr., be provided the opportunity to move on to other duties and training.

Commanding officers and staff personnel be carefully selected to handle the proposed transitional operation at Lockbourne and at the air installation to which the transfer of Negro airmen would be made. The reply signed by the Assistant Secretary indicated that the Air Force was not ready to take these steps as was understood. The matter would be studied."

Mr. Evans stated that for six months the Air Force did proceed with an exhaustive staff study. However, Evans' office had only remote knowledge of their actions. The Air Force had convinced itself that it would be in the interest of the military's efficiency not mentioning humane considerations, rights and the like to proceed almost identically as contemplated in the memorandum and moreover to proceed immediately.

During the early years of the Korean War, the US Air Force had Black pilots assigned to integrated units. There were Black air force flight nurses assigned to medical evacuation squadrons that were integrated. They were responsible for giving patients blood transfusions, treating them for shock and performing minor surgical procedures. A Lt. Drisdale from West Point, TX was assigned to the 801st Medical Evacuation Squadron, 374th Troop Carrier Wing (C-54 Sky master Aircraft). The 11th Evacuation hospital in Wonju, Korea had some Black personnel assigned. Many of the air force units in Japan and Korea had Black personnel assigned. The air force probably led the way in integrating their units.

General Mathew Ridgeway and the Integration of 8th US Army, Korea

General Ridgeway as the commanding general in Korea had some personal views about the integration of the armed forces. He had received recommendations from his subordinate commanders on the subject. Major General William Kean, Commanding General, 25th US Infantry Division, Korea stated that he believed that White and Negro troops should be integrated and that from a human and military perspective it was inefficient to segregate soldiers.

General Ridgeway's views were similar to Keans'. He had planned to request authorization from General Mac Arthur and the Pentagon, Washington, DC to begin integration of the military in Korea. Ridgeway realized that integration could help the army whereas each soldier would be given an opportunity to perform their skills on an equal basis. He said it was un-American and un-Christian to teach and downgrade the Black soldiers as if they were unfit to associate with the White soldiers or to accept leadership.

There were some senior officers who were against Ridgeway's recommendations to integrate the military in Korea. The Pentagon officials approved Ridgeway's plan to integrate the troops. The Washington officials believed that it was the right time to integrate and it would have a tremendous effect upon the US Army in future years.

General Ridgeway plans included the immediate deactivation of the 24th Infantry Regiment and the integration of the military personnel of the following units: 3rd Battalion, 9th Infantry Regiment, 3rd Battalion, 15th Infantry Regiment, 64th Tank Battalion, 77th Engineer Combat Battalion and other all Black Units. Ridgeway recommended that the 24th Infantry Regiment be replaced with the 14th Infantry Regiment which was stationed in Japan. He also recommended that there be established a quota of Blacks in the desegregated units and reassign the majority of Black troops to White units. The future replacements to the Far East Command would be a 10 per cent total established. Ridgeway stated in his plans that the National Guard possibly should not be desegregated right away, especially during the War. There were a few National Guard units that did initiate some menial efforts to integrate those units that were called to active duty and sent to Korea in 1952.

General Ridgeway's concerned efforts and actions to integrate the military in Korea started a gradual but determined compliance by all services and commanders to implement the integration order. Some of the positive actions that occurred were:

The Los Angeles Sentinel Newspaper reported that the US 8th Army, Korea had assigned 23 White replacements to fill requirements in the 24th Infantry Regiment I and R platoon. On 13 April 1951, Black soldiers were assigned to the 19th Infantry Regiment, 17 Blacks to the 24th Infantry Division Medial Battalion, one Black to the 24th Infantry Division's Headquarters Company, and 22 Blacks to the 24th Infantry Division's 3rd Engineer Battalion. Ironically four years later in July, 1955, I would be assigned to Company A 3rd Engineer Battalion, Munsan –Ni, Korea as a platoon leader. I was the only Black Commissioned officer assigned to the 3rd Engineer Battalion. There was one Black warrant officer, Chief Wilson.

The 25th US Infantry Division in 1951 and 1952 began to integrate some Black soldiers in various units. There were Black soldiers present in the 35th Infantry Regiment, 2nd Engineer Battalion, Medical Company, Ordnance Battalion, and the division's Military Police Company.

The 936th Field Artillery Battalion and the 7th Infantry Regiment had integrated. On 27 August 1951 the 14th Infantry Regiment officially replaced the 24th Infantry Regiment in the 25th Infantry Division. The predominantly White 89th Tank Battalion began to integrate around November 1952. A Black soldier assigned to the Battalion was PFC Richard Lancaster, Marietta, OH.

I have often stated during my lectures on segregation in the military services that during WW II and the Korean War, the real American minority was the Black American. Because today's designated minorities, Hispanics, Native Americans and Asians (except the famed 442nd Combat Unit) were able to be assigned to White units.

In 1950 there was an artillery unit present in Korea that had a personnel racial composition of 25 per cent White soldiers and 75 per cent representing the following ethnic groups who are considered minorities in 2003. They were Hawaiians, Samoans, Mexican Americans, Portuguese, Indians, Koreans and Japanese.

When General Ridgeway issued the order for integration of military units, the racial diverse battalion of America's so called minorities today responded in an excellent manner. The 555th Field Artillery Battalion had some African American soldiers assigned in the summer, 1951 to Batteries B and C. One Black soldier assigned was Cpl. James Shaw, Ogden, UT to C Battery. Later some Black soldiers were assigned to the Headquarters and Service Battery. A Black soldier, Pvt. Jim Brown was assigned to Battery B as a cook.

The 5th Regimental Combat Team Tank Company had its first Black enlisted soldier assigned in 1951. He was PFC Augustus Campbell who was assigned to a 25 man tank platoon. When Campbell participated in his first battle action with the platoon, he demonstrated outstanding courage in the performance of duty. PFC Campbell, an efficient gunner loaded his gun chamber and tripped the breach block cover into the firing position and opened the breach to remove the shell after the firing of the fun. He accomplished the procedures in a most exemplary manner, and was commended by his platoon leader.

The 5th Regimental Combat Team was assigned its first Black officers in 1951. He was 2nd Lt. Clarence H. Jackson, E Company. In 1949 Jackson was assigned to the US Army Infantry School, Ft. Benning, GA and was the only Black student in his class. He integrated the officers training course at Ft. Benning and was selected to become the first known Black to command White troops in combat. He was assigned to the 5th RCT when the unit was stationed near Chin Dong-Ni and Kusong, Korea. He performed dauntlessly during a combat action and was awarded the Silver Star Medal. The second Black officer assigned to the 5th RCT was Lt. B. T. Morris, of Houston, TX who was a rifle platoon leader. When Jackson returned to civilian life, he became one of the first Black teachers in the Houston, TX school district.

The Marine Corps and Integration

In January 1951 the Marine Corps had on its active roles two Black officers and 1,605 enlisted men. As of January 1953 there were ten Black officers and 14,479 enlisted personnel. The Marine Corps decided to integrate Black Marines in the First Provisional Marine Brigade during the fighting in the Pusan, Korea perimeter in August and September, 1950. Some Black Marines were integrated into the First Marine Division in Korea.

The 7th Marine Regiment an organic element of the 1st Marine Division in Korea. The 7th Regiment received some Black Marines. Col. Oliver Smith was responsible for this action; because when the Korean War commenced there was a 54 man Black service unit that was integrated throughout the command. Later there were 1,000 Black Marines serving in integrated units in the military occupations of cook, truck driver and infantryman Col. Smith stated:

> "The Black personnel did everything well because they were integrated and they were good people who did a good job. Two of the Negro marines received the

Navy Cross. There were also awarded some Silver Star and Bronze Star Medals. There were no complaints about their performance of duty.'

An article in the Washington Post newspaper 27 February 1951 stated that the 7th Infantry Regiment had one Negro soldier in command of a White squad of a Grave Registration Unit. The 7th Marines had a Black platoon leader assigned to Company B and he was Lt. William K. Jenkins.

WOMEN and INTEGRATION

During the Korean War, there were some Air Force African American women assigned to some units. Some served as nurses. There were some Black Army nurses who served in Korea, and there were WACS who served in Japan and Okinawa. They served as clerks, laboratory technicians and signal corps operators. There were no known Black female Marines who served in Korea. The Navy had floating hospital ships, the USS Repose, Consolation and Haven positioned in the Pusan, Korea harbor. I was able to confirm my research notes about the Navy's non-presence of Black women in Korea when I visited the Navy's Historical Research Center, Navy Yard in Washington, DC. The Marine Corps Historical Center could not provide me any information about the Black female marine presence in Korea because there were none.

The Secretary of the Navy on 20 August 1953 directed the complete elimination of all barriers to the free use of previously segregated facilities on government owned shore stations of the Navy

NATIONAL GUARD UNITS and INTEGRATION

In the early 1950's the Department of Defense adopted the policy of subjecting National Guard units and personnel under federal regulations to anti-discrimination and integrating during the period of federalization or call to active status. The individual states would continue to determine the status quo and only a few National Guard Army units integrated. There were some National Guard units present in Korea in 1951 that began to integrate their units. They also experienced some unique problems.

Oklahoma's National Guard

Oklahoma's 45th Thunderbird Division served six months in Korea; but when it arrived in Korea, there were no African Americans assigned to the Division. The Division did not integrate its units when General Ridgeway began to integrate the Far East Commands in 1951. On 31 October 1951 the Division had one Black enlisted soldier assigned, by March 1952 the Division had 10 Black officers, 2 Warrant officer and some enlisted men assigned to the Division.

When the 45th Division deployed from Korea to the United States, there were 30 Black officers, and 2,215 Black enlisted soldiers assigned to the Division. The Division was given personnel fillers from inactive reservists and regular Army troops while the Division was in Korea.

There were two Black National Guard units that served in Korea. They were the 231st Transportation Truck Company, Baltimore, MD, and the 715th Transportation Truck Company, District of Columbia National Guard.

The first National Guard unit to arrive in Korea was the 715th Transportation Truck Company which arrived in Pusan, Korea on January 5; just two days prior to the Alabama National Guard all White 107th Transportation Company. The 715th had a mission to haul ammunition for the 2nd

logistical command and provide support to the 1st Marine Division when requested. The 715th had moved large amounts of tonnage and troops. While supporting the front line troops, the 715th Truck Company's men were exposed to combat conditions and did not execute a withdrawal movement or "Bug Out".

Many of the 715th's vehicles were WW II rebuilt trucks and their maintenance personnel were tasked with keeping their fleet operable at all times. The 715th Truck Company remained in Korea until the end of the War and the armistice was signed. Their performance was exemplary under some adverse conditions. In March 1952, the 715th began to receive replacements other than Black troops or soldiers.

There were some National Guard units in Korea where it members expressed their views on integration. Major Vernon Sikes, Headquarters 227 AAA Group, Florida said,

> "As the coordinating and assignment officer for all units in our Pusan, Korea area and a southerner, I believe integration would work and I approve the overall operation."

1st Lt. Joseph Bracey, Company Commander, 715th Transportation Truck Co. said that when he was in Korea he saw the Army begin to integrate. When it happened Bracey stated he had left another unit and assumed command of the 715th on 1 February 1952. Bracey said,

> "The 715th Transportation Truck Co. went from 100 per cent Black to about 60 per cent White and when I left Korea in May, 1952, I was the only Black Officer in the Company."

1st Lt. Charles Rice, Executive officer, Reconnaissance Company, 45th Infantry Division (Oklahoma) said in March, 1952 that his unit received seven Black soldiers and several were assigned to each platoon and one to Headquarters and was a very smooth transfer.

When qualified replacements arrived in Korea, units would shift from 100 per cent Black to 60 per cent White and 40 per cent Black within a four month period. Many significant historical events occurred in Korea during the period 1950-1953. But there was one historical event that changed an undesirable policy of 'America the Beautiful" and that was a segregated military that discriminated against the minority of that day, Black Americans. It is unfortunate that our democratic nation was practically forced to integrate its military services in a combat environment in Korea but it was a blessing in disguise. President Truman stated the following during a speech at Howard University, Washington, DC in June 1952:

> "General Mathew Ridgeway should be credited for the integration of Blacks and Whites in his Command in the Far East."

APPENDIX

A KOREAN WAR VETERANS' STORY

Approximately forty-five years ago I had the opportunity to meet a very nice family who welcomed me to their home. I will always cherish the kindness of Mrs. Ruth Garnett and her family. As a young lieutenant in the Army, I met her oldest son while visiting their home in Washington, DC. He shared with me some of his experiences during the Korean War and gave me some advice that did help me as a platoon leader. It never occurred to me that one day this same outstanding and brave veteran of the Korean War, Sgt. Norval (Bobby) Lacy, would give me an interview for this book. He was most eager to share with me in more detail his combat experiences in Korea and also some interesting events about his life after the War.

Norval Lacy is a graduate of St. Cyprians and Armstrong High Schools in Washington, DC. After high school, he volunteered for the US Army. Lacy completed his basic training at Fort Jackson, SC and his first assignment was to the 710th Tank Battalion 11th Airborne in Fort Campbell, KY. He attended a leadership school and was selected as the soldier of the month. His Unit also participated in a training exercise at Fort Drum, NY.

Later he was reassigned as an Infantryman to Company B, 1st Battalion 23rd Infantry Regiment, 2nd US Infantry Division. Lacy arrived in Korea in 1951, just after the 2nd Division had suffered a serious loss at Heartbreak Ridge. The Division was in reserve.

Sgt. Lacy informed me that his first combat experience was during a patrol at "Old Baldy Mountain" area. As a squad leader his squad was given a mission to capture a small knoll on the mountain ridge that was occupied by enemy forward observers with machine gun emplacements. Sgt. Lacy and his men moved cautiously to a creek area. Suddenly, they were exposed to intense mortar fire directed along the creek and he was hit by mortar shell fragments which seriously wounded him in the arms and legs. Lacy became unconscious and later in the night he awoke and was hearing some noise and North Korean soldiers talking as they were approaching the direction where he lay. He kept his eyes closed and was still as possible. A North Korean soldier lowered his rifle with fixed bayonet and punctured Lacy in the chest area, a few inches from his heart. It is believed that the North Korean soldier was double checking to be sure that he was dead.

The next morning, Sgt Lacy remembers lying on a stretcher in a jeep until he blacked out again. Later he awoke in a field medical facility and observed some medical personnel wearing a cowboy type hat with a flap. He believes they were from Norway. Lacy was evacuated to a hospital in Japan and stayed there for a considerable time. Then he was flown to Andrews Air Force Base, MD and from there to Valley Forge Military hospital for his final recuperation. When he was released from the hospital, he was assigned to a missile unit stationed at Fort Detrick, MD. While in Maryland he attended a leadership school at Fort Meade, MD.

In 1954, Lacy was transferred to Germany and was assigned to a Post office facility at Rhein Main, Frankfurt. He returned to the United States in 1955 and was honorably discharged from the Army.

Sgt. Norval Lacy's civilian career has been productive and rewarding for him personally. He has been employed with the District of Columbia government, Andrews Air Force Base hospital and the Smithsonian National Zoological Park. He was able to attend job related schools and received an associate degree. Lacy's initiative and excellent job performances contributed to his attainment of a Civil Service position rating of GS-13 as a management officer. He retired from 43 years of government service which include his military service, in 1993.

Since his retirement, Lacy has enjoyed assisting senior citizens and other people who are in need of assistance and moral support. His sincere interest in people and a pleasant personality characterizes this outstanding Black Defender of the Korean War as a concerned civic minded individual.

THINGS THE MAJORITY (NON BLACK) NEWS MEDIA

"DID NOT TELL ME"

An Afro American newspaper reported that a Black segregated US Army Band played the Marine Corps' Hymn as a White combat unit of the First Marine Division landed in Pusan, Korea.

The Pittsburgh Courier newspaper stated that in 1950 a soldier from North Korea was using a Black Face as a way to infiltrate into the United Nations lines. Some troops of the 24th Infantry Regiment thought this individual who appeared to be "colored" was a friendly soldier. An officer of the 24th Infantry Regiment said he saw what appeared to be a Black soldier.

A Black newspaper reported that in March, 1952 Jesse Teverbaugh was denied admission to the Quantico Marine Base theater on a complimentary goodwill pass. After he informed the NAACP of the incident, he was accompanied to the theatre by Clarence Mitchell, NAACP Director of the Washington, DC Bureau for a conference with the manager. An apology was offered by the manager and Teverbaugh was admitted on a non-segregated basis. Ironically, Teverbaugh had earned a Silver Star for his heroic actions in combat during the War.

Corporal Columbus Samuels received the Silver Star Medal for operating the artillery liaison switchboard throughout the attack despite enemy fire directed toward his position.

Captain Harold A. Jenkins was awarded the Silver Star Medal for heroism by James C. Evans, Civilian Aide to the Secretary of Defense at ceremonies held at North Carolina A and T College where Jenkins was a faculty member.

The 45th National Guard Division in Oklahoma was one of the all White Guard Units that integrated during the Korean War. Lieutenant Charles Rice, Executive Officer, 45th Reconnaissance Company stated that the first Black soldier assigned to his Company was Private First Class Ozell Johnson and that he performed heroically during a combat action against the Chinese in 1952.

When the 231st Transportation Truck Company, I Corps landed at Pusan, Korea, the Commander of the Unit was Captain Bedford Bentley, a World War II Veteran.

Daniel Lee, Washington, DC enlisted in the Army at 16 years of age. He was an expert marksman and tanker. He was present in the Korean War and later he attended Tennessee State University.

Wor ku Gurmu a native of Ada Shoa Province, Ethiopia was wounded in his right leg and thigh in a battle during the Korean War. When he returned to Ethiopia, Emperor Haile Selassie decorated him with the Ethiopian Gold Battle Medal.

Robert L. Holeman, Memphis TN was wounded three times in combat actions in Korea. While being held a Prisoner of War, he was rescued by an Australian regiment.

Robert L. Holeman, Memphis TN was wounded three times in combat actions in Korea. While being held a Prisoner of War, he was rescued by an Australian regiment.

Sgt. Harold James, 24th Infantry Regiment, Gary IN was the recipient of the Silver Star medal for heroism in action.

It was reported that Sgt. James E. Johnson was killed in action in September, 1951 and he was from Virginia.

Sgt. John H. Jones, Baltimore, MD received the Silver Star Medal for heroism in the vicinity of Wonchon-Ni, Korea. He was a Tank commander assigned to the 3rd US Infantry Division.

First Lieutenant George Minor, Jr. from Norfolk, VA was a platoon leader assigned to M Company, 9th US Infantry Regiment. He was awarded the Bronze Star Medal for Meritorious service in Korea. His Citation read,

> "At all times Lt. Minor had a successful Unit and was concerned about the welfare of his men far above his own safety and conduct while directing supporting fire for friendly forces, he displayed an extremely aggressive attitude and superior leadership qualities."

Corporal Delus P. Mosley, 24th Infantry Regiment was the recipient of the Distinguished Service Cross for heroism.

Master Sgt. Wayman Ransom, 24th Infantry Regiment was the recipient of the Distinguished Service Cross for heroism.

First Lieutenant Harry E. Sutton, Bronx, NY was a platoon leader assigned to the 3rd US Infantry Division. His platoon was assigned a mission to protect a ridge in defense of the 3rd US Infantry Division on the eastern flank of a beachhead. The Chinese attacked the position and Sutton's men responded to the assault by continuing to defend their position.

Sgt. Ulysses Yarber, of St. Louis, MO was reported as listed as a POW. (Prisoner of War)

Oliver Young, of St. Louis, MO was reported listed also as a POW.

PICTURE CAPTION

Author's 3rd Platoon A Company 3rd Engineer Battalion, 24th Infantry Division, Korea, 1955.

THE BLACK PRESENCE IN THE KOREAN WAR 1950-1953　　　　　　　　119

PICTURE PAGE

BIBLIOGRAPHY

PRIMARY SOURCES

Manuscript Collection

    Manuscript Division, Library of Congress
    NAACP Collection

Moorland Spingarn Research Center, Howard University, Washington, DC

    Colonel Campbell C. Johnson Papers

National Archives, Washington, DC

    Military Pension Files, RG 15, Adjutant General Office
    National Guard Bureau, Record Group 168

Journals

    Alliance Advocate
    American Journal of International Law
    Army and Navy Journal
    Combat Forces Journal
    Commentary
    Congressional Record
    Journal of American History
    Military Review
    National Medical Association
    Naval War College Review
    Negro History Bulletin
    Negro History Journal
    Proceedings of the US Naval Institute of Naval History

Newspapers

    Afro American (Baltimore and Washington)
    Air Force Times
    Arizonal Informant (Phoenix)
    Army Times
    Baltimore Sun
    Black Chronicle (Oklahoma)
    Capital Guardian (District of Columbia National Guard)
    Chicago Defender
    Chicago Tribune

Cleveland Call and Post
Kansas City Call
Los Angeles Sentinel
Louisville Defender
Michigan Chronicle
Navy Times
New York Times
Norfolk Journal and Guide
Pentagram News
Philadelphia Inquirer
Pittsburgh Courier
Prince Georges Journal (Maryland)
Rangers
St. Louis American
St. Louis Argus
St. Louis Post Dispatch
Times Herald
USA Today
Washington Post
Washington Times

Magazines

Airman
Crisis
Disabled Veterans
Ebony
Jet
Life
Negro Digest
Newsweek
Saturday Evening Post
Scholastic
Soldiers
Time
USAA
US News and World Report

Interviews

Lacy, Norval V., Conversation with Norval Lacy, interviewed by Robert E. Greene, February 22, 2003, Severn, Maryland

Lowery, Jr., George, Conversation with George Lowery, Jr. interviewed by Robert E. Greene, July 2002, Severn, Maryland

Personal Notes

Class Lectures, unpublished and published manuscripts and photographs from the library of Robert E. Greene.

SECONDARY SOURCES

Books

Air Force History and Museum Program. *The US Air Force In Korea Steadfast and Courageous. FEAF Bomber Command and The Korean War 1950-1953,* PAMPHLET
Washington, DC: Air Force History and Museum Program, 2000.

Allan, David ed. *Battleground Korea, The Story of the 25th Infantry Division.* Tokyo: Toppan, 1952.

Alexander, Bevin. *Korea The First War We Lost.* New York: Hippocrane Books, 1993.

Alexander, Joseph H. *Battle of the Barricades US Marines in the Recapture of Seoul.* Washington, DC: Marine Corps Historical Center, 2000.

Anderson, Burton F. *We Claim the Title.* California: Tracey Publishing Co., N.D.

Appleman, Roy. *East of Chosin: Entrapment and Breakout In Korea, 1950.* 1987.

Appleman, Roy E. East of Chosin: *Entrapment and Breakout In Korea, 1950* Texas: College Station Texas A & M University Press, 1987

Appleman, Roy E. The US Army in the Korean War: South to the Naktong, North to the Yalu (June –November, 1950) Washington, 1961.

Army Times Editors, *American Heroes of Asian War.* New York: Dodd Mead and Co., 1969.

Berebitsky, William. *A very Long Weekend, The Army National Guard In Korea. 1950-1953.* White Mane Publishing Co., 1996.

Berry, Craig. *The Chosen Few: North Korea, November – December 1950.* Paducah, KY. Turner Publishing Co., 1989.

Bertrand, Lawrence. Dogging Their Steps Some Military Engagements of the 9th Infantry Regiment in Korea. 1950 – 1951, CA.

Blair, Clay. *The Forgotten War..* New York: Time Books, Random House, 1987

Boetcher, Thomas D. *First Call The Making of the Modern US History 1945-*

1953. Boston: Little Brown and Co., 1992.

Bowers, William T., Hammond, William and Mac Garrigle, George L. *Black Soldier, White Army The 24th Infantry Regiment In Korea.* Washington, DC: Center of Military History US Army, 1996.

Browing, John R. *Chosen Sky The Air Battle For Korea.* Virginia: Dulles, Brasseys, 2000.

Bruer, William B., *Shadow Warriors the Great War in Korea.* New York: John Wiley and Sons, 1986

Bussey, Charles M. *Firefight at Yechon: Courage and Racism in the Korean War.* Nebraska, Lincoln: University of Nebraska Press, 2002..

Carroll, Elmo, Dean. *Bayonet a History of the 7th Infantry Division.* 1951.

Catchpole, Brian. *The Korean War 1950-1953.* New York: Carroll and Graf Publishers, 2001

Chapin, John C. Fire Brigade US Marines In the Pusan Perimeter. Washington DC: Marine Corps Historical Center, 2000.

Chinnery, Philip D. Korean Atrocity Forgotten War Crimes 1950 – 1953. Annapolis, MD: Naval Institute Press, 2000.

Clark, Mark W. *From The Danube To the Yalu.* New York: Harper Brothers Publishers, 1954.

Coleman, J. D. Wonju: *The Gettysburg of the Korean War.* Virginia. Dulles, Brassey's Inc. 2000.

Cowdrey, Alfred E. *US Army In Korean War The Medic War.* Washington, DC: The Center for Military History, 1987.

Cowart, Glenn C. *Miracle in Korea: The Evacuation of X Corps From the Hungnam beachhead.* Columbia: University of South Carolina Press, 1992.

Dailey, Edward L. *Mac Arthur's X Corps In Korea: Inchon to the Yalu, 1950.* Paducah, KY: Turner Publishing Co., 1999.

Davies, S. J. *In Spite of Dungeons.* Hodden, Stoughton, 1955.

Davis, Benjamin O. Jr. *An Auto-biography Benjamin O. Davis, Jr., American.* Washington, DC: Smithsonian Institution Press, 1991.

Dolacater, Max. *History of the Third Infantry Division in Korea.* Tokyo: Toppan Printing Co., 1954

Donnelly, William M. *Under Army Orders the National Guard During the Korean War.* Texas: College Station. Texas A & M University Press, 2001.

Donnelly, William. *We Can Do It. The 503ʳᵈ Field Artillery Battalion In the Korean War.*

Dvorchak, David. *Battle For Korea a History of the Korean Conflict.* Pennsylvania: Combined Publishing, 2000.

Evans, James C. *Counsellor to Secretary of Defense.* Washington DC: July, 1970.

Evans, James C. *Integration in the Armed Services a Progress Report.* Washington, DC: Office of the Assistant Secretary of Defense. Manpower and Reserve, 1955.

Fehrenback, T. R. *The Fight for Korea from the War of 1950 to the Pueblo Incident.* New York: Grosset and Dunlap, 1969.

Fehrenback, T. R. *This Kind of War.* Washington, DC: Brasseys, 1998.

Foner, Jack E. *Blacks and the Military In American History.* New York: Praeger Publishers, Inc. 1974.

Francis, Charles E. *The Tuskegee Airmen.* Boston: Bruce Humphries Inc., 1955.

Futrell, Robert R. *The US Air Force in Korea.* Washington, DC. US Air Force, 1983,

Gardner, Lloyd. *Korean War.* New York: Quadrangle Books, 1972.

Gardner, Michael R. *Harry Truman and Civil Rights.* Illinois: Carbon dale, Southern University Press, 2002.

Godson, Susan H. *Serving Proudly a History of Women in the US Navy.* Annapolis, MD Naval Institute Press, 2001.

Goldstein, Donald M. and Maihafer, Harry J. *Korean War.* The Story and Photographs. Washington, DC: Brassey, 2000.

Greene, Robert E. *Black Defenders of America 1775 – 1973.* Chicago: Johnson Publishing Co., 1974.

Greene, Robert E. *Black Defenders of the Persian Gulf War Desert Shield Desert Storm a Reference and Pictorial History.* R. E. Greene Publisher. 1991.

Greene, Robert E. *Physicians and Surgeons of Color Real Image Models for Youth and Adults.* Maryland: Fort Washington. R E. Greene Publisher, 1996.

Greene, Robert E. *Who Were the Real Buffalo Soldiers? Black Defenders of America.* Maryland: Fort Washington. R. E. Greene Publisher, 1994.

Gropman, Alan L. *The Air Force Integration 1945 – 1964*. Washington, DC: 2nd Edition Smithsonian Institution Press, 1998.

Gugeler, Russel A. *Combat Actins In Korea*. Washington, DC: Center of Military History US Army, 1987.

Halliday, Jim and Cummigs, Bruce. *The Unknown War*. Pantheon Books, 1988.

Hammel, Eric M. Chosin: *Heroic Ordeal of the Korean War*. California, Novato, Presidio Press, 1990.

Harris, William Warner. *Puerto Rico's Fighting 65th US Infantry from San Juan to Chorwan*. California: San Rafael, Presidio Press, 1965.

Hastings, Max. *The Korean War*. New York: Simon and Schuster, 1987.

Heller, Francis H. *The Korean War*. Kansar: Lawrence, Regents Press, 1997.

Hermes, Walter G. *US Army In the Korean War Truce Tent and Fighting Front*. Washington, DC: Government Printing Office, 1966.

Hickey, Michael. *The Korean War. The West Confronts Communism*. New York: The Overlook Press, Peter Mayers Publishing, Inc. 1989.

Higgins, Marguerite. *War In Korea: The Report of a Woman Combat Correspondent*. New York: Garden City Doubleday, 1951.

Hill, Jim. *The Minute Man in Peace and War*. Pennsylvania: Harrisburg. The Stackpole Co., 1964

Hine, Darlene Clark, *Black Women in White. Racial Conflict and Cooperation* in *the Nursing Profession, 1870 – 1950*. Indiana, Bloomight: Indiana University Press, 1989.

Hoyt, Edwin Palmer. *Pusan Perimeter: Korea !950*. New York: Stein and Day, 1984.

Hoyt, Edwin Palmer. *Bloody Road to Panmunjom*. New York: Stein and Day, 1984.

Hur, Sonja Vegdahl and Ben Seunghwa Hur. *Culture Shock: Korea*. Oregon: Portland Graphic Arts Center Publishing Co., 2001.

Hurd, Charles. *The Compact History of the American Red Cross*. New York: Hawthorne Books, 1959.

Jacobs, Bruce. *Korea Heroes The Medal of Honor Story*. New York: Berkley Books, 1982.

Johnson, Charles Jr. *African American Soldiers in the National Guard.* Connecticut: West Port, Greenwood Press, 1992.

Johnson, Jesse J. *A Pictorial History of Black Soldiers in the US (1619-1969).* Hampton, VA 1973.

Kaufman, Burton Ira. *Korean Conflict.* Connecticut: Westport, Greenwood Press, 1999.

Kellet, Anthony. *Combat Motivation the Behavior of Soldiers in Battle.* Boston: Kluwen, 1982.

Knox, Donald. *The Korean War an Oral History Uncertain Victory.* New York: A Harvest Book. Harcourt Inc., 1991.

La Bree, Clifton. *The Gentle Warrior, General Oliver Prince Smith, USMC.* Ohio: Kent State University Press, 2001.

Lanning, Michael Lee. *The African American Soldier,* New Jersey: Carol Publishing Group, 1997.

Lech, Raymond B. *Broken Soldiers.* Illinois: Urbana University of Illinois Press, 2000.

Leckie, Robert. *Conflict The History of the Korean War.* New York: DA Capto Press, 1996.

Lee, Irvin H. *Negro Medal of Honor Men.* New York: Dodd Mead & Co., 1967.

Lewis, Vickie. *Side by Side. A Photographic History of American Women In War.* New York: Stewart, Tabori and Chang, 1999.

Lindsey, Cordell. *Step by Step. Across The Pond.* Pennsylvania, Pittsburgh, Dorrance, 1996.

Lowe, Peter. *Korean War.* New York: St. Martins Press, 2000.

Lucas, Ernestine G. *Wider Windows of the Past, African American History From a Family Perceptive.* Iowa: Decorah. The Arandsen Publishing Co., 1996.

Macgregor, Morris J. Jr., *Integration of the Armed Forces 1940-1965.* Washington, DC: Center of Military History, 1981.

MacKasian, Carter. *The Korean War 1950-1953.* Wisconsin: Osceola, Osprey Publishing Co. 2001

MacDonald, Callum A. *Korea The War Before Vietnam.* New York: The Free Press, Mac Millan, Inc. 1986.

Mahon, John K. and D. Romane. *Army Lineage Series Infantry Part I:* Regular Army. Washington, DC: Office of the Chief of Military History, 1972.

Malkasian, Carter. *The Korean War 1950-1953.* Great Britain: Osprey Publishing Limited, 2001.

Marcus, Harold G. *Ethiopia A History of Ethiopia.* California: Berkley: University of California Press, 2002.

Marquis, Publication. *Who's Who In the West 10th Edition.* Chicago, Who's Who Marquis Publications, 1970.

Marshall, S. L. A. *The River and The Guantlet.* Connecticut, West Port: Greenwood Press Publisher 1953 (Reprint 1970)

Martin, Russ. *The Last Parallel a Marine's War Journal.* New York: Fromm International, 1999.

McGee, Charlene E. *Tuskegee Airman. Biography of Charles E. McGee Air Force Fighter Combat Record Holder.* Boston: Branden Publisher, 1999.

Medal of Honor Recipients 1863-1963. 88th Congress 2nd Session Committee Print Washington, DC: US Government Printing Office, 1962

Mesko, Jim. *Armor In Korea A Pictorial History.* Texas: Carrollton Squadron Signal Publication, 1984.

Miller, John Jr. Carroll, Owen J. and Tuckley, Margaret E. *Korea 1951-1953.* Washington, DC: Center of Military History. Department of the Army, 1989.

Mitchell, George C. *Mathew B. Ridgeway, Soldier, Statesman, Scholar, Citizen.* PA, 2002.

Munroe, Clark C. and May, Joseph R. *The Second United States Infantry Division In Korea. 1952.*

Nalty, Bernard C., *Stalemate US Marines From Bunker Hill to the Hook.* Washington, DC: US Marine Corps Historical Center, 2001.

Nalty, Bernard C. *Strength For the Fight, A History of Black Americans In The Miltary.* New York: Mac Millian, Inc. The Free Press, 1986.

Nelson, Harold W. Jacobs Bruce, Bluhin J. and Raymond K. Eds. *The Army.* Virginia: Arlington. The Army Pictorial Foundation, 2001.

Office of the Assistant Secretary of Defense, Manpower, *Integration and the Negro Officer in the Armed Forces of the United States of America.* Washington, DC: US Government Printing Office, 1962.

Omori, Francis. *Quiet Heroes Navy Nurses of the Korean War 1950-1953 Far East Command.* Minnesota: St. Paul, 2000.

Owen, Joseph R. *Colder Than Hell A Marine Company at Chosin Reservoir.* New York: Ivy Books. Ballantine, 1996.

Paige, Glenn D. *The Korean Decision.* Free Press, 1968.

Pasley, Virginia. *21 Stayed, The Story of the American GI's Who Chose Communist China, Who They Were and Why They Stopped.* New York: Farrar, Straus & Cudaky, 1955.

Pettigrew, T. Jr. *The Korean Incident.* New York: Vantage Press, 1963.

Pincher, Chapman. *Traitors: The Anatomy of Treason.* New York: St Martin's Press, 1987.

Powell, Colin. *My American Journey.* New York: Random House, 1995.

Price, Scott T. *The Forgotten Service In the Forgotten War: The US Coast Guard's Role in the Korean Conflict.* Maryland: Annapolis, US Naval Institute Press, 1979.

Rees, David. *Korea The Limited War.* New York: St. Martin's Press, 1964.

Ridgeway, Matthew B. *The Korean War.* New York: Double Day Co. Inc., 1967.

Rishell, Lyle. *With A Black Platoon In Combat A year In Korea.* Texas: College Station: Texas A & M University Press, 1993.

Rogers, John K. ed, *The 8th Bomb Squadron, Korea 1952. January – July.* Japan, Tokyo: Toppan Printing Co., 1952.

Russ, Martin. *Breakout: The Chosin Reservoir Champaign, Korea 1950.* New York: Fromm International, 1999.

Sandler, Stanley. *Segregated Skies All Black Combat Squadron of World War II.* Washington, DC: Smithsonian Institution Press, 1992.

Seventh Infantry Division In Korea. Atlanta, Georgia, Albert Love Enterprises, 1954.

Shaw, Henry I. Jr. and Donnelly, Ralph W. *Blacks In the Marine Corps.* Washington, DC: History and Museum Division, Headquarters, US Marine Corps, 1988.

Sherwood, John Darrell. *Officers In Flight Suits The Story of American Air Force Fighter Pilots In Korean War.* New York: New York University Press, 1996.

Simmons, Edwin H. *Over The Sea Wall, US Marines at Inchon.* Washington, DC: Marine Corps Historical Center, 2000.

Skordiles, Kimon. *Kagnew The Story of the Ethiopian Fighters In Korea.* Japan: Tokyo Radio Press, 1954.

Slater, Michael. *Hills of Sacrifice The 5th Regimental Combat Team (RCT) In Korea.* Kentucky: Paducah: Turner Publishing Co. 2000.

Soderbergh, Peter A. *Women Marines In The Korean War Era.* Connecticut: Wesport Praeger Publishers, 1994.

Stanton, Shelby L. *America's Tenth Legion: X Corps In Korea, 1950.* California: Novato, 1989.

Stapleton, Bell. *Fourth Squad.* New York: Collier Magazine (January 13, 1951)

Sterner, Doris M. *In and Out of Harms Way A History of the Navy Marine Corps.* Washington: Seattle Peanut Butter Publishers, 1997.

Stillwell, Paul ed. *The Golden Thirteen Recollection of the First Black Naval Officers.* New York: Berkely Books, 1973.

Stokesbury, James L. *A Short History of the Korean War.* New York: William Morrow Co., 1988.

Storey, Robert and Eunk Yong Park. *Korea.* California, Oakland: Lonely Planet Publisher, 2001.

Stubbs, Mary Lee and Connor, Stanley R. *Army Lineage Series. Army – Cavalry Part I: Regular Army and Army Reserve.* Washington, DC: Office of the Chief of Military History US Army, 1969.

Sawyer, Robert K. Major. *Military Advisors In Korea: KMAG In Peace and War.* Washington, DC: Center of Military History US Army, 1988

Third Infantry Division, *Third Infantry Division In Korea.* Japan, Tokyo: Toppan Co. Limited, 1953.

Toland, John. *In Mortal Combat Korea 1950-1953.* New York: William Morrow and Co., Inc. 1991.

Tucker, Spencer C. *Encyclopedia of the Korean War, A Political, Social, and Military History*. New York: Check mark Books, 2002.

US Army Center of Military History Brochure. *The Korean War Years of Stalemate. July 1951-July 1, 1953*. Washington, DC: Center of Military History n.d.

US Army Center of Military History Brochure. *The Korean War The Outbreak 27 June – 15 September 1950*. Washington, DC: The Center of Military History, n.d.

US Army Center of Military History Brochure. *The Korean War Restoring The Balance. 25 January - 8 July 1951*. Washington, DC: Center of Military History. n.d.

US Army Center of Military History Brochure. *The Korean War - The UN Offensive, 16 September – 2 November 1950*. Washington, DC: The Center of Military History, n.d.

US Army 1st Cavalry Division. *The First Cavalry Division In Korea*. Georgia: Atlanta, Albert Love Enterprises 1950.

US Army 24th Infantry Division. *24th Infantry Division, A Brief History, The Story of the 24th Division's Actions In the Korean Conflict*. 1953.

US Army 25th Division. *Battleground Korea: The Story of the 25th Infantry Division*. 1951.

US Army 45th Division. *The Thunderbird, A 45th Division History, The Story of the 45th Division's Actions in the Korean Conflict*. Japan: Tokyo Toppan Print Co., 1953.

US Army Service Forces Manual. *Training Leadership and The Negro Soldier*. Headquarters Army Service Forces. Washington, DC: US Government Printing Office, 1944.

US 103rd Congress, Thurgood Marshall Associate Justice of the Supreme Court Memorial Tributes in the Congress of the US House Document 103-244. Washington, DC: US Government Printing Office, 1944.

US 107th Congress. 2001 – 2002 Official Congressional Directory 107th Congress. Washington, DC: US Government Printing Office, 2001.

US Government. *Three Wars of Lt. General George E. Stratemeyer: His Korean War Diary*, 1999.

US Government. *United States Air Force In Korea 1950 – 1953.* 1983

US Marine Corps 1st Division *Chosin Reservoir*. Washington, DC: US Government Printing Office, 1951.

US Martine Corps. Combined Lineal List of Officers on Active Duty in the Marine Corps 1 January 1953.

Utz, Curtis. Assault From The Sea. The Amphibious Landing at Inchon. Washington, DC: Naval Historical Center. Dept. of the Navy, 2001.

Varhola, Michael J. *Fire and Ice The Korean War 1950-1953.* Iowa: Savas Publishing Co. 2000.

Voss, Charles W. "Men and Vehicles in Korea" *Army Information Digest 7,* No. 10 (October 1952): 17 – 22.

Wakin, Edward. *Black Fighting Men In US History.* New York: Lothrop Lee & Shepard Co. 1971.

Warnock, A. Timothy ed. *The USAF In Korea A chronology 1950-1953.* Program and Air University Press.

Westover, John G. Combat Support In Korea. Washington, DC: Combat Forces. Presidio Press, 1955.

White, William. *Captives of Korea.* New York: Charles Scribner Co., 1985.

Wilkerson, Frederick ed. *Directory of Graduates, Howard University, 1870-1963.* Washington, DC: Howard University 1963.

Williams, Juan. *Thurgood Marshall American Revolutionary.* New York: Three River Press 1998.

Wills, Morris R. *Turncoat: An American 12 years in Communist China.* New Jersey: Englewood Cliffs. Prentice Hall 1968.

INDEX

A

Abbott, Jesse F., 50
Aberat, Gulitat, 100
Abitewi, Abitte, 98
Absent Without Leave, 106
Acts of Courage, 102
ADA Shoa Province, Ethiopia, 116
Adams, Clarence, 75, 76
Adams, Edward, 32
Adams, Louis, 32
Adams, Raymond J., 77
Adams, Thessalonia, 79
Adell, Allen, 32
Adkins, Legree, 32
Air Force Flight Nurses, 109
Ainsworth, Jess W., 49, 50
Alabama National Guard, 112
Allen, Aris T., 58
Allen, Clifford, 72
Allen, Charles, 50
Allen, Donald, 32
Allen, Floyd, 50
Allen, Homer, 65
Allen, Russell, 40
Allen, Walter, 38
Allen, Warren, 32
Allen, Warren E., 29
Alexander, James L., 65
Alexander, William H., 65
Alligator Jaws, 101
Allison, Thomas G., 37
Almond, General, 5
Almond, Edward M., 26
Alston, Eugene, 38
Alston, James H., 82
Alston, John, 45
Alston, Leslie, 37
Alston, Marion, 32
Alton, Alexander M., 65
Alton, Ozal, 50
Amaker, William Patrick, 79
American Red Cross, 6
American Transport Ship Blatchford, 100
Amos, Benjamin, 65, 82
Andargue, Asfaw, 98, 102
Anderson, Alvin, 72
Anderson, Eric, 82
Anderson, Frederick, 82
Anderson, Henry, 50
Anderson, Herman, 50
Anderson, James, 82
Anderson, Jessie, 32
Anderson, Lyonel, 50
Anderson, Norman, 50
Anderson, Ralph, 47, 50
Anderson, Theophilius, 38
Andrade, Anthony, 32
Andrews, Air Force Base, 114, 115
Andrews, James, 38
Andrews, Robert, 50
Anelege, Teguegu, 97
Anthony, Joseph, 79
Appendix, 114
Arceneaux, Lucian, 72
Ard, Norman, 38
Arizona: Lodge of Free and Acceptance Masons, 80
Armed Forces Radio Network, 60
Armed Forces Service Mobile Radio Service, 43
Armed Forces Medical Journal, 71
Armstrong, Charles, 50
Armstrong, Morris, 38
Armstead, Wilbert, 40
Army Review Board, 106
Army Segregation Policy, 107
Arnold, Eugene, 32
Arrington, Clark, 50
Arrington, Elbert, 79
Arrington, Robert W., 65
Arrington, Thomas, 65
Asfaw, Zenebe, 101
Ashe, Thomas, 45

Ashlya Airbase, 6
Aspin, Les, 28
Aster, Ayanna, 100
Atkins, George, 71
Atkins, Thomas, 45
Augneten, Admasu, 99
Austin, Charles, 82
Australia, 3
Australian Regiment, 116
Avent, Cleveland, 50
Avery, Jackson, 38, 50
Avery, Joseph P., 79
Ayele, Bezabih, 101
Ayers, Paul, 82

B

Bagey, C., 82
Bailey, Anton, 64
Bailey, Elmer, 50
Bailey, Levi, 50
Bailey, Willie, J., 50
Bakele, Melaku, 99
Baker, Captain, 18, 19
Baker, Clarence, 45
Baker, Isaac, 30, 32
Baker, Newton, 11
Baker, S. E., 82
Baker, Sylvester, 38
Balleg, Emanuel, 82
Baltimore Afro American Newspaper, 38
Bandung, Indonesia, 7
Banks, Earl, 77
Banks, George, 65
Banks, Nathaniel, 45
Banks, Nelson, 32
Banks, R. L., 72
Banks, Travis, 79
Barber, James, 50
Barber, Julius, 72
Barbour, Charles 38
Barge, Wendell, 82
Barnes, Joseph, 72
Barnes, Richard, 72
Barnes, Shelly, 82

Barnwell, Jerome, 82
Barrett, George, 50
Barrow, Robert O., 50
Barton, George E., 49
Barton, Richard, 32
Bass, George T., 50
Bass, Joseph T., 79
Battle of Bloody Ridge, 7
Battle, Edward 50
Battle, George, 40
Battle, James, 38
Battle Mountain, 12, 15
Battle of Mandaeri, 98
Battle of Pork Chop Hill, 7
Baty, Willie J., 82
Baxter, Douglass, 79
Baylor, Page, 72, 77
Baughans, Phillip James, 79
Beamon, Olga, 50
Bean, Edward, 50
Beaver, John, 65
Beck, David, 50
Bedley, Bethel, 32
Belachew, Y., 99
Belcher, Willie J., 50, 82
Belgium, 3
Bell, Colin, 50, 65
Bell, Emma, 55
Bell, John, 32
Bell, Will, 82
Bellman, Arthur, 50
Benefield, William, 23, 82
Benford, Wilbert, 50
Benn, William, 77
Bennett, Fred, 65
Bennett, Joe D., 38
Bennett, Percy, 79
Berthoud, Kenneth H., 50
Berry, Jesse, 50
Berry, William, 50
Best, Chase, 50
Beverly, Phillip, 82
Bell, Lawrence, 79
Bentley, Bedford, 116
Benefield, Chester M. 26
Benefield, William, 19

Berhanu, Tariku, 102
Berkenash, Kehede, 101
Berry, Benny, 77
Berry, George, 65
Beverly, William, 32
Bey, Floyd, 77
Bibbs, Charles, 50
Bibbs, Charles K., 82
Bibbs, James, 38
Bibbs, Sammie, 38
Bibleway Church, 107
Biggs, Bradley, 50, 65
Billingsley, Al, 50
Billingsley, Billy, 50
Billips, Albert, 72
Bivens, George, 32
Bivens, William N., 82
Black Combat Units, In Korean War Action, 25
Black Face, 116
Black, Gordon, 51
Black, Joe, 72
Black National Guard Units, 112
Black Pilots, 109
Black Sheep Fighter Squadron, 60
Blackley, Elvin, 51
Blackman, Laurence, 51
Blackwell, Roy, 51
Blair, Clay, 27
Blair, Russell, 13
Blair, Russell Melvin, 19
Blakley, Willis, 82
Bland, William, 51
Bland, William R., 40
Blizzard, Thornton, 51
Bloody Ridge, 37
Bloody Ridge Mountain, 91
Blount, Howard, 51
Blount, Paul, 44
Blow, Richell, 51
Boatwright, Daniel, 31, 32
Body, Melvin, 82
Bogan, Steven, 65
Bolden, Leroy, 51
Bolling, Jesse B., 79

Bolton, C., 72
Booker, Arthur, 51
Booker, Walter, 79
Bond, Rapier, 65
Boone, Albert, 65
Boone, Gordon, 51
Boone, Webster, 40
Borge, Wendell, 65
Borum, James, 77
Bourne, Earle, 51
Bowen, Samuel, 82
Bowers, J. W., 72
Bowie, Jimmie, 40
Bowser, Corporal, 65
Boyd, Howard A., 59
Boyd, James G., 42, 51
Boyd, Oscar, 51
Boyd, Percy, 51
Boyd, Robert, 72
Boyd, Vernon F., 65
Boykin, Cornelius, 51
Bracy, Joseph, 40, 44, 113
Bradley, Omar N., 27
Branch, James, 51
Brandon, Ewing, 51, 65, 72, 82
Brasfield, PFC., 29
Bratton, Clyde, 51, 65
Brewer, Nicodemus, 79
Brewer, Herbert L., 51
Brickhouse, George H., 51
Brimm, Frank, 51
Brinkly, Charles F., 48
Broadus, Walter, 79
Brocks, Nelson, 51
Brooks, George, 40
Brooks, Horace G., 82
Brooks, John, 51
Brooks, Joseph T., 51
Broom, George, 82
Briscoe, Albert, 82
Briscoe, Herman, 40
Briscoe, Richard, 32
British Battalion, 35
Britt, Henry C., 19
Brock, James, 47
Brooks, Morris H., 65

Brooks, Robert, 72
Brown, Alvin, 5
Brown, Cassell, 83
Brown, Charles, 42
Brown, Daniel, 51
Brown, Earl, 51, 77
Brown, Emerson, 40
Brown, Everett, 51
Brown, Flora, 55
Brown, George, 51
Brown, George Jr., 77
Brown, Harold, 72
Brown, James, 32
Brown, James J. Jr., 51
Brown, Jennings, 51
Brown, Jesse L., 83
Brown, Jim, 111
Brown, Joel, 51, 65
Brown, Joseph, 51
Brown, L. C., 51
Brown, Lee, 65
Brown, Leo B., 65
Brown, Lewis, 38
Brown, Linkin, 51
Brown, Luther, 51, 83
Brown, Mack, 51
Brown, Richard, 51
Brown, Robert, 45, 51
Brown, Robert L., 65
Brown, Tommie L., 46
Brown, William, 77
Brown, William E., 51
Brownsville, Texas, 28
Bryant, Charles, 65
Bruckett, George, 51
Brumfield, Charles, 38
Bryant, William L., 83
Bryant, Willie, 83
Buchanan, Billy J., 72
Buchanan, William, 51
Buckner, Henry, 43, 77
Buckner, Rudy, 42, 77
Buford, David, 32
Briggs, Eugene, 79
Bug Out Boogie, 13
Bugout Unit, 12

Bulbula, Benijam, 99
Bulli, Mulugetta, 96,101
Bullock, Laura A., 51
Bumbray, Edward, 65
Burney, Clifford, 38
Burrough, Roy, V., 40
Burse, Thomas, 32
Bush, Homer, 32
Bussey, Charles M., 26
Bussey, Charles, 15, 17, 18, 20, 21, 23, 24, 42
Butler, James, 40
Butts, William, 79
Burke, Maurice J., 44
Burnette, Elwood, 65
Burton, Edward, 51
Burns, Joseph, 72
Burton, George, 51
Bynum, George, 32
Byrd, Clayton, 79
Byrd, Llewellyn, 32
Byrd, Thomas R., 65

C

Cade, Melvin, 40
Callahan, Leonard, 65
Calvin, Arthur, 38
Camp, Allen, 65
Camp Kokuru, 6
Camp McNealy, 6
Camp Stoneman, 29
Campbell, Augustus, 111
Campbell, Booker T., 72
Campbell, Leroy, 51
Campbell, Mack, 32
Campbell, Veronice, 72
Campbell, Vernon L., 51
Campbell, Vernon Lee, 77
Campos, Victor, 32
Canada, 3
Cannon, Charles, 65
Carberry, Bernard, 51, 65
Carey, Edward, 48
Carey, James, 46
Carey, Jeffries, 40

Carlisle, David, 15, 16, 23, 25, 28, 42
Carman, Archie Jr., 79
Carpenter, Robert C., 83
Carr, Antonio, 47, 51
Carr, Winston, 79
Carrell, James, 32
Carrington, Edward Melvin, 72
Carroll, George, 51
Carroll, Henry, 42
Carter, Charles, 51
Carter, Earl, 51
Carter, Eldridge, 29
Carter, Jed E., 51
Carter, Ninevah, 51, 72
Carter, John H., 83
Carter, Lawrence, 51
Carter, Morgan, 47
Carter, Theodore, 43, 44
Cash, John, 15
Ceasar, Edward, 44
Chambers, Booker T., 65
Chambers, Carl, 46, 51
Chambers, Walter, 72
Chambliss, Johnson, 65
Chambliss, Johnson, 51
Chapel, George, 29
Chapmn, Floyd, 51
Charles, Alvin, 38
Charlton, Charles, 51
Charlton, Cornelius, 26
Charlton, Cornelius H., 83-84
Cheaney, George, 51
Cheatham, Eugene, 51
Cheatman, Willie, 72
Cheeks, Robert H., 79
Cherry, Albert H., 65
Cherry, Carlisle Ferdinand, 65
Cherry, Ferdinand Carlise, 51
Chief Liason Groups, UNC, 101
Chillis, James F., 72
Chipori, Korea, 83
Chappelle, Dewey, 51, 83
Chorwon, Korea, 98, 100
Chosin Reservoir, 13, 62
Christopher, Curtis W., 79

Christian, Howard, 51
Christian, Willie, 38, 39
Clark, Arthur, 51
Clark, Claude, 77
Clarke, David, 32
Clark, James, 65
Clark, John, 83
Clark, Leroy, 83
Clark, Mark, 6, 143
Clark, Mark W., 27, 101, 103
Clark, Verdell, 40
Clark, Walter, 40
Clarke, Bruce C., 103
Clarke, Frederick, 51
Clay, Alex, 79
Clay, Alex C., 65
Clay, Arthur, 51
Clay, Morris, 45
Clearborn, Edward, 84
Clement, Kenneth W., 58
Clemmons, Joseph, 84
Cleveland, Clinton, 32
Cliette, Albert, 32
Coates, Isaac, 52
Cockayne, John, 32
Coffee, Robert J., 72
Cole, George, 52
Cole, Hardy, 39
Cole Joseph, 40
Coleman, Alfred, 52
Coleman, Eugene, 32
Coleman, Everett, 52, 72
Coleman, Samuel, 52
Coleman, Willie, 32
Coles, Charles, 51
Coles, Earl, 51
Coley, Timothy, 39
Collins, Arthur, 84
Collins, Dovie, 55
Collins, John E., 65
Collins, Lawton J., 27
Collins, Norman, 32
Collins, Ralph, 52
Collins, Virl, 32
Collins, William, 79
Columbia, 3

Colvin, Don H., 72, 77
Compt, Richard, 52
Congo, John, 52
Congressional Armed Forces Committee, 108
Congressional Medal of Honor, 18, 23
Conley, Benjamin, 72
Conover, David, 52
Cook, Charles, 72
Cook, Robert L. 84
Cooley, Timothy, 52
Cooper, Charles R., 84
Cooper, Thomas W., 84
Copeland, David, 52
Copeland, Wallace, 72
Coplin, Robert B., 39
Corley, Colonel, 18, 19, 20
Corley, John T., 16, 27
Cornelius, Patrick, 77
Corum, William, 52
Costa, Wongele, 101
Coston, Charles, 72
Cotton, Henry, 52
Cotton, Melvin, 77
Court-martial, 104, 105
Court-martial cases, 106, 107
Court-martial Charges, 106
Courts, Curtis, 32
Covington, Clarence, 52, 72, 77
Covington, Edward, 52, 72
Coward Place, 75
Cox, Embre, 39
Cox, James, 52
Cox, John, 66
Cox, Sherbert, 52
Cox, William, 72
Craigwell, Ernest J., 84
Cramer, Henry G., 84
Cravin, Oliver P., 84
Crawford, Norman, 34
Crawford, Thomas, 72
Crawford, Walter, 29
Credle, Lewis, 84
Crocker, Bernard, 43
Crockett, Woodrow, 52

Cromartie, Julian E., 84
Cromwell, Norman, 52, 65
Culpepper, Geneva, 52
Cunningham, Earl, 45
Curry, Emmanuel, 52, 66
Curry, Maurice, 77
Curry, William, 52
Curtis, Fred D., 66
Curtis, Fred Jr., 66
Curtis, Lawrence, 52

D

Dalits, 14
Daniels, Curtis L., 77
Daniels, Hillard, 52
Daniels, Sherman, 30, 32
Daniels, Tommy, 45
Daniels, William, 66
Davenport, Kathryn, 7
Davidson, Cecil, 52
Davis, Benjamin, Jr., 109
Davis, Carl, 39
Davis, George, 52
Davis, Freeman, 52
Davis, Herbert, 42, 52
Davis, James, 32, 52
Davis, Judd, 52
Davis, Leroy, 77
Davis, Richard, 32, 71
Davis, William H., 84
Dawson, Eugene, 46
Dawson, George, 40
Dawson, Matthew Jr., 52
Dawson, Richard, 40
Dean, Alan P., 52
Dean, Major General, 54
Death Sentences, 106
Deberry James L., 66
Defectors' Profiles, 75
Defraffinreed, Paul, 32
Dejenie, Lt., 98
Denmark, 3, 5
Dennis, Merrill, 39
Denson, E. B., 52
Department of Defense, 112
Derrell, Al, 52

Derrell, Al, 52
Destroyer Mansfield, 65
Deveaux, John H., 52
Dewey, Lee A., 77
Dias, Herculaneo, 32
Diaz, Joseph, 39
Dickerson, Harvey, 66
Diggs, James L., 52
Dill, Earl, 84
Dilver, James A., 79
Dingle, Booker, 52
Dinwiddie, Rudolph, 84
Dishonorable Discharge, 105
Dissie, Kenwood, 52
District of Columbia Gov't, 115
Dixon, David R., 52
Dixon, Edward, 52
Dixon, Harold, 66
Dixon, Howard, 52
Dixon, James W., 34
Dixon, Julian C., 22
Dolphy, Alice H., 52
Dolvin, Welborn, 21
Donahoe, Alphonsus J., 109
Donley, Ray, 84
Dotson, Robert, 72
Dotson, Wylie, 84
Douglass, Edward, 84
Douglas, Harold, 52
Dowdy, Paul R., 66
Downing, Alvin J. 49, 52
Dozier, Johnny, 39
Drennan, Richard, 71
Drisdale, A., 52
Drisdale, Lt., 109
Drummond, Edward, 49, 52
Dryden, Charles, 53
Duckworth, Charles, 52
Duckworth, Overton, 84
Dudley, Arthur C., 84
Dudley, Roscoe, 52
Duggan, H., 84
Duncan, Walter, 84
Dunn, A., 52
Dunn, John, 45

E

Easterling, Jeremiah, 46
Eckles, Clarence, 53
Edmondson, James, 53
Edmondson, James E., 66
Edwards, Alphonso, 84
Edwards, Calvin, 53
Edwards, Carl, 84
Edwards, Fenton, M., 53
Edwards, James A., 66
Edwards, William, 53
Eichelberger, William Y., 66
Eighth Bomber Squadron, 62
Eight Hundred First Medical Evacuation Squadron, 109
Eight Hundred Second Engineers Aviation Bn., 44
Eight Hundred Third Regional Post Engineer Units, 9
Eight Hundred Eleventh Engineer Aviation Bn., 9
Eight Hundred Twenty Second Engineer Aviation Bn., 9, 44, 64
Eight Hundred Forty Ninth Quartermaster Petroleum Supply Co., 9, 44
Eight Hundred Sixty Second Transportation Port Co., 9
Eight Hundred Sixty Six Transportation Port Co., 9, 43
Eighth Station Hospital, 67
Eighth US Army, 4, 36, 44, 101, 103, 105, 108, 109, 110
Eighteenth Bombardment Group, 54
Eighteenth Fighter Bomber Wing, 84
Eighty Second AAA Bn., 35, 36
Eighty Ninth Tank Bn, 21, 110
Eisenhower, Dwight, 108
Elledge, John A., 37
Eleventh Airborne, 114
Eleventh Evacuation Hospital, 109
Eleventh Marines, 4

Ellis, Calvin, 53, 84
Ellis, Norman E., 66
Ellis, Stacey, 39
Elmore, Daniel, 53
Elsberry, Joseph, 84
Elizabeth State College, NC, 55
Emerson, Amos, 85
Enfield, NC, 79
England, 5
Engleman, Harvey, 33
English, Tony, 45
Eritrea, 93
Escarela, Jose, 33
Estell, Lawrence, 33
Ester, Horace, 53
Ethiopia, 3
Ethiopian Awards and Commendations, 102
Ethiopian Battle Honors, 103
Ethiopian Chaplains, 101
Ethiopian Chief UN Liasion Officer, 102
Ethiopian Citations, 103
Ethiopian Expeditionary Force, 96, 107
Ethiopian First Com. 99, 100
Ethiopian Fourth Com., 100, 101
Ethiopian Gold Battle Medal, 116
Ethiopian Heavy Weapons Platoon, 101
Ethiopian Kagnew Bns, 96, 102, 103
Ethiopian Letters of Commendation, 103
Ethiopian Nurses, 101
Ethiopian Profile, 93
Ethiopian Second Com. 99, 100, 102
Ethiopian Third Kagnew Bn, 100
Ethiopian UNC Liaison Group, 101
Evans, Hosea L., 79
Evans, James, 33, 53
Evans, James C., 109, 116
Evans, James D., 85

Evans, James W., 66
Evans, Robert, 39
Evans, Ruppert, 53
Executive Order 9981, 108
Eyob, Lt., 97

F

Fahy, Charles, 109
Fair, Benjamin, 53
Fairfax, John, 46
Faison, Malcolm, 53
Far East Air Force, 4
Far East Air Force Bomber Command, 4
Far East Air Force Combat Cargo Command, 4
Farmers, Baldwin, 39
Farnsworth, E. E., 101
Farrell, Carlton, 45
Farrell, Corporal, 53
Fassett, James E., 53
Feeny, Nick, 53
Felder, Delon, 46
Felder, Donald, 33
Fennell, Bernis, 66
Fereber, Robert, 331
Ferguson, Timothy, 45
Ferenbaugh, Major General, 31
Fesenbaugh, C. B., 97
Fetherson, James, 43
Fields, James, 33
Fields, Lawrence, 85
Fifteenth Field Artillery Bn, 36
Fifteenth Infantry Regiment, 8, 27, 67, 110
Fifteenth US Army Band, 9
Fifth Air Force, 4, 6, 49, 50 84
Fifth Infantry Regiment, 86
Fifth Marine Regiment, 4, 31, 38, 64
Fifth Regimental Combat Team Tank Com., 111
Fifty-first Fighter Interceptor Wing, 57

Fifty First Military Police Criminal Investigation Detachment, 8
Fifty First Signal Bn, 48
Fifty Fourth Transportation Heavy Truck Co., 8
Fifty Fifth Engineer Treadway Bridge Co., 8
Fifty Fifth ETB, 64
Fifty Fifth Ordnance Ammunition Co., 8
Fifty Fifth US Army Band, 9
Fifty Sixth Military Police Co., 88
Fifty Sixth US Army Band, 9
Fifty Seventh Ordnance Recovery Co., 8
Fifty Eighth Armored Field Artillery Bn, 5, 8 26, 40
Fifty Eighth Quartermaster Salvage Co, 8
Fifty Ninth Medical Dispensary Unit, 8
Fighter Squadron, 32, 83
Finch, Lester, 66
First Battle of the Naktong Bridge, 7
First Battalion 24th Infantry Regiment, 11, 14
First Ethiopian Kagnew Bn, 96, 97, 98
First Marine Division, 4, 62, 63, 64, 111, 112, 116
First Provisional Marine Bridge, 111
First US Cavalry Division, 4, 17, 36, 45, 50, 74, 79, 86
First US Infantry Division, 18
Fisher, Clyde, 45
Fisher, Robert L., 53
Fitalla, Gifar, 102
Fitz, Robert, 46
Fitzgerald, Leon C., 53
Five Hundred Third Field Artillery Bn., 8, 35, 35,36, 37, 71, 72, 88, 107
Five Hundred Fifth Quartermaster Reclamation and Maintenance Co., 8
Five Hundred Sixth Quartermaster Petroleum Supply Co., 8
Five Hundred Twelfth Military Police Co., 8
Five Hundred Thirteenth Transportation Truck Co., 8
Five Hundred Fourtheeth Transportation Truck Co., 8
Five Hundred Fifteenth Transportation Truck Co., 8, 43
Five Hundred Nineteenth Veterinary Food Inspection Detachment, 8
Five Hundred Twenty-ninth Quartermaster Petroleum Supply Co., 8
Five Hundred Thirty-ninth Transportation Truck Co., 8
Five Hundred Fortieth Transportation Truck Co., 8, 47
Five Hundred Forty-first Transportation Truck Co., 8
Five Hundred Forty-sixth Engineer Fire Fighting Co., 45, 88
Five Hundred Forty-eighth Engineer Service Bn, 8
Five Hundred Forty-ninth Quartermaster Laundry Co., 8, 45
Five Hundred Forty-ninth Veterinary Food Inspection Service, 8
Five Hundred Fifty-first Transportation Truck Co., 10, 45
Five Hundred Fifty-third Transportation Heavy Truck Co., 8
Five Hundred Fifty-fifth Field Artillery Bn., 111
Five Hundred Fifty-Fifth Parachute Infantry Bn., 27

Five Hundred Fifty-sixth Transportation Co., 8
Five Hundred Fifty-eighth Medical Collecting Separate Co., 8, 45
Five Hundred Sixtieth Medical Ambulance Co., 8
Five Hundred Sixty-third Medical Ambulance Co., 8
Five Hundred Sixty-Fourth Military Police Co., 45
Five Hundred Sixty-fifth Military Police Bn., 67
Five Hundred Sixty-seventh Medical Ambulance Co., 45, 46
Five Hundred Sixty-seventh Military Police Co., 8
Five Hundred Sixty-eighth Medical Ambulance Co., 8, 46
Five Hundred Seventieth Engineer Water Supply Co., 8
Five Hundred Seventy-first Engineer Dump Truck Co., 8
Five Hundred Seventy-third Engineer Platoon Bridge Co., 8
Five Hundred Seventy-sixth Engineer Service Co., 8
Five Hundred Seventy-seventh Ordinance Co., 8
Five Hundred Eightieth Quartermaster Co., 46
Five Hundred Eighty-fourth Transportation Truck Co., 8
Five Hundred Ninety-fifth Engineer Dump Truck Co., 8, 46
Flack, Lawrence, 77
Fleming, Isaac, 53
Flemming, Olander, 52
Fletcher, Henry, 33
Flournoy, Travis, 39
Flowers, Horrie Jr., 85
Floyd, Albert J., 53
Floyd, William, 40
Flying Parsons, 84
Ford, Algin, 53
Ford, Alton C., 53
Ford, John, 33, 53
Ford, John H., 53
Fordham, Herbert, 66
Forside, Spencer, 85
Fort Benning, GA, 29, 39, 41, 111
Fort Campbell, 114
Fort Detrick, 114
Fort Drum, 114
Fort Harrison, 53
Fort Jackson, 114
Fort Knox, KY, 41
Fort Lewis, 34
Forty-first Infantry Regiment, 10
Forty Infantry Division, 4
Forty-second Transportation Truck Co., 8, 68
Forty-fifth Infantry Division, 4
Forty-fifth Military Police Co., 47
Forty-fifth National Guard Division, 116
Forty-fifth Thunderbird Division, 112
Forty-sixth Transportation Truck Co., 8
Forty-eighth Fortress Bomber Wing, 59
Forty-eighth Transportation Truck Co., 8
Forty-ninth Bomber Wing, 55, 61, 62
Forty-ninth Fighter Bomber Wing, 59, 61
Forty-ninth Transportation Truck Co., 8, 48
Foster, Albert, 33
Foster, Clyde, 79
Foster, Henry, 85
Foster, James, 53
Foster, Milton, 79
Foster, William, 85
Foster, Willis, 42
Four Hundred Second Transportation Truck Co., 8

Four Hundred Third
Construction Co., 8
Four Hundred Seventeenth
Engineer Aviation Brigade, 64
Four Hundred Forty-second
Combat Unit, 110
Fourth Battalion, Thirty-second
Regiment, 96
Fourth Fighter Interceptor Wing
F 86 Jet Base, 60
Fourth Kagnew Co., 99
Fourth Ranger Co., 29, 30
Fourteenth Infantry Regiment,
51, 110
Fox, Corporal, 77
Fox, Frank, 72
Fox, Gerald, 45
Fralish, Major, 35, 36
France, 3, 5
Frank, Earl, 53
Frankfurt, 114
Frazier, Daniel, 45
Frazier, William, 50, 66
Freeland, Walter, 53
Freeman, Bernard, 53
Freeman, Frank, 85
Freeman, Frank P. 66
Freeman, James, 33
Freeman, Oswald, 77
Frost Bites, 14, 66, 71, 72, 106
Frost, Paul, 29
Fulcher, Malcolm, 85
Fuller, Henry, 45
Fulton, Jesse L., 66
Fulton, Robert, 33
Fulton, Wesley, 53
Furnace, Oliphant, 39
Furnish, Stanley, 71

G

Gabriel, Hosea, 53
Gainer, Leon S. Jr., 85
Gaiten, Leon, 53
Galington, Oliver, 33
Gardner, Tinnie, 85

Garland, Lester, 33
Garnett, Ruth, 114
Garrett, Moses, 53
Garrett, Percy, 53, 66
Gebeyiou, Workneh, 99
Gebressadick, Lemma, 101
Geddes, Leander, 85
Gelatta, Fekensa, 100
General Legal Office, 106
General Macrea, 96
Germun, Gerard, 33
Getahan, Assefa, 99, 101, 102
Gethers, Charles, 38
Gibbs, Ozie, 53
Gibson, Albert, 39
Gibson, Clarence, 53
Gibson, Culver, 33
Gibson, James, 45
Gibson, Lewis C., 85
Gibson, Robert, 53
Gifar, Pvt., 97
Gifu, 15
Gilbert, Donald, 53, 72
Gilbert, Leon, 105
Gilbert, Lt., 104, 105
Gilbert, Nathaniel, 66
Gilbert, Raymond, 34
Giles, Pressley, 85
Gilipse, Vonica, 72
Gill, Columbus, 53
Gillespie, Bailey, 53
Gillis, Edward, 39
Ginn, Harvey, 39
Girifin, Claude, 39
Gist, Harry, 53
Givens, Kenneth Marcell, 66
Gizan, Merid, 97, 102
Glisple, Vunice Lee, 77
Gloryland Gospel Singers, 43
Glover, Lawrence, 85
Glover, Richard, 31, 33
Goff, Willie, 85
Goins, Joe Jr., 53
Golden, Arthur, 40
Golston, Obie, 45
Gomes, Dannie, 43

Goode, John, 85
Gooding, Zacharis, 85
Goodman, John F., 72
Goodman, William B., 85
Goodwin, Elmore, 77
Gorden, Harvey, 53
Gordon, Frances A., 66
Gordon, Andrew, 33
Gordon, Clarence, 39
Gorham, Willie V., 47
Gorman, Mattie Lee, 76
Gorman, Walter, 76
Gott, William, 45
Gould, John, 33
Gourdine, Jack, 85
Gourdine, Jack M., 53
Grady, Elmer J., 72
Graham, Annie E., 53
Graham, Charles, 53
Graham, Earl, 33
Graham, John J., 53
Graham, Walter, 85
Granger, Lester B., 109
Gransberry, Freddie, 85
Grant, Earl, 85
Grant, Bellie Sgt., 48
Grant, Hiram C. Jr., 85
Grant, Hiram C. Sr., 85
Grant, Joseph C., 85
Grant, Lawrence, 53
Grant, Thomas, 72
Grasty, Isaac, 33
Grave Registration Unit, 111
Gravely, Sam Jr., 53
Graves, Morris, 45
Graves, Robert E., 85
Graves, William, 40
Gray, George, 85
Gray, James, 85
Gray, Mildred, 55
Gray, Walter, 33
Grayson, Oliver, 53
Green, Bob, 20
Green, Curtis, 53
Green, Doxie, 53
Green, Herman, 33

Green, John, 71
Green, Leon A., 86
Green, James W., 72
Green, Louis, 66
Green, Raubie, 54
Green, William, 40, 49
Greenberg, Jack, 106
Greene, James, 85
Greene, Lawrence, 58
Greene, Milton, 54
Greene, Robert, 16
Greene, Theodore, 39
Greene, Vernon, 40
Greene, William, 54
Gregg, John, 52
Greer, Edward, 38, 86
Greenwood Memorial Park Cemetery, 80
Gregory, Alfred, 79
Griffin, Arthur, 40
Griffin, George, 66
Griffin, James, 54
Grier, Alonzo, 77
Gross, Abraham, 54
Gross, Gary, 40
Gude, James, 33
Guebre, Heffede, 102
Guinyard, Warwick, 45
Guria, John, 33
Gurmu, Worku, 116
Gussie, Charley, 86

H

Hadley, Joseph L., 54, 86
Hague, Owen E., 54
Haile, Ballette, 99
Haile, Bellete, 100
Haile, Meshesha
Haile, Mesheta, 98
Haile Selassie Military Academy, 98
Haile, Sgt., 101
Hailemariam, Fasika, 100
Hairston, James C., 86
Haith, Edward, 45

Hale, Ernest, 79
Hale, Randolph, 79
Hall, Carl, 33
Hall, Edgbert W., 72
Hall, Elanton, 54
Hall, Herbert, 54
Hall, James, 54
Hall, James L. 54
Hall, William, 66, 72
Hamilton, Charles, 54
Hamilton, Joseph, 54
Haman, Korea, 91, 92
Hamhung-Hungnam Perimeter, 7
Hampton, Thomas, 72
Hampton University, 42, 68
Handy, John W., 54
Handy, Raymond, 77
Handley, Danny, 77
Haneda Air Base, 6
Haptemikael, Teklu, 100
Hardin, Harold, 66
Hardy, Clifton, 54
Hardy, Jim, 33
Hargrove, Jessie, 54
Hargrove, William, 33
Haridong, Korea, 102
Harlan, John C., 72
Harper, Everett, 54
Harper, James, 66
Harrell, Julius P., 54
Harris, Artheris M., 77
Harris, Ellsworth, 33
Harris, George, 66
Harris, Herbert W., 72
Harris, James B., 86
Harris, James R., 54
Harris, John, 54, 58
Harris, Ltc., 5
Harris, O'Neil, 39
Harris, Rachell, 54, 86
Harris, Smith, 72
Harris, William, 33
Harris, William, J. 54
Harrison, Arthur, 54
Harrison, Herman, 33
Hart, Curtis, 54

Hart, H., 54
Harvey, James, 33, 86
Harvey, Oscar S., 40
Hastic, William, 5
Hawaiians, 111
Hawkins, Gus, 28
Hawkins, Frances, 66
Hawkins, Willie, 33
Hayes, Arthur, 54
Hayes, George, 86
Hayes, Payton, W., 60
Headen, Emanuel, 54
Hearn, Charles F., 54, 72
Heartbridge Ridge, 37, 98, 114
Henderson, Archie, 40
Henderson, Edward, 66
Henderson, James, 23
Henderson, James W., 86
Henry, John, 40
Henry, Joe, 47
Henry, Luther, 54
Herdon, William J., 86
Herman, Edgar J., 54
Herring, John O., 86
Hickman, Allen R., 66
Hickman, Pfc., 86
Hicks, Carl, 40
Hicks, David, 54
Hicks, Harry, 54
Hicks, James, 54, 86
Hicks, James B., 22
Hicks, James L., 42
Hicks, John L., 86
Hicks, Wesley, 54
Hicks, William, 54
Higgenbotham, McBert, 33,86
Higgins, Marquerite, 18
Highsmith, Rudolph, 66
Hill, Oscar, 86
Hill, Roland, 33
Hill, James, 40
Hill, Jesse, 54
Hill 151, 30
Hill 160, 66
Hill 358, 99
Hill 400, 100

Hill 605, 98
Hill 612, 98
Hill 1073, 97
Hillery, Harold, 49, 54
Hinnant, Ned, 80
Hinson, David, 54
Hinton, Albert Jr., 55
Hinton, Albert S., 55
Hinton, Carl, 55
Hinton, Charles, 45
Hinton, Dorothy, 55
Hinton, Edgar, 54
Hinton, Edgar J., 73
Hinton, Gale, 55
Hinton, Lelia, 55
Hinton, Leonard, 55
Hogan, James, 55
Hodge, Herbert, 73
Hodge, Roland, 33
Hodges, Edward Norman, 55
Hodges, Samuel, 66
Hodson, Milburn, 55
Hogan, Melvin, 66
Hoggalt, Henry, 40
Holden, Joseph, 41
Holder, James, 73
Holeman, Robert L., 86, 116
Holinger, William, 33
Holland, Floyd, 33
Hollard, Horace, 55
Holley, Eldern, 86
Holley, J., 31, 33
Hollis, Levy V., 86
Holloway, Jesse J., 66
Holmes, Fred, 44
Holmes, Oliver W., 86
Honore, Arthur J., 55
Hoover, Herbert, 104
Hopkins, James, 40
Hosey, Lee, 33
House Committee on Un-American Activities, 76
Houston Texas Riot, 11
Howard, Bennie, 33
Howard, David, 55
Howard, Joe W., 77

Howard, John, 29
Howard, Mayo, 86
Howard University, 113, 79
Howard, William, 55
Howe, John P., 55
Howell, Clifton, 80
Hudgin, Lester, 40
Hudner, Thomas, 83
Hudson, George, 55
Hudson, Theodore B., 66
Huff, Edgar, 55
Hughes, Herbert, 66
Hughes, Roosevelt, 86
Huhanggol, Korea, 98, 102
Hull, John, 86
Humbord, Robert D., 66, 86
Humphrey, John, 55
Hunter, Chester W., 66
Hurley, Marshall, 38, 86
Hungnam Perimeter, 39
Hurd, Charles, 40
Hurd, James, 49
Hursey, Elijah, 77
Hutton, Preston Lee, 66
Hyman, Walter, 55

I

Imperial Bodyguard, 99
India, 3
Indians, 111
Indian Field Ambulance Unit, 30
Ingram, Kenneth, 87
Ingram, Robert, 40
Inspector General, 104, 105
Integration of US Military Services In Korea, 108
International Red Cross, 6
Irgetu, Teshome, 96, 102
Iron Triangle, 7, 100
Irving, Dennie, 80
Irving, James, 66
Irving, James E., 55
Isaac, Dennis, 56
Isaac, Willie, 55
Isheta, Hallemarial, 102

Italy, 3
Itami Air Base, 6
Ivey, John, 45
Ivy, Woodson, 80
Ix Corps, 96

J
Jackson, Andrew, 55
Jackson, Bernard J., 77
Jackson, Carol J., 55
Jackson, Charles, 55
Jackson, Clarence, 86
Jackson, Clarence H., 111
Jackson, Donald, 55
Jackson, Earl, 33
Jackson, Ellis, 73
Jackson, Emery L., 86
Jackson, Herbert 86
Jackson, Herman, 31, 33
Jackson, Howard, 38
Jackson, Jasper, 55
Jackson, Johnny, 66
Jackson, Levi, 55, 66
Jackson, Levi A., 26
Jackson, Levi Jr., 86
Jackson, Lonnie, 86
Jackson, Robert, 39
Jackson, Timothy, 55
Jackson, William, 73
Jackson, William Jr., 55
Jackson, Winston, 33
James, Daniel Chappie General Jr., 55
James, Frank, 73
James, Harold, 116
James, Harvey, 49
James John 67, 86
James Joseph, 41
James, Lt., 11
James, Robert, 50
Jamison, Charles, 86
Janifer, Robert, 55, 86
Japanese, 111
Jasper, William, 39
Jeffrey, Clarence, 55

Jeffries, James Earl, 67
Jenkins, Constance, 55
Jenkins, Elmer, 77
Jenkins, Glenn, 33
Jenkins, Harold, 67
Jenkins, Harold A., 116

Jenkins, Louise, 55
Jenkins, Monroe, 86
Jenkins, William K., 55, 112
Jennings, Thomas, 67
Jett, Richard, 73
Jeter, Frank, 73
Jiggetts, Julius, 55
Johns, Louis D., 55
Johnson, Albert E., 67
Johnson, Alfred, 56, 67
Johnson, Alphonso, 71, 73
Johnson, Andrew, 49, 67
Johnson, Arthur L. Jr., 54
Johnson, Bernard H., 56
Johnson, Bruce, 33
Johnson, Calvin W., 55
Johnson, Campbell C., 24
Johnson, Charles A., 86
Johnson, Clarence, 77
Johnson, Cornelius, 87
Johnson, Edgar, 87
Johnson, Emmet, 33
Johnson, Harold, 32
Johnson, Henry, 56
Johnson, James 80
Johnson, James E. 117
Johnson, John, 80
Johnson, Junior, 56
Johnson, L. E., 34
Johnson, Leonard, 67
Johnson, Leroy, 56
Johnson, Leroy Jr., 87
Johnson, M., 56
Johnson, Marvin, 56
Johnson, Milton, 31, 32
Johnson, Norman R., 77
Johnson, Ozell, 116
Johnson, Prince, 87
Johnson, Ostell, 45

Johnson, Ray, 67
Johnson, Robert E., 87
Johonson, Robert Jr., 56, 73
Johnson, Roy, 67
Johnson Faulkner, Ruth, 56
Johnson, Sidney, 49, 56
Johnson, Thomas, 39
Johnson, William, 40
Jones, Aaron, 87
Jones, Albert, 87
Jones, Arthur, 87
Jones, Calvin, 77
Jones, Charles, 80
Jones, David, 80
Jones, Davis, 56
Jones, Eddie, 87
Jones, Edward, 45
Jones, Edward L., 56, 87
Jones, Frank, 73
Jones, Harry, 39, 56
Jones, Henry, 87
Jones James, 45
Jones, James C., 56
Jones, John, 32
Jones, John H., 87, 117
Jones, John L., 56
Jones, Leroy, 67
Jones, Louis, 56
Jones, Robert, 56, 87
Jones, Robert E., 87
Jones, Sidney, 40
Jones, Sam, 87
Jones, Victor, 40
Jones, William, 39. 45
Jordan, Lloyd B., 67
Jordan, Clyde B, 87
Jordan, George W., 56
Joseph, Walter, 67
Judd, Denner, 56
Judge Advocate Board of Review, 106
Julius, Victor, 32

K

Kagnew, 96

Kagnew Patrol, 99
Kassahun, Abele, 97, 102
Kay, James Howard, 16
Kay, John Robert, 16
Kean, General, 110
Kean, William, 109
Kean, William, B., 27
Kearney, Clarence, 56, 80
Kearns, Abraham, 73
Kebbede, Major, 98
Kebbede, Colonel, 103
Keeton, James, 56
Keiler, Mike, 18, 21
Keiser, General, 35
Keiser, Lawrence B., 34
Kelker, Samuel, 77
Kelly, Arthur, 67
Kelly, Dupree, 67
Kelly, Joseph, 32
Kenate, Bayesa, 102
Kendrix, Elijah, 39
Kennerly, Johnnie, 56
Kenny, Howard, 58
Kenny, Norman, 39
Killed In Action, 79
Kimble, Nealy, 43
Kimbrough, David, 73
Kimpo Air Force Base, 6, 61, 84, 88
King, Charles, 40
King, Ernest, 39
King, Frank, 31, 32
King, Irving, 56
King, James, 87
King, James C., 56
King, Richard, 87
King, Robert, 56
King, Ross, 56, 67
Kirkland, George W., 56
Kmag, 3
Knight, John W., 56
Knowlton, William A., 24
Knox Class Destroyer, 83
Knox, William, 8y
Korean History, 1
Korean War Veterans' Story, 114

Koreans, 111
Kum River, 86
Kumhwa, 98
Kumhwa, 100
Kunuri, Korea, 85
Kusong, Korea, 111
Kyer, Myer B., 87

L

Lacy, Norval, 67, 114, 115
Lamar, Wilfred, 87
Lancaster, Richard, 110
Land, Elmore, 32
Lane, Jesse, 87
Lane, Sam, 39
Langston University, 68
Lanier, William, 32
La Prince, Joseph, 87
Larkins, Walter, 87
Lavell, Geoffrey, 35
Lavor, Frank, 56
Lawes, William, 56
Lawrence, William, 56, 87
Lay, L. B., 56
Leary, Fred, 32
Lee, Daniel, 116
Lee, David, 56
Lee, Ellison, 67
Lee, Frank, 49, 56
Lee, Nosey, 32
Lee, John, 56
Leggs, Ralph, 32
Lehman, Paul D., 56
Lenon, Charles, 56
Lenon, Chester, 19, 42, 87
Lenon, Chester J., 26
Leonard, Francis, 67
Lesser, Leo, 56
Lester, David C., 56
Lesure, David, 32
Le Tellier, Carroll N., 20, 21
Lett, Philip, 56
Lewis, A., 56
Lewis, Charles, 32
Lewis, Clinton, 56

Lewis, Gordon, 32
Lewis, Harold, 23, 24
Lewis, Harold O., 16
Lewis, P. E., 88
Lewis, William, 49
Lewis, William, H., 56
Lewis, William Jr., 73
Lee, Wyman J., 87
Lida, Charles, 72
Life, Moses, 40
Life Sentences, 106
Lightfoot, Willie, 56
Lilley, J., 56
Lincoln University of PA, 104
Lindberry, Wendell, 56
Lind, James F., 105
Line Kansas, 7
Linson, William, 56
Little, Herman H., 80
Little, James H., 56
Little, Oscar, 56
Lloyd, Reginald, 40
Lockbourne Air Force Base, 109
Lockett, Lindsey, 77
Lockinour, James Albert, 67, 77
Locklear, Joseph, 40
Lofton, Harry F., 56
Lofton, Matthew, 32
Logan, Herman, 80
Long, George, 88
Long, James, 56
Long, Juanita, 56
Long, Nathaniel, 56
Lonon, James, 88
Lopes, John, 40
Los Angeles Sentinel, 110
Louis, Joe, 50
Loundes, John, 32
Love, George, 88
Love, Jack, 56
Lowery, Eddie C., 88
Lowery, George Jr., 88
Lowery, Lewis, 40
Lowery, Robert Lee, 56
Lowery, Shirley, 88
Lucus, Ernest, 32

THE BLACK PRESENCE IN THE KOREAN WAR 1950-1953

Lucas, James, 88
Lucas, Levin, 56
Lucas, Levin J., 67
Luckman, Charles, 109
Lundy, Richard E., 67
Luxembourg, 3
Lyle, John, 56
Lyles, Edward H., 73
Lyles, Paul, 32
Lynn, Archie, 57
Lyons, L. J., 47
Lyon, Lt., 11
Lyons, Louis, 88

M

Mac Arthur, Douglas, 5, 20, 27, 67, 88, 104, 106, 107
Mac Calla, Thomas, 57
Mac Grow, John, 57
Mack, Herbert Ulysses, 80 88
Mack, William, 88
Mackall, Gabriel, 34
Mac Kenzie, Colonel, 16
Mackey, Carlos, 57
Mackey, Walter, 67
Macklin, Harold F., 57
Macklin, Leonard, 67
Macklin, Leonard W., 57
Maddox, Horace, 73
Maddox, William, 80
Makkois, Workinew, 101
Makonnen Teferi School, 96
Mamo, Lt., 100
Mamo, Wolde, 102
Mandaeri, Korea, 102
Mango, Thad, 45
Marine Corps, 4
Marine Corps Historical Center, 112
Marine Corps and Integration, 111
Marine Corps Hymn, 116
Marrow, Henry, 88
Marsh, John Jr., 15
Marsh, John O. Jr., 28

Marshall, Joseph, 39
Marshall, Norma, 104
Marshall, Silia, 17
Marshall, Thurgood, 106, 107
Marshall, Thurgood and Military Justice, 104
Marshall, William, 104
Martin, Albert J., 80
Martin, Darwin, 105
Martin, James, 73
Martin, James E., 67
Martin, Joe H., 57
Martin, John, 57
Martin, Joseph J., 57
Martin, Laurence, 57
Martin, Paul G., 77
Mason, Jacob, 32
Mason, James, 39
Mason, Howard, 57
Martin, Lloyd J., 67
Mason, Walter H., 57
Massie, Charles E., 88
Mathena, Erin B., 88
Mathis, William, 32
Matthew, Walter, 88
Matthews, Ralph, 57
Matthews, Raymond, 67
Maxwell, Hurdle, 57
McBride, Cleaven, 32
McCain, Robert, 77
McCaine, Douglas, 80
McCall, Nathaniel, 67
McClain, Theodore, 88
McClary, Jake, 39
McClean, Leslie, 32
McClease, George W., 67
McClendon, Herbert, 80
McClure, Amos, 73
McCormick, Robert L., 80
McCray, Robert, 88
McCullough, Edmond, 77
McCullough, Thomas, 57
McDaniel, Armour, 57
McDaniel, Delmar Theodore, 80
McDavid, Edward D., 88
McDavid, Emmett, 73

McEachin, Archie, 39
McGarrity, Claude, 88
McGee, Charles E., 57
McGee, Charles F., 88
McGhee, Monroe, 57, 67
McGowan, George, 71
MacGrow, John C., 57
McGruder, Henry, 67, 88
McIntosh, Charles, 48
McKindra, Wilson, 67
McLaurin, Henry E., 67
McLeod, Harold, 57
McLure, Amos, 77
McManus, Luther, 88
McMullen, David, 47, 57
McMurren, Howard, 58
McPheeters, William, 88
McPherson, William, 32
McShan, Laurence, 71
McWee, Nathaniel, 58
McVey, Clifton, 58
Medal of Honor Recipients, 83, 91
Medical Doctors, 58
Medical Reports Category, 102
Meekins, Walter R., 67
Mellon, James, 88
Merrills, Marauders, 19
Metropolitan Baptist Church, 75, 84
Mexican Americans, 111
Meyers, Alexander, Jr., 60
Meyers, Johnnie, 88
Meyers, Lionel, 73
Miatt, Philip A., 59
Micael, Feshima Gebre, 100
Michaelis, John, 18
Mickael, Gebresus, 102
Midgett, Alexander, 77
Military Academy of Haile Salassie, 96
Military Court of Appeals, 105
Milton, James A., 80
Miller, Clarence A., 67
Miller, Donald, 59
Miller, Horace, 59
Miller, James A., 58
Miller, John D., 59
Miller, Ned, 32
Miller, Richard, 59
Miller, Richard K., 73
Miller, Robert, 88
Miller, Rudolph, 59
Miller, Russell, 59
Mills, Wilbert, 68
Minn, Earl Jr., 59
Minor, George, 117
Minter, Donald L., 73, 77
Missing In Action, 77
Mitchell, Clarence, 116
Mitchell, Dorothy, 7
Mitchell, George, 32
Mitchell, James, 88
Mitchell, Johnnie, 88
Mitchell, Robert, 59
Mobley, Belton, 59
Mobley, Thomas, 68
Moffett, William, 59
Molson, George, 32
Monte, James, 32
Moore, Arthur, 68
Moore, Charles, B., 59
Moore, Edward, 59, 88
Moore, Fred, 39
Moore, Hercules, 77
Moore, James, 78, 88
Moore, John O., 59, 78
Moore, Marcus, 59
Moore, Robert, 60
Moore, Stanley, 60
Moore, Thomas, 88
Moore, William, 68
Moorman, Clinton, 88
Montgomery, Herbert, 59
Montgomery, Hubert, 88
Morgan, Albert, 78
Morgan, Early G., 89
Morgan, John, 45
Morgan State University, 72, 78
Morris, B. T., 111
Morris, George, 89
Morris, John C., 89

Morro, Lema, 97
Morrow, James, 68
Mosely, James, 60
Mosely, Clarence, 60
Morgan, Thomas, 60
Motley, Thomas, 60
Morton, Benjamin, 47
Mosley, Delus, 117
Mosley, Samuel W., 89
Moss, Dennis, 46
Mountain, Robert, 59
Mullin, Walter, 89
Mundang-Ni, 98
Murdock, Ralph, 40
Murphy, Audie, 18
Murphy, John D., 80
Murray, Charles, 29
Myers, Alexander, 45

N

NAACP, 104, 106, 116
NAACP's Legal Counsel, 107
National Guard, 110, 113
National Guard Units and Integration, 112
Nann, William, 89
Naval Historical Research Center, 112
Neal, Harold, 73
Negatou, Belayneh, 101
Neel, Gordon, 32
Nelson, H., 60
Nelson, John H., 73
Nelson, Robert R., 60, 73
Newsome, Wilbert J., 60
Netherlands, 3
Newman, Richard, 32
New York, Herald Tribune, 18
New Zealand, 3
Nickens, John Jr., 68
Nickens, Royal, 45, 60
Nicholson, Thomas, 73
Ninth US Infantry Regiment, 14, 17, 25, 26, 34, 35, 52, 63, 66, 83, 84, 85, 91, 92, 110, 117

Nineteenth Bombardment Group, 56
Nineteenth Bomber Wing Far East Air Force, 49, 54
Nineteenth Combat Engineers, 63
Nineteenth US Army Band, 9
Ninety First Ordnance Medium Automotive Maintenance Co., 9
Ninety First Strategic Reconnaissance Squadron, 64
Ninety Second Infantry Division, 5, 26
Ninety Third Engineer Construction Bn., 9, 46
Ninety Fifth Transportation Car Co., 9
Ninety Sixth Field Artillery Bn., 8, 43
Ninety Ninth Pursuit Squadron, 53
Nine Hundred Thirtieth Engineering Aviation Unit, 43, 64
Nine Hundred Thirty Third Aircraft Artillery Automatic Weapons, Bn., 8
Nine Hundred Thirty Third Anti Aircraft Artillery (AAW), 8, 43, 44
Nine Hundred Thirty Sixth Field Artillery Bn., 110
Nine Hundred Thirty Ninth Aviation Group, 64
Nine Hundred Thirty Ninth Engineer Aviation Group, 43
Nine Hundred Forty Fifth Quartermaster Service Co., 9
Nine Hundred Ninety Ninth Field Artillery Bn., 5, 26, 45
Nixon, John, 46
Nixon, Oscar, 60
Nixon, President, 28
Nixon, Samuel, 32
Noel, Robert, 29
Norcom, Henry, C., 68

Norfolk Journal and Guide, 55
North Carolina A & T College, 116
Norway, 3, 114
Nunley, John, 32
Oakley, James 30, 32
O'Bannon, Julian, 89
Odom, Sidney, 89
Ogwin, Leon, 89
Oklahoma's National Guard, 112
Old Baldy Mountain, 114
Oliver, Daisy, 55
Oliver, Howard, 32
Oliver, Joe, 32
Oliver, Lee Earl, 56
One Hundred Seventh Transportation Co., 112
One Hundred Twelfth Army Postal Unit, 9
One Hundred Thirtieth Quartermaster Bakery Co., 9
One Hundred Eighteenth Control Detachment, 9
One Hundred Twenty First Evacuation Hospital, 60
One Hundred Fifty Fifth Station Hospital, 66, 67, 68
One Hundred Fifty Ninth Field Artillery Bn., 8, 17, 19, 25, 26, 38, 66, 86, 89
One Hundred Sixty Ninth Transportation Truck Bn., 9
One Hundred Eighty Seventh Airborne Regimental Combat Team (RCT), 29, 36
Fourteen Hundred One Engineer Combat Bn., 17
Onjin Peninsula, 11
Operation Big Switch, 74
Operation Clamour, 98
Operation Dauntless, 7
Operation little Switch, 70
Operation Ripper, 7, 30, 42
Operation Round up, 36
Operation Rugged, 7
Operation Tomahawk, 30

Ophee, Wilbur, 46
Outpost Uncle, 101
Outpost Yoke, 100, 101
Otis, Theodore, 45
Owens, Edison, 78
Owens, Lawrence, 89
Owens, S. A., 84
Owens, William J., 60

P

Page, Harry, 60
Paige, Matthew, 60
Palmer, Dwight, 109
Palmer, John, 60
Palmore-Sullivan, Anita, 76
Pangdangdon-Ni, 97, 102
Parham, Julius, 60
Parham, Robert, 60
Parker, Charles, 40
Parker, Frederick, 60
Parker, Frederick Jr., 49
Parker, John, 60
Parks, Nathan, 32
Parkins, Elgen, 60
Parks, Robert, 78
Paschall, Samuel, 45, 60
Patterson, Arthur L., 68
Patterson, Claude, 40
Patterson, Elbert, 43
Patterson, Lawrence, 60
Patton, Albert, 39
Patton, Legus, 68
Paulding, Craig, 30, 32
Payne, Baltimore, 78
Payne, Elmer, 60
Payne, Ethel, 7
Payne, Samuel, 32
Pemberton, Robert, 89
Peoples, Gladys, 75
Peoples, Hazael, 60
Peoples University, 74
Pender, Willie G., 89
Penn, George M., 44
Pentagon Officials, 110
Perin, Roosevelt, 60

THE BLACK PRESENCE IN THE KOREAN WAR 1950-1953

Perry, C., 2
Perry, Willie Lee, 68
Persall, Jack, 89
Person, Elijah, 40
Peters, Arnold, 60
Petersen, Frank E., 60
Petteress, James, 32
Pettigrew, Thomas, 42
Philips, Clyde W., 59
Phillips, Delia Mae, 52
Phillips, Otis, 89
Pickett, Ernest W., 60
Pickins, Guy, 89
Pigford, David, 60, 89
Pierce, John L., 60
Pierson, Edward, 60
Pikes, James, 60
Pikes, James jr., 68
Pile Driver Operation, 7
Pitt, Ellis, 45, 60
Pitts, Charles Jr., 68
Pittsburgh Courier, 22, 63, 116
Plater, James, 32
Plessy, Vs Ferguson, 4
Plowden, Paul, 89
Plowden, Warren, 68
Pohang Ambush, 66
Polk, Rudolph, 89
Pope, Paul W., 60
Pope, James, 32
Pope, Paul, 68
Pope, Rupert, 39
Porkchop Hill, 101
Porter, Anthony, 40
Porter, Samuel, 68
Portuguese, 111
Posey, Edward, 32
Posey, Hollis, 47
Postage Stamp, 107
Post Yoke, 98
Potter, Tomnas, 60
Potts, Edgar, 47, 60
Potts, Joe W., 60
Powell, Earl, 68
POW Singing Group, 71
POW Racial Discrimination, 71

Powers, Norman C. Jr., 73
Prather, Kermit, 78
Pratt, Silas, 60
Preece, Ellas, 71
President's Committee on Equality of Treatment and Opportunity, 108
President's Executive Order, 109
Preston, Cassius W., 89
Preston, Walter J., 89
Price, James, 45
Prince, Earl P., 60
Price, Willie, E., 68, 80
Prisoner of War Camps, 70
Prisoner of War Defectors, 74-76
Prisoners of War (POW's), 70
Pryde, Louis, 73
Pryor, Bernard, 32
Puerto Ricans, 5
Pugh, Anthony, 60
Pugh, Charles E., 89
Pugh, Curtis, 26
Pullin, George Jr., 60
Punch Bowl, 98
Pusan Perimeter, 7, 25
Pusey, Oscar, 68
Quantico Marine Base Theather, 116
Quaterman, William, 60
Queen, James, 31, 32
Queen, James, 32
Queen, S. M., 75
Quota, 110

R

Racalera, Jose, 32
Race Relations School, 15
Racial Segregation, 107
Ragland, Dayton, 60, 73
Rainey, Leon, 68
Randall, Joseph, 60
Randall, Morris, 61
Randall, Thomas, 40
Raney, William, 61
Rangel, Charles B., 89, 90

Rankins, George, 32
Rankins, M., 90
Ransom, Wayman, 117
Ratliff, Walter, 61, 90
Rauls, Henry, 40
Ray, Howard, 61
Ray, Moses, 61
Rayford, Lee, 61
Rebi, Getaneh, 100
Reconnaissance Company, Forty Fifth Infantry Division, 113
Red Cross Worker, 63
Reed, Benjamin D., 45
Reed, Cornelius, 68
Reed, James, 61
Reed, Milton, 61
Reed, Thomas, 80
Reeder, Joseph J., 68
Reese, Earnest, 33
Reeves, Andrew, 61
Reeves, Andrew H., 68
Reeves, Frank, 105
Rembert, Herman, 31, 33
Reported Military Wounded In Action, 65
Republic of Korea Military Ulchi, 102
Republic of Korea (ROK's) 32nd Regiment, 36
Republic of Korea The Order of Military Wharang with/without Stars, 102
Rest and Recuperation Leave, 6
Reynolds, Clarence, 61
Reynolds, Merle, 61
Rhee, Syngman, 3, 96, 113
Rhem Main, 114
Rhodes, Jonnie B., 80
Rhodes, William, 33
Rhodes, William, E. 30
Rhone, Ray, 33
Ribbi, Getane, 101
Rice, Albert W. D., 61
Rice, Charles, 113, 116
Richardson, Arthur L., 68
Richardson, Claudia, 61

Richardson, Ellis, 61
Richardson, Jack M., 61
Richardson, Vincent, 68
Ricks, Alvin, 61
Riddell, William, 33
Ridgeway General, 110, 111
Ridgeway, Mathew, 25, 99, 109, 113
Riley, Larry, 90
Rivers, Martin, 90
Rivers, Richard, 61, 68
Roand, Nathaniel, 40
Roberts, James, 61
Roberts, Leroy, 49, 61
Roberts, William, 90
Roberts, William M., 68
Robertson, Freddie L., 61
Robertson, Paul, 73
Robertson, Paul E., 68
Robertson, Smead, 31, 33
Robertson, Walter, 45
Robertson, William, 61
Robinson, Dean, 61
Robinson, Henry, 40
Robinson, Isiah, 68
Robinson, Leo Othis, 80
Robinson, Roscoe, 15
Rodgers, Leroy, 61
Roe, Maxio, 40
Rogers, Marion, 49, 61
Rogers, Montell, 33
Rogers, Sylvia L., 88
Rogers, Wesley, 39
Rogers, Phil, 61
Rogers, Harold Jr., 90
Rollins, Alfred G., 45
Roman, Charles, 40
Rosenblatt, Richard D., 24
Ross, Alfred, 90
Ross, Benjamin L., 68
Ross, Leon C., 73
Rothwell, Floyd, 72
Roulhac, Clifton J., 68
Roundtree, Louis, 90
Rowe, Willie, 78
Rowell, Earl, 68

Royal, Calvin, 73
Royal, James, 61
Royal, Nathaniel, 61
Rush, Judson, 105
Russ, Joseph, R., 101
Rutherford, Early Jr., 84
Russell, Arthur, 40
Russell, William, 68

S

Saint Cruix, 5
Saint John, 5
Saint Martin, Jude, 33
Saint Thomas, 5, 31, 33
Saint Thomas, Virgin Island, 63
Salik, Sgt., 100
Samoans, 111
Slam-Hyon, Korea, 102
Samson, Albert, 61
Samuel, Albert, 61
Samuel, Samuel, 46
Samuels, Columbus, 116
Samuels, Frederick H., 49, 61
Sanders, F., 61
Sanders, Grover, 61
Sangyang-Ni, Korea, 98
Sankey, Roosevelt, 73
Saunders, Hilton, 9
Savey, Clayton, 61
Sawyer, Johnny, 42
Sawyer, Leonard G., 61
Sawyer, Roosevelt, 61
Scarbor, James, 68
Schools, Melvin H., 90
Scoon, Pilton, 80
Scott, Amos, 73
Scott, Bernard, 34
Scott, Bernie, 61
Scott, Charles, 31, 33
Scott, Harold, 61
Scott, James, 73
Scott, James F., 61
Scott, Leonard, 77
Scott, Leslie, 68
Scott, Russell, 90

Scott, Thomas K., 61
Scott, Tommie, 90
Scott, Vernie, 90
Scroggins, Vernon, 61, 73, 78
Scruggins, Vernon, 61
Scars, Thomas, 90
Second Armored Division, 41, 63
Second Battle of Mandaere, 98
Second Battalion Twenty-fourth Infantry Regiment, 11, 12, 26
Second Engineer Bn., 35, 36, 110
Second Ethiopian Kagnew Bn., 96, 100
Second Kagnew Battalion, 98
Second Logistical Command, 96, 112
Second Ranger Co., 8, 30-33
Second US Infantry Division, 4 13, 25, 26, 34-36, 47, 64, 66, 67, 69, 71, 72, 74, 76, 80, 83, 86, 88, 90, 96, 98
Secretary of the Navy, 112
Sedgewick, Ferdinand, 78
Seggars, Angel, 101
Selassie, Haile, 95, 96, 116
Selected Black Units That Served in Korea, 29
Selden, Benjamin, 68
Sellers, Leroy, 42
Sellers, Thomas F, 6
Sendeku, Taddese, 100
Sengstacke, John H., 109
Seoul, 7, 11, 25
Seven Hundred Fifteenth Transportation Truck Co., 9, 44, 112, 113
Seven Hundred Twenty Sixth Transportation Truck Co., 9, 44
Seven Hundred Fifty Eighth Battles, Coat of Arms and Decorations, 41
Seven Hundred Fifty Eighth Light Tank Bn., 40
Seven Hundred Fifty Eighth Heavy Tank Bn., 41
Seventh Day Adventist, 45

Seventh Infantry Battalion, 97
Seventh Marine Regiment, 66, 79, 99, 111, 112
Seventh Transportation Truck Bn, 48
Seventy US Infantry Division, 4, 13, 31, 41, 29, 52, 60, 65, 72, 89, 103
Seventeenth Infantry Regiment, 60, 64, 80 89
Seventeen Regimental Combat Team, 30
Seventeenth South Korean Regiment, 12
Seventy Transportation Truck Co., 8
Seventy Eighth Tank Bn., 9, 40
Seventy First Chemical Smoke Generator Co., 8
Seventy Fourth Engineer Combat Co., 42, 77, 82
Seventy Fourth Transportation Truck Co., 8
Seventy Seventh Engineer Combat Co., 16, 18, 19, 24, 25, 42
Seventy Sixth Anti Aircraft Artillery Automatic Weapons Bn, 8, 43
Seventy Third Engineer Combat Bn., 8, 48
Shackleford, Kenneth, 39
Shade, William, 33
Shafter, William R., 10
Shane, Thomas, 39
Sharp, Clements, 90
Sharpe, A. L., 78
Shaw, James, 111
Shaw, Thomas 61
Shaw University, 61
Shelly, Jesse, 61
Shelton, Edward T., 61
Shelton, Robert, 43
Sheperd, Robert, 71
Shirley, Harry, 62
Shirley, Theophilius, 62

Shitta, Wolde Yohannes, 100-102
Short, James, 62
Short, Leon, 62, 68
Shuffer, George, 14, 15, 62
Shuttlesworth, Leroy A, 62
Sikes, Vernon, 113
Simmons, Charles, 61
Simmons, Charles F., 90
Simmons, Joseph, 61, 90
Simmons, Robert L., 90
Simmons, Stephen, 55
Simmons, Tyrone, 73
Simms, William, 33
Simons, Calvin, 61, 68
Simpson, George L., 43
Simpson, Jack, 61
Simpson, James, 78
Simpson, Orville L., 80
Singleton, Alonzo, 90
Singleton, Arthur, 61
Six Hundred Eleventh Port Co., 8
Six Hundred Forty Sixth Ordnance Co., 9
Six Hundred Ninety Sixth Ordnance Ammunition Co., 9, 44
Six Hundred Nineteenth Ammunition Co., 9
Six Hundred Sixteen Air Base Wing, 62
Six Hundred Sixty Fifth Transportation Truck Co., 9
Six Hundred Thirtieth Ordnance Ammunition Co., 9, 46
Six Hundred Thirty Sixth Ordnance Ammunition Co., 9
Six Hundred Twenty Fourth Transportation Co., 46
Sixteenth US Army Band, 9
Sixth Infantry Marine Bn., 57
Sixtieth Transportation Truck Co., 8
Sixty First Field Artillery Bn, 34, 35
Sixty Fourth Bn., 8

Sixty Fourth Heavy Tank Bn., 5, 62, 71, 87, 110
Sixty Fourth Infantry Regiment, 11
Sixty Fourth Tank Bn., 5, 26, 40, 41
Sixty Fifth Engineers, 20
Sixty Fifth Ordnance Ammunition Co., 8
Sixty Fifth Puerto Rican Infantry Regiment, 4, 5, 26
Sixty Fifth Regimental Combat Team, 17
Sixty Ninth Ordnance Ammunition Co., 48
Sixty Ninth Transportation Truck Co., 8
Sixty One Hundred Sixty First Air Bomber Wing, 60
Sixty One Hundred Twenty Seventh Air Terminal Group, 55, 61
Sixty One Hundred Forty Seventh Tactical Control Squadron, 55
Sixty Seventh Fighter Bomber Squadron, 57
Slaughter, Melvin O., 68
Sloan George, 62
Sloan, John T., 62
Sloan, Robert H., 68
Sloane, Charles C., 26
Small, Wheeler, 30
Small, William, 33
Smedley, Benny, 39
Smiley, Ernest, 62
Smith, Albert L., 73
Smith, Clarence, 41
Smith, Elijah, 73
Smith, Gerald, 80
Smith, Herbert, 29
Smith, James B., 90
Smith, James H., 40
Smith, John L., 47
Smith, Lawrence, 29
Smith, Leroy, 68

Smith, Martin, 62
Smith, Nicholas, 90
Smith, Norman, 62
Smith, Oliver, 111
Smith, Raymond, 68
Smith Robert, 33
Smith, Roy L., 80
Smith, Scherrell, 33
Smith, Sherman, W., 90
Smith, Sumerrell, 33
Smith, Thomas, 62
Smith, Thomas J., 62
Smith, Willie, 45, 62
Smith, William C., 68
Smith, Wortham, 90
Smithsonian National Zoological Park, 115
Soloman, Robert B., 21
Solomon, Curtis, 62
South Carolina National Guard, 16
South Carolina State College, 60
South Korea Presidential Unit Citation, 103
Snowden, William R., 62
Spain, 5
Sparks, Frank C. Jr., 62
Speaks, Joe F., 62, 90
Spearman, Oscar, 62
Special Services Club, 7
Speller, Joseph D., 68
Spence, Vernon, 62
Spriggs, Harold, 68
Springs, Claude, 90
Spruell, James, 40
Spencer, Russell, 90
Spivey, Joe, 62
Spivey, John, 73
Squires, Howard, 33
Stanfield, Charles R., 90
Stanley, William Milford, 73
Staples, Willie C., 47
Starks, Edward, 62
Stephen, Samuel, 62
Stephens, Richard, 62
Stephenson, Robert L., 62

Sterling, George W., 49, 62
Sterling, Hayward, 68, 69
Stevens, Richard, 62
Stevens, Henry, 73
Stevenson, Olden C., 69
Stevenson, Robert, 62
Stevenson, William H., 109
Stewart, Ossie D., 62
Stewart, Charles, 62
Steward, James, 80
Stewart, Linwood, 69
Stewart, William, 62
Stills, Bardett, 62
Stokes, Ahren, 69
Stone, Garfield, 62
Stone, Lillian, 62
Stover, David, 62
Strong, Leroy, 62
Strothers, Samuel Roscoe, 90
Strothers, Stewart, 33
Stubbs, Norman, 90
Submarine Combat Pin, 84
Suggs, John J., 49, 62
Sullivan, LaRance, 75-76
Supple, James O., 55
Sutton, Harry, 39, 90
Sutton, Harry E., 27, 117
Sutton, Ralph, 31, 33
Sweden, 3
Swinney, Talmadge, 90
Symington, W. Stuart, 109
Sykes, Leroy, 73

T

Taft, Marvin, 62
Taft, Thaddeus, 62
Taliaferro, James, 62
Taliaferro, Oscar, 62
Tammons, Herbert, 39
Tanaker, Clarence, 62
Tapp, Marvin, 62
Tate, Billie, 33
Tate, Carl, 69
Tatum, Pfc. 86
Taylor, Charles, 34
Taylor, Claudius, 62
Taylor, Earl W., 78
Taylor, James, 33
Taylor, Karl W., 78
Taylor, Luther R., 62
Taylor, Maxwell, 101
Taylor, Melvin, 71
Taylor, Nathaniel, 62
Taylor, Ordie, 62
Taylor, Ray, 69, 90
Taylor, Richard, 62
Taylor, Ulysses, 62
Tennelle, Baron Lee, 62
Tennesse State University, 116
Tenth US Cavalry, 10
Terrell, John, 33
Terrick, Johnnie, 91
Terry, Luther, 91
Terry, Willie, 91
Tessem, Tamarat, 101
Tessema, Mellesse, 99
Tessama, Nigga, 102
Tessmma, Tamarat, 102
Testfaye, Wolde, Sadic, 102
Testgaye, Wolde Sadic, 102
Teverbaugh, Jesse, 91, 116
Thailand, 3
Theus, Wade, 63
Thimaya, T. S., 74
Things The Majority News Media Did Not Tell Me, 116
Third Air Rescue Squadron, 55
Third Bn. Fifteenth Infantry Regiment, 26, 39
Third Bn. Five Hundred Fifth Parachute Infantry Regiment, 18-19
Third Bn. Ninth Infantry Regiment, 8
Third Bn. Twenty Fourth Infantry Regiment, 11-13, 25, 42
Third Bn. Thirty First Infantry Regiment, 13
Third Bomber Wing, 64
Third Bn. Thirty Fifth Infantry, 13

Third Engineer Bn, 110
Third Kagnew Bn., 96, 101
Third US Infantry Division, 4, 25, 38, 79, 84, 87, 90, 91, 92, 117
Third US Marine Division, 50
Third Wing B-26 Bomber, 53
Thirteenth Air Force, 49, 55, 56
Thirty Eighth Field Artillery Bn., 11, 34-35
Thirty Eighth Infantry Regiment, 10, 35-36, 66, 68
Thirty Eighth Parallel, 7, 11
Thirty Fifth Infantry Regiment, 26, 60, 63, 110
Thirty Fifth Fighter Interceptor Aerial Defense Unit, 56
Thirty Fifth Fighter Group, 52
Thirty First Infantry Regiment, 13, 55, 68, 82, 89, 90
Thirty First Reconnaissance, 49
Thirty Fourth Infantry Regiment, 64, 84
Thirty Ninth Medical Dispensary Co., 8
Thirty Second US Infantry Regiment, 63, 96, 99-100
Thirty Seventh Field Artillery Bn., 35, 37
Thirty Sixth Regiment Nineteenth North Korean Division, 30
Thomas, Bernard, 40
Thomas, Charles E., 46
Thomas, Clinton, 63
Thomas, Curtis, 62
Thomas, George, 33
Thomas, Herbert, 69
Thomas, H. W., 63
Thomas, James 63
Thomas, James Jr., 78
Thomas, Jesse, 63
Thomas, Philip, 63
Thomas, Rodney, 73, 78
Thomas, William, 33
Thompson, Albert S., 63, 91
Thompson, Alvin, 58

Thompson, James D., 63
Thompson, John C., 91
Thompson, Lee, 48
Thompson, Robert, 69
Thompson, Ronald E., 42
Thompson, Silas, 63
Thompson, William, 26, 91
Thorn, Arthur, 63
Thornton, Theodore, 78
Three Hundred Fifteenth Air Division, 4, 57
Three Hundred Fifty First Field Artillery Regiment, 34
Three Hundred Nineteenth Engineer Bn., 16
Three Hundred Ninety Sixth Transportation Truck Co., 47
Three Hundred Seventy Fifth Chemical Smoke Generator Co., 8
Three Hundred Seventy First Infantry Regiment, 27
Three Hundred Seventy Fourth Carrier Wing, 109
Three Hundred Seventy Sixth Engineer Construction Co., 8, 46
Three Hundred Sixty Fifth Infantry Regiment, 16
Three Hundred Sixty Seventh Infantry Regiment, 16
Three Hundred Thirty Second Fighter Group, 17, 26
Throiner, Carl 5, 63
Thurman, Reuben, 78
Tiano Indian, 5
Tilahublan, Pvt., 101
Tiller, Willie, 44
Tillman, Robert, 63
Time Magazine, 39
Toatley, Ulysses, 49, 63
Toppins, Bernie, 44
Towns, Otis, 69
Townsend, Floyd, 63
Trial Judge Advocate, 105
Tribble, Alfred, 91
Troop Rotation System, 6

Trox, Sammie, 63
Trudeau, Arthur, 103
Truman, Harry, 3, 5, 104, 108
Truman, President, 3, 11, 105, 109, 113
Tucker, Orrie, 33
Turner, Andrew, 63
Tuskegee University, 61
Twelfth Field Artillery Bn., 24, 37
Twentieth US Air Force, 62-64, 49, 54
Twenty Eighth Transportation Truck Co., 8
Twenty Fifth Chemical Decontamination Unit, 8
Twenty Fifth US Infantry Division, 4, 25, 42, 45, 61, 63, 110
Twenty Fourth Infantry Regiment, 8, 10, 18-21, 25-28, 50, 105, 107, 110, 116
Twenty Fourth Infantry Regiment Heavy Mortar Co., 21
Twenty Fourth US Infantry Division, 4, 17, 45, 74-75, 77, 80, 110
Twenty Fourth Regimental Combat Team, 50
Twenty Seventh Infantry Regiment, 14
Twenty Seventh Tank Recovery Ordnance Bn, 47
Twenty Third Infantry Regiment, 34-35, 37, 67, 114
Twenty Seventh "Wolfhound" Regiment, 14, 18, 61
Two Hundred Eighty Ninth US Army Band, 9
Two Hundred Fiftieth Laundry Detachment, 9
Two Hundred Ninety First US Army Band, 9
Two Hundred Thirty First Transportation Truck Co., 9, 40, 116
Two Hundred Twelfth Military Police Co., 6, 9
Two Hundred Twenty Seventh AAA Group, 113
Two Hundred Sixteenth Medical Detachment, 9
Tyce, Donald, 73
Tyson, Bobby, 63

U

Union Methodist Church, 107
Union of South Africa, 3
United Kingdom, 3
United Nations Command, 3
United Nations Command Cemetery, 100
United States, 3
US Air Force Far East Command, 49
US Army Heavy Weight Boxing Champion, 67
US Army Nurse Corps, 50
US Army Infantry School, 111
US Army Quartermaster Post, 7
US I Corps, 41
US Navy, 4
US Navy Nurse Corps, 4
US Tenth Corps, 48
US Virgin Islands, 5
USS Collett, 83
USS Consolation, 112
USS General Butner, 29
USS General William Mitchell, 34
USS Haven, 112
USS Jesse Brown, 83
USS Juneau, 61
USS Leyte, 83
USS Lind, 61
USS Missouri, 60, 63, 90
USS Nelson Walker, 71
USS Pickerel, 84
USS Repose, 112
Utah Line, 7
Valentine, Lionel, 63

Valery, Cleveland, 33
Valley Forge Military Hospital, 114
Vandunk, William, 33
Vanfleet, General, 103
Vann, Russell, 34, 91
Vails, Robert, 33
Vaughn, James, 63
Venable, Walter, 63
Verner, I., 63
Victor, Julius, 33
Victoria, 10
Vietnam, 21
Vincenti, Ray, 63
Virginia State College, 79

W

Wacs, 112
Wade, Virgil, 33
Wade, William, 63
Waiters, Thaddeus, 63
Waites, Leroy, 91
Waldemarian, Mano, 101
Walden, Emerson Coleman, 59
Walden, Roger, 18
Walden, Rogers S. 27, 63
Waldertekee, Tiggu, 101
Waldetensye, Tefera, 97-98, 102
Walker, Edward, 91
Walker, Frank, 73
Walker, Hardon B., 91
Walker, Horace, 63
Walker, James, 33, 63, 91
Walker, Moses, 63
Walker, Robert L., 91
Wallace, James W., 63
Wallace, Jesse, 92
Wallace, Willard, 63
Wallace, William, 29, 43, 61
Walls, Corporal, 39
Walter, Andrew, 63
Walton, Shirley M., 63
Walwyn, David, 92
Wandemu, Negatu, 97, 102
Wanzo, Lois, 63

War Correspondent, 63
Ward, Albert, 63
Ward Arthur L., 49, 63
Ward, Joseph L., 80
Wardell, George, 39
Warden, Leonard, 63
Ware, William, 92
Warford, Louis, 73
Warmley, James, 29
Warr, Wilmer, 63
Warren, Bonnie, 63
Warren, Charles A., 92
Warren, John D., 63
Warren, Samuel, 78
Warren, Vernon, 73, 78
Warring, Wilbert M., 73
Washington, Charles, 92
Washington, Charles L., 80
Washington, John W., 63
Washington, Johnnie C., 39
Washington, Levi, 63
Washington, Louis, 61
Washington Post, 111
Washington, Raymond, 63
Washington, Sullus, 63
Washington, Thomas, 63
Washington, William, 33
Waters, C. W., 92
Watkins, Charles M., 40
Watkins, Robert, 33
Watley, Harry, 63
Watson, Edward, 46, 63
Watson, Thomas, 38
Weaker, Henry, 48
Weathersbee, William, 33
Webb, Burke, 30, 33
Webb, George, 49
Webb, George W., 63
Webster, Walter, 73
Welch, Lt., 38
Welde, Kassaye, 98
Wedgeworth, James, 45
Wellison, George, 63
Wells, Joseph, 33
Wells, June, 7
Wells, Paul, 20

West, Donald, 33
West, First Sergeant, 30
West, George Jr., 78
West, Lawrence, 33
West Point, 16
West, Ramon, 33
Wheldon, Don M., 73
Whening, James, 63
Whisonant, Frank, 63
White, Albert, 40
White Archie, 63
White, Gyre, 63
White, John O., 63
White, Leroy, 33
White, Leslie, 80
White, Percy, 92
White Replacements, 110
White Servicemen, 105-106
White, Walter, 92, 104, 106
White, William, 43
White, William C., 75-76
Whitehead, David, 92
Whitehurst, Pfc., 29
Whitmore, Clarence, 63
Whitemore, Joseph, 33
Whitten, Charles F., 63
Wickes, William, 63
Wiggins, Charles, 92
Wiggins, Rosalie H., 63
Wilburn, Vincent, 33
Wiley, K., 92
Wilkerson, Albert L., 73
Wilkerson, Eldred, 40, 63
Wilkerson, Jerry, 63
Wilkins, Hiram, 43, 63
Williams, Aikins, 33
Williams, Anderson, 40
Williams, Archie, 64
Williams, Eldridge, 49, 64
Williams, Edward, 64
Williams, Edward J., 49-50
Williams, Fred, 64
Williams, George, 92
Williams, Isaiah, 37
Williams, James, 92
Williams, James C., 46

Williams, Lawrence, 31, 33
Williams, Lonnie W., 42
Williams, Louis, 39
Williams, Maurice, 80
Williams, Ozzie, 45
Williams, Richard D., 18
Williams, Richard W., 26-27
Williams, Robert, 78
Williams, Robert L. 64
Williams, Roosevelt, 74
Williams, Samuel 45
Williams, Wilbur, 43, 64
Williams, Wilkes, 64
Williams, Willie, 64
Williams, William, 64
Williamson, Otis, 33
Wills, Lowell, 64
Wise, John E., 64
Wilson, Bernard, 74
Wilson, Chief, 110
Wilson, Clarence, 64
Wilson, Henry, 33
Wilson, James, 42
Wilson, Lawrence, 92
Wilson, Leon, 64
Wilson, Leroy, 64
Wilson, Major, 64
Wilson, Ozzie, 64
Wilson, Theodore, 40
Wilson, Theodore A., 64
Wilson, William, 33
Winans, Herman L., 64
Wincheny, Robert, 64
Winchester, Eugene, 64
Windon, Joseph Clifton, 78
Winfield, Jacob E., 64
Wingers, William, 92
Wingfield, B. L. 46
Winkfield, John, 92
Winters, William W., 92
Woddard, Isaiah, 33
Wofford, Kenneth O., 49, 64
Wogan, William, 105
Wolbong-Ni, Korea, 88
Wolde, Kasaye, 102
Woldemanuel, Tafara, 101

Woldenmichael, Manno, 98
Women and Integration, 112
Wondimagegenehu, Tilaye, 99
Wonju, Korea, 109
Wood, Thomas, 64
Woodard, Bennie, 64
Woodhouse, Melvin J., 74, 78
Woodmore, Henry, 39
Woods, Jacob, 64
Woodson, Morris, 80
Woodward, Leroy, 39
Wooten, James A., 64
Wonchon-Ni, Korea, 87
Wondee, Immeru, 101
Worknew, T., 101
Wounded in Action Statistics, 69
Wright, C. C., 78
Wright, C. L., 74
Wright, Jack, 64
Wright, James Jr., 64
Wright, Perry, 64
Wright, William
Wuhan University, 74
Wyatt, Robert Lee, 78
Wynn, Ellison, 29, 92
Wynn, Ellison C., 26
Wyman, Lee, 64

X

X Corps, 5, 26, 36, 41, 43-44

Y

Yalu River, 91
Yarber, Ulysses Sherman, 64, 78, 117
Yayi, Jeru, 100
Yechon, 42
Young, Crenshaw, 44
Young, Huey, 64
Young, John, 64, 92
Young, Oliver, 117
Youngblood, Franklin, 40
Yongsan, Korea, 85
York, PA, 105

Z

Zampier, Alphonse, 64
Zampier, Alphonse Sr., 64
Zampier, Gladys, 64
Zenebe, Asfaw, 102
Zuckert, Eugene, 109